CURIOSITY AND PILGRIMAGE

Also by Christian K. Zacher

CRITICAL STUDIES OF SIR GAWAIN
AND THE GREEN KNIGHT
(co-editor, with D. R. Howard)

CURIOSITY and PILGRIMAGE

THE LITERATURE

OF DISCOVERY

IN FOURTEENTH-

CENTURY ENGLAND

Christian K. Zacher

THE JOHNS HOPKINS UNIVERSITY PRESS   Baltimore and London

This book has been brought to publication with the generous assistance of the Andrew W. Mellon Foundation.

The Johns Hopkins University Press, Baltimore, Maryland 21218
The Johns Hopkins University Press Ltd., London
Library of Congress Catalog Card Number 75-36929
ISBN 0-8018-1778-1

Library of Congress Cataloging in Publication data will be found on the last printed page of this book.

For my parents,
Eugene Robert Zacher
and Catherine Keeler Zacher,
with love and with gratitude
for a life of lilacs and piñon

CONTENTS

ACKNOWLEDGMENTS

Over the last few years when colleagues, students, and bemused relatives have asked what I was "working on," my reply has been that I was writing about the interplay between two contrary impulses or forces in late-medieval English life and literature: the itch to explore (a vice then called *curiositas*) and the sanctioned practice of pilgrimage. If that odd word moved them, other questions followed, and I would offer a synopsis of my idea. I received enough frowns, pointed criticisms, and recommendations for further reading that I kept refining the presentation of my idea, trying out parts of it at scholarly conventions, and shoring it round with that sense of security new discoveries in the card catalog and the buttressing of more footnotes always give. Then too, during all this infusing I received some complimentary but uncritical enthusiasm for my contentions. Fortunately, sound critics outnumbered enthusiasts, and their suggestions and cautious encouragement have helped shape this into what I hope is a useful contribution to medieval studies. This hope is rooted in my belief that the conflict discernible between medieval pilgrimage and curiosity is an important one and has not been investigated before, and that two of the three works written in fourteenth-century England I have chosen to verify my perception—Richard de Bury's *Philobiblon* and John Mandeville's *Travels*—have undeservedly received next to no attention as literature.

John M. Steadman and William F. Munson carefully read and guided this work in its first awkward stages. Robert M. Estrich corrected many mistakes of fact and, as he has done for so many before me, gave generously from his accumulated knowledge of medieval culture. Stanley

J. Kahrl, Walter Scheps, Alan Brown, James R. Kincaid, John B. Gabel, and for a time, Arthur C. Cawley, colleagues at Ohio State, heard me out and made useful criticisms. E. Talbot Donaldson, Thomas D. Hill, Russell A. Peck, and Stephen J. Manning kindly read the manuscript at different stages and offered valuable suggestions; I thank them again. Francis Lee Utley and Donald R. Howard have been most influential in this entire effort. To the former, whose death impoverished us all, I owe what only frequent contact with a learned medievalist offers. To Donald Howard I am specially indebted for both the immersion in medieval literature that led me to begin this book and the years of instructive prodding that have come now to seem like one continuous conversation.

My wife, Judith, a surgeon by trade, is by some medieval definitions a hopeless victim of *curiositas* and because of that, and much else, has been infected with the whole endeavor from the start.

Judith Feil, Joel Hermann, Andrea Lunsford, Barbara Parker, and especially JoAnn Gutin of The Johns Hopkins University Press helped greatly in the final preparations of the manuscript. And I am thankful to The Ohio State University College of Humanities for the financial assistance provided one summer, which granted me more time to read, write, and evolve this study.

Columbus, Ohio
April 1975

CURIOSITY AND PILGRIMAGE

CHAPTER I. A NEW SENSE
OF THE WORLD

*I have often said that man's unhappiness arises
from one thing only, namely that he cannot
abide quietly in one room.* —Pascal, Pensées

Curiosity began in Eden: having eaten the
forbidden fruit from the tree of knowledge, Adam and Eve were put
out of the garden. Ever since, mankind has been wandering in time,
engrossed by this world yet aware of the promise of heaven. This
Christian commonplace, which described man as a stranger and pilgrim, homeless in the world and in pursuit of Celestial Jerusalem, has
stressed the innumerable risks he faced in enduring his exile. Distracted by the world and inquisitive about God's creatures, he merely repeated the sin of his first parents, departed from the straight and
narrow road, and jeopardized his soul's salvation. As one of the earliest Christians expressed it, man must decide between this world and
the homeland of the Father; the choice is either *mundus* or *patria*
(1 John 2:16). Medieval Christians gave considerable attention to the
many implications of these alternatives—the comparable value of
scientia and *sapientia*, the proper use of knowledge and worldly
things, the possibility and value of human progress. How closely
should the homeless Christian study this world he inhabits? To what
uses should he put the experience and knowledge obtained in his wayfaring?

To show fully how such questions were faced would mean (among
other things) chronicling the rise of experimental science or assessing

the history of man's motives for geographical exploration. But my aim is more limited. I intend to examine medieval attitudes surrounding the scriptural antithesis between this world and the next by concentrating on the convergence of two ideas, curiosity and pilgrimage. Generally defined, the temptation of *curiositas* referred to any morally excessive and suspect interest in observing the world, seeking novel experiences, or acquiring knowledge for its own sake. (Since *curiositas* had exact medieval connotations long gone from our now neutralized word "curiosity," I will use the Latin term where there is a need to stress its theological meaning, then dispense with it and use the English term otherwise.) *Curiositas* was a vice related to pride and sloth, and by the late Middle Ages it gradually came to be seen as a threat to pilgrimage, that distinctively medieval mode of religious travel. Pilgrimage was a theological idea and a cultural phenomenon—but above all it was a religious institution, a devotional practice which let pious Christians travel through the physical world only because their destinations were places sanctified by spiritual, otherworldly associations. Throughout the Middle Ages, theologians looked on *curiositas* as a phase of original sin, which made all men wanderers in the fallen world; curiosity about this inferior world would prevent a man from reaching that other land of the Father. As a form of religious worship, pilgrimage allowed men to journey through this present world visiting sacral landscapes as long as they kept their gaze permanently fixed on the invisible world beyond. It excluded from sight and undue speculation that same arena of interest *curiositas* tempted men to enter.

Without really using the term in its exact, opprobrious medieval sense, critics discussing pilgrimage will observe on occasion that pilgrims at times traveled about out of sheer curiosity. Less frequently, scholars treating *curiositas* will mention incidentally that this class of medieval travelers was particularly vulnerable to that vice. Of course, many activities other than pilgrimage were labeled curious in the Middle Ages; complaints about pilgrimages were often directed against evils other than curiosity; and warnings against curiosity as a temptation to pilgrims do occur, occasionally, early in the Middle Ages. But no one to my knowledge has carefully investigated what I find to be an important cultural fact—that by the late Middle Ages, and as far as I can tell certainly in the fourteenth century, the devotional practice and the vice had become closely identified with one another. By

Chaucer's lifetime pilgrimages were being criticized as undertakings prompted by curiosity. Doctrinal pronouncements, royal decrees, pulpit warnings, popular adages, and the serious literature of the age were making the connection and discovering a personage who was an unsettling spiritual and historical contradiction: the curious pilgrim. At the close of the Middle Ages pilgrimage had gradually become little more than a mask concealing natural human yearnings to explore other lands—the journey itself, more than the sacred goal, became the objective of men's travels. Pilgrimage survived the Middle Ages, diminished much in piety. *Curiositas* too survived, no longer the medieval affliction of moral peril but a generally prized stimulus for post-medieval travelers and inquirers. By the Renaissance, although curiosity was still considered a vice by some, it was also widely thought of as a harmless and even virtuous motivation.

In tracing the gradual impingement of curiosity on pilgrimage and the eventual predominance of the one over the other, I plan to discuss first the treatment of *curiositas* in Christian teaching and then the changing meanings and motivations of medieval pilgrimage. Afterward, I will turn to an analysis of three literary works from fourteenth-century England that reflect a cluster of issues growing out of the associations between *curiositas* and pilgrimage. Richard de Bury's *Philobiblon*, ostensibly a learned book-collector's defense against specific charges of *curiositas*, actually turns out to be a spirited apologia for the curious man's secular pilgrimages into the world of books. Chaucer's *Canterbury Tales* is a work in which pilgrim piety is confronted by *curiositas* in almost all its imaginable ramifications and in which the social order ideally symbolized by pilgrimage is shown to be threatened by the questionable motivations of many of the pilgrims. And Mandeville's *Travels* begins as a pilgrim's manual but ends as a monument to worldly inquisitiveness. Of the three, the *Travels* makes the most apt conclusion for this study, since it presents in sharp outline the conflict between the traditional goal of the pilgrim and the multitude of worldly goals sought by the wandering, questioning explorer of the next and succeeding centuries.

But, having chosen to deal with these three works in this order, I concede that neither the choice nor the order makes a great deal of difference to the line of my argument. An analysis of *The Cloud of Unknowing*, Hilton's *Scale of Perfection, Piers Plowman,* Petrarch's

Secretum, or any of several actual European pilgrimage itineraries of the fourteenth and fifteenth centuries would substantiate the same conflicts I find in these works. However, I do think that my choice of works written in the dominant languages of medieval England—de Bury wrote in Latin, Chaucer in English, and Mandeville presumably in Anglo-French—suggests more strongly the wide cultural awareness of the conflict than a focus on three Middle English texts would. I believe, as many do, that considering their importance as literary languages, Anglo-Latin and Anglo-French are too often neglected in medieval English studies; as D. W. Robertson, Jr., puts it, they have "a legitimate place in English literary history. The tendency to relegate [them] to a vague realm of cultural background seldom brought into direct focus has no justification."[1] But what is most important is that each of these three books combines the idea or metaphor of pilgrimage with the secular urge that makes men want to go investigate the world, and while each is certainly "about" more than the clash I dwell on, all three nevertheless illustrate the progressive secularization of pilgrimage and the gradual redefinition of curiosity.

There are differences among the three works in style, genre, and intent—as well as in the attitudes each author adopts toward *curiositas*—but taken together they form a rich index of a new sensibility, a new feeling about the world. Bishop de Bury's epistolary defense of books is written in the fashionable Latin *cursus* style of the day, and that style is one his enemies as well as most rhetoricians would have described as *curiosus*: superfluous, extravagant in figures, excessively ornate. It is probably like the "heighe style" Harry Bailly asks the Clerk, another Oxford figure, to forgo at the start of his tale. De Bury's prose style reinforces what his actual and metaphoric pilgrimages to libraries and booksellers more openly reveal: his thirst for books is a curious urge, a lifelong journey he himself charactrizes as a spiritual quest. The book is his shrine.

De Bury's *curiositas* is apparent in his rhetoric and in the objectives of his pilgrimages. But John Mandeville's pilgrimage is a real, not a figurative one, and at least the first part of his journey is religious. Yet the second half is not a pilgrimage; it is a voyage through the real and imaginary world beyond Jerusalem, a curious venture entirely. The routes out there are really plotted inside Mandeville's head; indeed, what Mandeville did was read others' pilgrimage and travel books and compose his own. De Bury lived for books, lived in them, was surrounded by them. Mandeville collapsed a shelf of them into one, a novel and unusual book, reshaped as a fiction (for he never went to half the places he claimed)—and it was his pilgrimage-exploration account, not the books of actual pilgrim diarists and Asian travelers, that Europeans avidly read for centuries. Both writers were bookbound, the one to books as incitements to curious discovery, the other to books as experience out of which he created an excitement about new lands and peoples, a new sense of the earth, fully populated with the known and the possible, a new circumnavigable globe which other curious travelers soon went out to circle.

While de Bury is all words and Mandeville all eyes, Chaucer's pilgrims are all talk. They tell the tales Chaucer has filled his own book with. In their tale-telling they manifest the vice and delight of curiosity; and they perhaps just make it to journey's end. The norms of devout pilgrimage are embedded in the *Canterbury Tales*; but these pilgrims are set on telling stories about one another, quarreling, prying, backbiting, breaking bonds. They do what *curiositas* could make pilgrims do and ignore what Becket implicitly and the Parson overtly have to say about the meaning of pilgrimage. Chaucer looked upon the practice of pilgrimage, by his time a curiosity-ridden institution, with what seems to have been a skeptical eye. I do not mean that Geoffrey Chaucer had nothing at all of the *curiosus* in him. Everywhere in his writings one can spot the characteristics which, placed in a focus different from my present one, would associate him with the likes of Mandeville and de Bury: his aerial voyage in the *House of Fame*, his observant eye in the *General Prologue*, his love of books and perhaps of travel, his sense of the past, his obvious familiarity with alchemical and astrological matters, his skillfulness with the voyager's astrolabe, and much else. Indeed, in the *Canterbury Tales* itself the narrator's pose is that of a returned pilgrim—and the whole work is a feat of memory, as Donald R. Howard reminds us[2]—so we expect him to offer us tales, exaggerate, even lie. R. W. V. Elliott's description of the *Tales* could apply as well to parts of Mandeville: it is filled with "worlds of faerye, mythology, and wonder as marvelous as anything in the dream-visions, worlds in which animals talk, ladies change shape, rocks disappear, magic horses and rings function, and fairies walk."[3]

Chaucer knew what *curiositas* was and what pilgrimage had come
to represent. Of course, I recognize Chaucer the humorist, the ironist,
the dramatist, and acknowledge the presence of numerous other
themes and concerns in the *Tales*, but I also think—and urge it as a
major consideration—that as moralist and artist Chaucer presents in
the work an argument against the desultory effects of pilgrim curiosity and for the stability of the institution in its true sense. Apart from
whatever else led Chaucer to decide on a pilgrimage as the frame for
his tales, I believe he used the pilgrimage to show how the divisive
curiosity it could engender and play upon mirrored the abundant social
and political disorders that beset England in the late fourteenth century. Having read Mandeville, aware of both the traditional injunctions
against curiosity and the growing advocacy of it, Chaucer might have
easily joined together his characters and their tales in some form less
pointedly pious in its historical suggestiveness than pilgrimage. He
could, in other words, have written another *Decameron*. If such a
possibility crossed his mind, he discarded it, or, to borrow C. S.
Lewis's word, "medievalized" it, just as he had earlier medievalized
Il Filostrato. I am claiming then that the author of the *Tales*, himself
an intellectual and a traveler with what appears to be an insatiable
curiosity, is a conservative spokesman for the orthodox spiritual values
of pilgrimage. He need not have been a Lollard to hold this conviction.
And, in fact, if my interpretation of his view of pilgrimage is right,
Chaucer's complex perception of the curiosity that pervaded pilgrimages of his day probably tells us as much as any other contemporary
testimony about the phenomenon.

To read the *Philobiblon*, the *Canterbury Tales*, and the *Travels* is
to sense that excitement about new ideas, terrestrial exploration, and
the natural world that permeates late-medieval thought as it never did
earlier in the age. The significant impact of curiosity as a motivation
on pilgrims and their evolution into figures like the travelers in these
three fourteenth-century books presses on us at least two interrelated
questions. Why does this phenomenon happen in the fourteenth century? Is this current of new feeling tied to the immediate origins of
modern humanism? I have no complete answers to these questions,
only some intimations, most of them derived from the fairly unanimous view of a number of scholars whose understanding of certain

fourteenth-century developments corroborates my sense of forward
movement in the period that results from the convergence of curiosity
and piety.

The familiar labels that literary critics and intellectual historians
recently have affixed to the fourteenth century suggest in themselves
several reasons why we should not be surprised to see venerable institutions (like the pilgrimage) and human motivations (like curiosity)
undergoing redefinition. The century has been called an age of adversity, doubt, discord, crisis, uncertainty, self-criticism, pessimism, and
questioning. Certainly, leaps from selected facts to generalizations
about "the age of" make us uncomfortable; in speaking of any century—the fourteenth no less than others—discriminations must be
made between any two countries, and careful scrutiny has to be given
to decades, even decisive years and days. But, while these caveats are
as commonly noted as they are ignored, the cultural historians who
have most influenced my thinking are those who do generalize about
the age without either burying or belaboring pertinent facts.

Throughout the fourteenth century Europe as a whole experienced
a widespread political, economic, and religious turbulence, the causes
and effects of which were mixed. The papacy gone from Rome for
generations, heading toward the Schism; two great national powers
and their allies sporadically battling till they achieved a century of
total war; a vicious plague sweeping in amid other tribulations at mid-
century (and followed by recurring outbreaks); temporary and long-
lasting civil rebellions among the lowest and middle classes of society
in different countries—these well-known catastrophes obvious allow
us (as they did contemporaries) to declare fourteenth-century Europe
an age of adversity. Men of intellect faced or retreated from the awesome uncertainties; those who reacted by testing a range of earlier
beliefs and values in various spheres of intellectual activity seem most
responsible for the broad, curious, experimental, skeptical outlook
that de Bury, Mandeville, and Chaucer share. What David Knowles has
called "the breakdown of the medieval synthesis" occurred in this
century, and although to do so risks distorted simplification, I am
going to emphasize the thinking of only a few philosophers and scientists who were caught up in that breakdown and its results.

The fate of the thirteenth-century confidence in the union of faith
and reason and belief in the comprehensibility of all knowledge has

been learnedly studied, especially so, I think, by Knowles, Gordon
Leff, R. W. Southern, and Heiko A. Oberman.[4] Following upon the
formal and informal renunciations of the schoolmen in the late thirteenth century and the disputes between conservative enemies of
Averroistic doctrine and the champions of empiricism led by Grosseteste and Bacon, key thinkers like Duns Scotus and Ockham began to
separate the study of philosophy from theology. The result was that
such influential fourteenth-century thinkers as Henry of Ghent,
Thomas Bradwardine, and Gregory of Rimini (along with Scotus and
Ockham) "joined in returning to the older view of theology as the
preserve of scriptural truth, concerned with elucidating the articles of
faith and fortifying its adherents."[5] Man's mind cannot prove or dis-
prove matters of faith, they argued; the provinces of each are distinct.
With this division made, it was further alleged that all we can know
through reason as certain truths are things and individuals, not uni-
versals or abstractions. The Ockhamists (at least the more radical ones)
asserted that "the universe neither needed nor was susceptible of explanation; it could be experienced, but not understood."[6] This nominalist stance was revolutionary in its emphasis on individual experience, observation, and the speculative scientific approach. John
Mandeville in his curiosity embodies this attitude. In Gordon Leff's
words, Scotus had taken "the momentous step of leaving man no
certain knowledge other than that derived from experience and the
operation of reason."[7] If it is an overstatement to say that men like
de Bury, Mandeville, and Chaucer now lived with "the great new intellectual fact of the later Middle Ages: the divorce between faith and
knowledge based on natural experience,"[8] the period was typified by
what Oberman calls the "phenomenon of crisis," and "the discovery
of the inductive method as the basis for reliable scientific conclusions"
figured crucially in both the waning of the Middle Ages and the birth
pangs of the modern era.[9] The complicated new problems of the age
and the omnipresent instability, as Robert E. Lerner has suggested,
are perhaps "graphically illustrated by the fact that the *summa* or
summary, which had been a favorite compositional form of the thirteenth century, was replaced in the fourteenth century by the tract.
This characteristic form of writing was addressed to particular, often
practical, questions and written from all conceivable points of view,
conservative and progressive."[10] Chaucer's collection of tales is neither

summa nor tract; and of course it is not a theology textbook or a
philosophical argument, although Chaucer criticism abounds with
attempts both to compare it to a unified, integrated *summa* and to
see it as a series of discrete tract-like pieces. Neither approach is
wholly acceptable, but the fragmentation, incompleteness, and multiple points of view of the collection may well owe something to nominalist habits of mind. The individuation and "realism" of some portraits in the *General Prologue* likewise may reflect the nominalist
influence on late-medieval portraiture that Panofsky detected[11]—
but then not all of Chaucer's portraits are so composed.

Recent studies of nominalism should make us more wary of making
too much of late-medieval scholastic movements, more ready to see
the proliferating tracts as complements to the earlier *summae* and not
rejections of them, and more cautious about ignoring the basic continuity of medieval and early modern thought.[12] Nevertheless, it is
likely that a thirteenth-century thinker who called himself a philosopher or a theologian might find his discipline splintered a century
later, and he might turn, as many did, to natural science and a miscellany of related studies. De Bury himself dabbled in several areas of
inquiry, as his book reveals; the Merton College scholars whose dinner-
table discussions he sponsored and moderated were a mixed lot—
mathematicians and physicians as well as preachers, lawyers, and
philosophers. Mandeville was reputed to be a physician as well as a
knight-traveler. And of course Chaucer the poet and professional
administrator wrote a learned treatise on the astrolabe (giving acknowl-
edgment to two Oxford scholars). This diversity of new explorations,
especially in the sciences, caused by the developing sense that a single,
whole explanation of creation was no longer attainable and by a
larger set of social uncertainties, had a number of effects on the new
studies and students. Much of the scientific study (aside from the
mechanical inventions that experimentation produced) was purely
theoretical, speculative, and often conducive to critical self-question-
ing. In other words, it was tainted with *curiositas*, and self-doubt was
a normal effect; any rigid moralist could quickly ascertain that, and
many did. According to Marshall Clagett, Nicole Oresme, the famous
French theoretician of Chaucer's generation, had a habit of deprecat-
ing his own arguments about physical theory and cosmography with
"a rather 'probabilistic' tone" of self-doubt, and Clagett believes

Oresme "was affected by the probabilistic and skeptical currents that swept through various phases of natural philosophy in the fourteenth century." Oresme in fact said of his scientific conjectures, "I indeed know nothing except that I know that I know nothing."[13] (Mandeville, perhaps less learned or maybe just more audacious, shows no doubt about the *possibility* of sailing around the earth, only an awareness that the time and matériel required might make it impractical.) Doubt and continuous questioning, however, usually feed one another, and the same endless curiosity that the new skepticism at first induced kept the questioning alive. Joseph R. Strayer, writing of the promise of the fourteenth century, argues that the obvious pessimism and instability of the age should not blind us to the important advances in technology, science, and political organization that Western Europeans made. "It was the existence of alternative explanations and the controversies which they caused which made science an intellectually rewarding study."[14] Curiosity is epidemic and endless.

Earlier the question was posed—Why does this attitude toward travel and curiosity arise so noticeably in the fourteenth century?—and perhaps enough has been said now to suggest why. The other, related question, whose resolution I hope will grow inferentially from my entire study, is whether curiosity has anything at all to do with the origins of modern humanism. If I am right in linking certain aspects of fourteenth-century thought and scientific endeavor with curiosity—seen by these same thinkers as a temptation but also as a conscionable impulse for investigation—then indeed the books by de Bury, Mandeville, and Chaucer and the intellectual environments they flourished in are signs of an incipient humanism.

To be sure, the continuing debate over the meanings of the term has been as fierce and intricate as debates about, for example, what allegory is and when the Renaissance "began." I have no elaborate new theory to propound, but I think three scholars, R. W. Southern, Beryl Smalley, and Paul Oskar Kristeller, have provided useful definitions of the term that characterize a budding humanism in fourteenth-century England. Their evidence, assumptions, and emphases differ from one another, but they also differ strikingly from those customarily offered by most historians. Roberto Weiss, for instance, believes the first real humanists were mostly Italians, scholars "who studied the writings of ancient authors without fear of supernatural anticiceronian warnings, searched for manuscripts of lost or rare classical texts, celebrated the works of classical writers, and attempted to learn Greek and write like the ancient authors of Rome."[15] This one widely shared definition of humanism—which would appear to exclude from the ranks Chaucer, de Bury, Mandeville, and even much of Petrarch—leads Weiss to diagnose fourteenth-century English humanism as a creature only partly alive, displaying "unmistakable symptoms of stagnation."[16] I am ultimately unpersuaded by the point of view of scholars like Weiss or even Peter Burke (whose criteria for judgment in *The Renaissance Sense of the Past*—the sense of anachronism, awareness of evidence, and interest in causation—ought to be applied to fourteenth-century English thought). Looking backward in time and northward over their shoulders toward England, they find the Middle Ages lacking in the ingredients of humanism they have already discovered elsewhere at a later time. Weiss maintains this posture in a later study, in which, indeed, he *is* generally correct in what he says about medieval antiquaries' motives:

> What led to the collection of antique objects during the Middle Ages was not their antiquity but their appeal to the eye or their rare or unusual materials, or simply because they were different, or even in some cases because they were thought to be endowed with magical powers. The antiques preserved in the treasuries of cathedrals were kept there because their materials or their craftmanship were considered precious, not because they were ancient.[17]

Nevertheless, even though the Italian-centered views are more moderated here than in his earlier *Humanism in England in the Fifteenth Century*, this historian's bias remains cisalpine and his focus the quattrocento.

R. W. Southern, in *Medieval Humanism*, presents a fresh and surely provocative approach to the whole question. He posits the succession of two forms of humanism, the earlier one "scientific," the later one "literary." "Scientific humanism" embraces, in part, that mélange of speculative scientific thought I have already described, although Southern sees it beginning in the twelfth century and ending in the early fourteenth and adds as its identifying features a belief in the dignity of nature and human nature and a reasoned trust in nature as an orderly, intelligible system. Southern finally thinks that literary humanism, what most Renaissance scholars mean when they talk of Humanism, is actually a fifteenth-century misunderstanding of scientific humanism.

> It was the product of disillusion with the great projects of the recent past. When the hope of universal order faded, the cultivation of sensibility and personal virtue, and the nostalgic vision of an ancient utopia revealed in classical literature, remained as the chief supports of humane values. Instead of the confident and progressive humanism of the central Middle Ages, the new humanism retreated into the individual and the past; it saw the aristocracy rather than the clergy as the guardians of culture; it sought inspiration in literature rather than theology and science; its ideal was a group of friends rather than a universal system; and the nobility of man was expressed in his struggle with an unintelligible world rather than in his capacity to know all things. When this happened the humanism of the central Middle Ages came to be mistaken for formalism and hostility to human experience.[18]

The curiosity of fourteenth-century thinkers that Leff, Knowles, Oberman, Strayer, and others have aided me in summarizing seems closely allied with the notion of scientific humanism. Leff, independently, has come to the same conclusion as Southern in his major study, *Paris and Oxford Universities in the Thirteenth and Fourteenth Centuries*. He believes the intellectual ferment in England, especially at Oxford, which was rich in scientific efforts throughout the fourteenth century, became impoverished "by the revival of literary humanism, which was once believed to have rescued culture from the barbarism of the Middle Ages. Whatever else the Renaissance may have achieved, it also led to the decline of medieval science and speculation and a hiatus in scientific and philosophical thought until the seventeenth century."[19] But other interpretations by other scholars make one ask whether the distinction between scientific and literary humanism is not a false, or at least an unnecessarily rigid, one. Beryl Smalley, examining different territory, has made a case for the existence of what she calls "proto-humanism" among a circle of fourteenth-century English clerics and laymen, many of whom were directly connected with de Bury—Thomas Waleys, John Ridevall, Robert Holcot, Nicholas Trivet, and others, whose chief writings spanned a period beginning about 1320 (when Southern's "scientific humanism" ought to have ended) and tapering off in the 1350s.[20] Her classicizing friars seem more "literary" than "scientific" in their aims and methods. Kristeller, working from yet different premises, has argued that the humanism of the early Italian Renaissance had three direct medieval antecedents: the *ars dictaminis* tradition, the study of grammar and poetry, and Byzantine Greek learning. Kristeller recommends that scholars thoroughly analyze these elements and the several marks of Renaissance humanism he exactingly defines.[21] I myself am convinced (and will try to demonstrate later) that de Bury, for one, reflects not only these antecedents but perhaps even the full-blown characteristics of such humanism. Only continued research into the influence of this remarkable group of thinkers and a testing of Southern's, Smalley's, and Kristeller's arguments will firmly establish new assumptions and criteria necessary for a revaluation of northern medieval humanism.

Yet it is clear that these theories cannot be casually blended together or simply borrowed conveniently and piecemeal to underpin claims that, for instance, Mandeville, de Bury, and Chaucer were humanists. I am not now prepared to make any such absolute claim; nor am I sure the vexing problem of the origins of "humanism," however it is defined, ever can be satisfactorily resolved. But the theories and beliefs I have singled out do underscore the eclectic and often hopelessly tangled nature of the intellectual traditions and new attitudes which affected these three writers. The curiosity that infects their works is there for many reasons; it *is* a phenomenon which needs explanation. Its presence raises questions that might be unnecessary if the three had lived a century later (or in another country); and the implications of this new urge to explore old books, remote parts of the earth, and a fellow-pilgrim's world seem to warrant attention to philosophical and scientific shifts of thought in and out of England in the fourteenth century. So I have chosen to anticipate these implications here instead of gathering them up at the end of this book because, insofar as they bear on assumptions I hold, they ought to precede my argument.

Although by the fourteenth century *curiositas* had overwhelmed pilgrimage, the institution did not die with the Middle Ages. Christians still journey to Lourdes, Fátima, and Our Lady of Guadalupe (now with or without Saint Christopher's guidance) to beseech the Virgin. They still worship in awe at Bethlehem and Jerusalem; and in this Holy Year 1975 pilgrims worldwide flock to Rome. Some visit Canterbury (more as tourists than pilgrims, for the shrine is gone). Just as the sin of *curiositas* can be found listed today in Father McGuire's *Baltimore Catechism*, pilgrimage has for many pious Christians retained the devotional meaning it had for Chaucer's Knight and Parson. However, as the distinctly medieval form of travel which ideally had a religious focus and symbolic value, and which tolerated the dangers of the traversed world because they justified the rewards of the goal, in short, as an acceptable way for Christians to go usefully through the world without succumbing to it, pilgrimage survived in importance only until other forms of travel geared to different motives superseded it. The traders who followed Polo's route into China, the explorers who scoured the oceans of the New World, and that modern figure, the tourist, were to later ages what the pilgrim had been to his.

The wave of complaints against pilgrimage in the late Middle Ages proved that the custom was decaying from abuse, but it also reflected human discovery of another world full of mysteries and riches at least more visible than those of Celestial Jerusalem, more novel than those of saints' shrines. Pilgrims outlived the Middle Ages and curiosity remained a vice beyond the Renaissance—but wayfarers in different dress now clogged the roads, and if their busyness seemed curious it was curious largely in the modern sense of the word. The remark made by an Italian pilgrim going to Jerusalem in 1502—". . . yearning after new things as a thirsty man doth for fresh water, I entered the Nile and arrived at Cairo"—is typical of this changing outlook on the world in the later Middle Ages. Yet the beginnings of that new perspective are already evident to Richard de Bury, Chaucer's pilgrims, and John Mandeville. Were I to choose a fourth figure to match these, out of the dozens to pick from I would choose an obscure but fascinating fourteenth-century Italian named Giovanni Dondi dell' Orologio, a friend of Petrarch's and, perhaps like the author of the *Travels*, a physician. In the spring of 1375, as an old man, Dondi made a journey, which he called a pilgrimage, south through Italy to Rome. Mandeville's *Travels* had already begun to captivate readers throughout Europe, and Chaucer in between trips to Italy was probably still pondering the idea for his own pilgrimage fiction. Dondi left a brief account of his journey (the manuscript is yet unedited), and I rely on Roberto Weiss for a summary of it. Weiss calls him an antiquarian; he is one, but he is more than that:

Already on the journey out he had not failed to note the more striking Roman ruins on his way. At Rimini he was impressed by the bridge built by Tiberius over the Marecchia and took good care to jot down the first and last words of one of its inscriptions. The arch of Augustus in the same town also met with his approval. At Cagli he did not fail to notice the remains of a Roman bridge, while near Spello he observed the 'Ruine duarum arenarum parvarum in modum Colixei'. The enthusiasm of Dondi was, however, bound to reach its highest peaks in Rome. Here he took copious archaeological notes, which he later shaped together and copied into the volume where he had assembled pieces by other humanists, as well as writings of his own. The result was not, as one might have hoped, an antiquarian itinerary of the town, but rather an account of those monuments which had caught his eye. . . . It is obvious that in Dondi the pilgrim made way entirely for the antiquarian, so that one may well wonder how much time he dedicated while in Rome to the visiting of churches and to pious practices, and how much to investigating what was left of the pagan city. [22]

What moved this pilgrim was *curiositas*. In fact he followed his friend Petrarch's advice perfectly. In an itinerary composed in 1358 for some other friends making a Holy Land pilgrimage, Petrarch told the travelers to see Italy first (especially Giotto's frescoes in Naples) and to look for antiquities as well as relics.[23] All these fourteenth-century travelers—Dondi, Petrarch, Petrarch's English acquaintance de Bury, Mandeville, and the Canterbury pilgrims—discovered new worlds in the past and beyond familiar horizons. These curious pilgrims had discovered our world.

CHAPTER II. *CURIOSITAS*

Let wise men seek out and study the height of the sky, the breadth of the earth, and the depth of the sea. Let them dispute about each, let them examine all, let them learn and teach as long as they want. What do they have for their efforts but toil, sorrow, and vexation of the spirit? . . . "God made man right, but he has entangled himself in an infinity of questions."—Innocent III, De miseria humanae conditionis

In our modern lexicon the words "curious" and "curiosity" have positive or at least morally neutral meanings. If someone says an idea or an object is curious, the worst he may be suggesting is that it is unexpected, strange, or perhaps in need of fuller explanation. We almost universally applaud curiosity, identifying it with imagination and with speedy development in children. And scholarship, of course, demands it. Our culture has freed (some few would say deprived) us of the evil and frightening connotations curiosity held for most Christians through the seventeenth century. A popular recent book titled *The Ulysses Factor: The Exploring Instinct in Man* excitedly claims that mankind has survived because of our individual and collective curiosity. Medievals might have been uneasy reading that

> the Ulysses type is interested in everything. The factor may promote intense concentration in action, and the preparation for action, for the purpose in hand, but the next purpose may be something quite different. It will always be related to the need to *know*, but it may be knowledge in a variety of fields. . . . The Ulysses factor is a complex of impulses in an individual prompting him to seek firsthand physical experience of something hitherto unknown (to him) that has aroused his curiosity.[1]

However, certain late Greek and Latin writers, followed by a vigorous and uninterrupted stream of Christian thinkers in the Middle Ages and the Renaissance, looked on the human impulse to know with less enthusiasm and much more anxiety. A number of scholars have thoroughly examined the classical and Christian attitudes towards curiosity—Don Cameron Allen, George Boas, G. K. Hunter, Eugene F. Rice, Jr., and Howard Schultz, among others.[2] Their researches into the varied sources for medieval views of the temptation of *curiositas* have underscored the relevance of Biblical comments on the uses of learning;[3] Christian moralizations of pagan myths about Prometheus, Pandora, Icarus, and Odysseus;[4] and especially the medievals' selective dependence on pre-Christian ethical pronouncements concerning the value and vanity of human knowledge. Pre-Christian philosophers were conscious of the potential good as well as potential evil involved in the human desire to know, and they made a distinction between *bona curiositas* and *mala curiositas*. The Greek moralist Plutarch, for instance, writing in the first century A.D., typifies the pagan attitude toward curiosity. If it leads a man to inquire into a neighbor's business, to be hungry for hearing and repeating news, tales, gossip, and novelties, to be ever searching out the ugly and the abnormal, then the impulse is misguided: it is *mala curiositas*. "What escape is there, then, from this vice?" he asks. The remedy is both self-knowledge and a resolve to channel that curiosity toward learning and science; study instead the phases of the moon, the workings of the sun, says Plutarch. Curiosity about people's private affairs is reprehensible; curiosity about the world should be encouraged.[5]

But from the beginning of the Christian era, moralists took a sharply different stance toward worldly learning and the human desire to learn. As Eugene Rice explains it, wisdom no longer was calmly seen as a naturally acquired human virtue but rather as an attribute of the Christian God in which men could participate only partially through grace. Christ was the new wisdom—*sapientia*—and, until the Renaissance again secularized wisdom, dissociating it from Christian revelation, orthodox medieval thinkers divided knowledge into two spheres—*sapientia*, knowledge of things divine, the attainment of God, the goal Christians must strive for (although only in eternity would they perfectly know it)—and *scientia*, human knowledge, speculative and faulty, inferior to *sapientia*.[6] The quest for *scientia*, now a subordinate and suspect study, was no longer seen as an innocent urge; and of course any investigation of the supernatural, *sapientia*, could ensnare one in the thickets of heresy. *Scientia*, it was agreed, might in theory aid one in attaining *sapientia*, but the dangers were too great and the chances of success too slight; curiosity must be repressed. Moreover, since the Edenic wish to know evil as well as good was the archetypal sin, it is no wonder Christian thinkers regarded sinful man's pursuit of *scientia* as a flirtation with *curiositas*.[7] The pursuit of knowledge itself was rarely called *curiositas*, but medievals knew from reading Peter Lombard's influential *Sententiae* that in pursuing knowledge man encountered along the way "plurimum supervacuae vanitatis et noxiae curiositatis."[8] Medieval thought is in one sense the history of attempts to harmonize *scientia* with *sapientia*, but despite various strong efforts made during the twelfth century and the marvelous scholastic syntheses, the prevailing orthodox point of view endured throughout the Middle Ages. When medieval moralists, philosophers, and scientists spoke of *curiositas*, they commonly had in mind a temptation, a vice, a sin, characterized by a fastidious, excessive, morally diverting interest in things and people.

Only after the Middle Ages, when, as Don Cameron Allen once said, God came to be seen as "a sort of director of research,"[9] did *curiositas* lose some of the terrifying connotations so alarming to the medievals. Certainly, for Renaissance thinkers no less than for their medieval predecessors, there was something mercurial and amorphous about the very nature of curiosity that precluded exact, absolute definitions of it; and good Christians were still reminded that energy expended on any investigation unessential to their salvation was sinful curiosity. Nevertheless, post-medieval Christians did revive the ancient separation between *bona* and *mala curiositas* that medieval moralists had done away with. The early-sixteenth-century humanist, Vives, believed curiosity was a laudable urge; it led men to make useful discoveries and to know the pleasure that comes from the conquest of ignorance. And, indeed, he felt that curious, serendipitous men would find their pleasure "constantly increasing, since some things seemed to follow from the finding of others, just as when the beginning of a thread is secured, it is found to be connected with another set of things quite different from those which were being examined." Of course, Vives, like Milton, admitted that curiosity misdirected by pride was wrong, but he and other Renaissance writers generally extolled curiosity for the rewards it brought man, especially the benefits of scientific discoveries.[10] The views of classical writers like Plutarch were again in circulation (Queen Elizabeth, for one, translated Plutarch's essay on curiosity into English). And the popular seventeenth-century Anglican divine, Jeremy Taylor, while reiterating the importance of self-knowledge, stressed the classical and unmedieval definition of curiosity, advising men not to be meddlesome and newsmongering and suggesting that they could better "scratch the itch of knowing" by studying terrestrial and heavenly phenomena.[11]

Since, as far as I can tell, medieval commentaries on the curiosity associated with pilgrimage never mention beneficent curiosity, only the malevolent destructive kind, it is not essential to my argument to sketch in any greater detail pagan and Renaissance opinions about *bona* and *mala curiositas*. Nor is it really necessary to characterize exhaustively the medieval view of *curiositas*. Certain dominant themes are repeated in all medieval treatments of the vice, and in truth, more pursuits than pilgrimage were thought curious. But three issues in particular require attention, inasmuch as they relate to the opposition between curiosity and the proper motives for pilgrimage. First was the belief that *curiositas* is a morally useless, dangerous diversion for wayfaring Christians. Moreover, it was seen as a vice that feeds on the senses (mainly sight) and affects one's entire intellectual outlook. Finally—and this seems most important for our understanding of the decline of pilgrimage—moralists thought *curiositas* signified a wandering, errant, and unstable frame of mind and was thus best exemplified in metaphors of motion and in the act of travel. And I believe we can discover the principal outlines of these features in orthodox medieval opinion by closely examining the works of a few representative spokesmen—chiefly Augustine's *Confessions*, Bernard of Clairvaux's *Steps of Humility*, and Thomas Aquinas's *Summa Theologica*.

In Book X of the *Confessions*, Augustine classifies his own sins according to the influential triad formulated by Saint John: *concupiscentia carnis, concupiscentia oculorum,* and *superbia vitae*. Augustine analyzes the temptations of the flesh by listing his failings in each of the five senses, and his sorrow for sins of the sense of sight moves him naturally into a discussion of the next major temptation, lust of the eyes. This temptation he calls *curiositas*, the "desire—cloaked under the name of knowledge and science—not for fleshly enjoyment, but for gaining personal experience through the flesh."[12] It is more complicated than lust of the flesh and thus more dangerous, because it begins as an appetite of the body, specifically of the eye, but culminates as an affliction of the mind. However, all the bodily senses encourage curious inquiry, not just the eye; as Augustine accurately observes, "we not only say 'See how it lights up' which the eyes alone can perceive, but also: 'See how it sounds; see how it smells; see how it tastes; see how hard it is.'"[13] Although lust of the eyes and lust of the flesh share the weakness of the senses, the flesh gives in to sin from motives of pleasure, but the curious eye and mind take delight in any experience, pleasurable or not.[14] The experience a *curiosus* seeks out and enjoys for its own sake serves no useful purpose, is relished to excess, and is irrelevant to moral growth and salvation.

There are two aspects of Augustine's analysis that deserve special emphasis. First of all, he has tried to distinguish two separate phases of curiosity. Man may be guilty of *curiositas* in simply looking around him at the things of creation. But it is worse to keep on looking, relishing the sight, thus becoming distracted from serious concerns by (to use Augustine's examples) staring dazedly at a lizard catching flies or a spider weaving a web. Here then is the major difference between Christian and pagan attitudes toward the vice: curiosity about the world of nature is a worthless endeavor; it is no less dangerous than curiosity about other people. Augustine's distinction between man's visual preoccupation with realia and the contingent idle speculation about what the eyes see resembles the traditional first two stages of Eve's sin—suggestion and delectation (later, in XIII, 21, Augustine compares curiosity to the poison of serpents); and once curiosity entraps a man, the vice, by its very nature, pushes its victim deeper into curious inquiry. The resemblance between these two phases and the stages of original sin further explains why the urge to scrutinize nature can be more treacherous for the Christian than the more obvious lusts of the flesh. For *curiositas* is subtler than simple suggestion, more difficult to detect and restrain, and it leads with insidious smoothness to pride.[15] Indeed, curiosity can shade so imperceptibly into pride in learning or pride in ability (just as it derives so naturally from lust of the flesh) that as a distinguishable element in the three-

part psychological process of sin or in other medieval schemata of
vices, it tended to get blurred with adjacent vices.

What Augustine also stresses is the intrinsic uselessness of curiosity.
To dwell at length on the movements of an insect is a moral waste of
time. Augustine mentions other frivolous distractions, all of them exercises that medievals continued to see as symptoms of curiosity: telling and listening to foolish tales, watching games, attending theatrical
performances (I, 10), and pursuing studies that are by nature fruitless
for salvation (sortilege, astrology, necromancy, sorcery—practices also
censurable on grounds of sacrilege).[16] In the same vein, in fact, Tertullian had condemned heresy as a result of the constant human wish to
hear speculations *nova* and *curiosa*, and he cited Paul's warning: the
people, "having itching ears, will heap up to themselves teachers according to their own lusts, and they will turn away their hearing from
the truth and turn aside rather to fables" (2 Timothy 4:3-4).[17] No
occupation or pursuit is justifiable unless it assists in the perfection
of morals. Because the value of all human activity depends on its
spiritual relevance, and because our vision should be inward and not
outward, Augustine is saddened to see that men go out "to admire
the mountains' peaks, giant waves in the sea, the broad courses of
rivers, the vast sweep of the ocean, and the circuits of the stars—and
they leave themselves behind" (X, 8). *Curiositas* diverts man's spiritual sight from otherworldly goals and distracts him with the spectacle
of worldly landscapes from contemplation of self. This was exactly
why Gregory the Great saw *curiositas* as a grave fault: men seeking to
gain knowledge of the world around them end up ignorant of themselves.[18]

Bernard of Clairvaux's expositions on *curiositas* probably should
be seen chiefly as part of the longstanding monastic outlook on learning and the uses of the created world, although the implications of
his views were as applicable to all Christians. Unlike Augustine's more
personal meditations on the many evils of curiosity, Bernard's warnings are addressed to orders of monks whom Benedict had lectured
long before on the temptations lurking within and without the
cloister walls. After periods of decay and reform, the monastic en-
closure of the twelfth century was still thought to be as much a refuge
from the outside world as it had been in Augustine's day. Monks could

still look upon the monastery as a model of paradise,[19] and the monastery continued to rest its foundations on the cardinal principle of *stabilitas*, a notion which epitomized that posture of order and strong government which the Benedictine Rule urged as a defense against a spiritually disordered outer world.[20] Like Benedict, Bernard repeatedly spoke of any infringement of this monastic rule as errancy. Symbolic of the instability of mind and body was that intolerable band of monks Benedict had labeled "gyrovagi," who wandered forever from country to country, living always outside the monastery, never settling in one place, "slaves to their own wills and to the enticements of gluttony."[21] Langland used this wandering cleric as a paradigm for curiosity in *Piers Plowman*; for him, for Bernard, and for many others these wanderers were virulent figures, since their waywardness and its concomitants infected other social ranks.

The world outside that the "gyrovagi" explored offered temptations enough, but the threats of disorder and waywardness within the monastery could be equally worrisome. As a monastic vice, *curiositas* at an early date had been fitted into the system of seven deadly sins by Cassian, Gregory, and other theologians and had been defined as an offshoot of sloth. Lazy hands and an idle mind left the monk exposed to other offenses—useless activity, aimless mental meandering, and speculation on matters unrelated to the perfection of religious life.[22] Yet by the twelfth century the amassed responsibilities of monasticism, including book-making, building up libraries, managing schools, maintaining communication with far-flung monastic centers, erecting cathedrals, and even advising popes (a favorite pursuit of Bernard's, in fact), had seriously weakened adherence to the root principle of *stabilitas* and had prompted renewed concern about the dangers of *curiositas*.[23] Bernard's obvious anxiety about the temptation reflects these new problematical functions of the monk.

In his *Steps of Humility*[24] Bernard repeats from the Benedictine Rule the twelve steps that the monk must climb to reach the knowledge of Truth—but in explaining these steps he seems to show keener interest in their counterparts, the twelve steps towards pride. *Curiositas* is the critical first step in the descent toward pride, and I think it is significant that Bernard devotes more space and polemic to it than to any of the other eleven stages. The conquest of curiosity is the last step before bliss, and surrender to it is the first step on the way to perdition. For Bernard, curiosity was, in Gilson's words, "the very

negation of Cistercian ascesis."[25] Bernard personifies curiosity with
the portrait of a monk who wanders with inquisitive eyes, his head
cocked expectantly and his ears perked up wherever he goes. To cure
this wandering of the eyes, which is an outward manifestation of inner
mental wandering, the monk must, as Benedict had already said, keep
"head bent and eyes fixed on the ground."[26] He may raise his eyes
only to ask help or offer it.

It is through the eyes, then, that the world and sin enter the mind,
and Bernard points to three infamous sinners whose eyes brought
about their fall. Women, not unexpectedly, provide the best monastic
exempla. Dinah sinned through curiosity in going out to see the
women of the region, and while out wandering she was raped (Genesis 34); as Bernard says to her, "Tu curiose spectas, sed curiosius
spectaris."[27] Eve's curiosity was much deadlier than Dinah's. God
gave her all necessary knowledge, but unsatisfied with knowing good
alone, she sought out the tree of the knowledge of good *and* evil.
Bernard (unlike Milton) declares that for Eve and the rest of us no
wisdom can be gained from knowing evil in addition to good—rather,
"sapere non est, sed desipere."[28] (Honorius of Autun described the
effects of Eve's error in slightly different terms, suggesting that before
original sin man knew good by experience and evil through knowledge, and afterward he knew evil by experience and good through
knowledge.)[29] Curiosity, in other words, doomed our first parents to
life in a world where the manifold temptations to all the senses could
only reinforce fallen man's inclination to curious inquiry. Once Eve
saw the apple of sin and relished the sight of it, it was easy for the
serpent to sharpen her desire and accomplish his task. Historically
prior to both these inquisitive women was Lucifer, Bernard's last
example. Unhappy with his full wisdom, he wandered far, "curiosius
inquirendo, irreverentius pervadendo,"[30] aspiring beyond and above
divinely appointed limits, upsetting the stability of heaven; finally
he assaulted God Himself and fell, damned forever to roam in exile
through the orbits between earth and heaven. Like the sins of Dinah
and of Eve, Lucifer's transgression began with the eyes; in succession,
he first curiously looked around, next unlawfully coveted, and then
proudly and fatally aspired.

Bernard intended these three curious sinners to be severe reminders
to the inquisitive monk of his own possible temptations and consequent
violation of monastic *stabilitas*. But each of the three figures revealed

different characteristics of the *curiosus*. Like Dinah, men and women could be guilty of curiosity not only by wandering about to visit neighbors and see the surroundings but also by wishing, like the Wife of Bath, to *be seen*. Eve's mistaken yearning for the knowledge of evil as well as good would remind Bernard's learned colleagues how varied and subtle were the risks of intellectual speculation; no doubt Bernard thought the daring conjectural approach to theology taken by his adversary Abelard in the *Sic et Non* was dangerously curious. And Lucifer's soaring curiosity at once reiterated this lesson and served to caution the worst of the *curiosi*, who explored much darker kinds of knowledge like the occult or the assortment of new Arabic-based studies.

Elsewhere in his writings Bernard expanded these remarks on *curiositas* and, as Augustine had done, underlined the double nature of the sin—lust of the eyes and intellectual lust—by dealing separately with each aspect. Thus, in a sermon on the Canticles, he described *curiositas* as one of three kinds of motivation found in those who make learning a livelihood. Those who seek knowledge merely from a desire to know ("ut sciant") offend through *curiositas*. That is sin enough, but those who seek knowledge in order to be known ("ut sciantur ipsi") sin further through *vanitas*. And even worse, there are those who acquire knowledge to sell it ("ut scientiam suam vendant").[31] Boastfulness and desire for financial gain are developed and more monstrous forms of a basic curiosity. Chaucer's Franklin, if not Chaucer himself, seems piously angered at the learned magicians of Orléans who charges squires like Aurelius dearly for their curious skills.

Plain curiosity of sight is the subject of Bernard's well-known epistle addressed to his fellow abbot, William of St. Thierry.[32] Bernard was enraged by the presence in the monastic cloister itself of the fantastic, distracting multitude of misshapen beasts and men, that bestiary of grotesques we associate with later medieval church art. These creatures, not so different from the monstrosities curious Mandeville will eagerly record on his Eastern journeys, require Bernard's exorcism:

> To what purpose are those unclean apes, those fierce lions, those monstrous centaurs, those half-men, those striped tigers, those fighting knights, those hunters winding their horns? Many bodies are there seen under one head, or again, many heads to a single body. Here is a four-footed beast with a serpent's

tail; there, a fish with a beast's head. Here again the forepart of a horse trails half a goat behind it, or a horned beast bears the hinder quarters of a horse. In short, so many and so marvellous are the varieties of divers shapes on every hand, that we are more tempted to read in the marble than in our books, and to spend the whole day in wondering at these things rather than in meditating the law of God. [33]

He summarily dismisses this unreligious ornamentation with "O vanitas vanitatum" and concludes: "De sumptibus egenorum servitur oculis divitum. Inveniunt curiosi quo delectentur, et non inveniunt miseri quo sustententur."[34] Because the monk here at prayer ignores his missal to "read" the sculpture, he risks the temptation of curiosity simply by coming into the cloister. Bernard's condemnation of the curiously wrought imagery also falls on the artists who created it, their superiors who permitted it, and the expense wasted on such useless decoration. Peter Cantor would upbraid designers and builders for the "superfluitatem et curiositatem vestium, ciborum et aedificiorum,"[35] and Bernard in another work said that too many ecclesiastical buildings were constructed "inquieta curiositate."[36] For anyone following the strict Bernardine point of view on these matters, it was never difficult to move from a condemnation of religious art as superfluous and harmful to monastic perfection to a broader attack against secular art as a horrifying moral distraction for all worshippers.[37] But it is sufficient here to stress that Bernard charged both fanciful church artisans and certain variously motivated scholars with *curiositas*. And his consistent emphasis on the separability of the two aspects of the vice—curiosity of the eye and of the mind—expressed with his typical verve and conservatism, had, like much that he wrote, a lasting influence on later medieval thinkers.[38] Augustine's fundamental analysis of the varying evils of curiosity underlay much of Bernard's own description of the vice; together with Augustine's admonitions, Bernard's view of the opposition between *curiositas* and *stabilitas* and his selection of Eve and Lucifer as types of curiosity established for succeeding centuries the main contours of this bothersome Christian problem. And in the century after Bernard, it is, as one might expect, Aquinas who synthesizes all earlier discussions of *curiositas*.

Whereas Augustine considered *curiositas* in its relation to lust of the eyes, and Bernard (though aware of its connection with the three temptations) placed it in a twelve-step series of monastic failings, Aquinas focused on it as the vice opposed to *studiositas*, a virtue descended from temperance. The Thomistic contrast of curiosity with this cardinal virtue was not novel, for *curiositas* had always been perceived as excess; besides, Aquinas ultimately saw all of the seven deadly sins as in one way or another offenses against temperance.

His comments on the vice show his reliance on the established views enunciated by previous moralists. Thus, he notes that lust of the eyes is spiritual concupiscence (as distinct from natural concupiscence or lust of the flesh). Echoing both Augustine and Bernard, Aquinas says this phrase can refer to the operations of the faculty of sight as well as to the things seen. (Like Augustine, he treats "sight" as synecdoche for all sense perception.)[39] He mentions Bernard's inclusion of curiosity in the twelve degrees of pride,[40] and he cites the opinion of Isidore and Gregory who, thinking along the lines Bernard followed, subordinated *curiositas* (with restlessness of the body, loquacity, and *instabilitas*) to sloth as a form of mental wandering (*evagatio mentis*).[41]

When he takes up the problem of curiosity directly,[42] Aquinas first admits that just as man's desires pursue the bodily pleasures of sex and food, so his soul has a natural yearning for knowledge, and here he quotes the opening line of Aristotle's *Metaphysics*: "All men naturally desire knowledge." Augustine and Bernard of course had recognized the normality of the desire to know and recommended self-control and obedience to *stabilitas* for those tempted. Aquinas also thought the desire must be checked by moderation, and for him *studiositas* (scholarly diligence tempered by spiritual vigilance) provided that check. He quotes Cicero to the effect that the desire for knowledge is one of the four movements of the mind and body requiring moderation, the other three being the movement of the mind toward excellence, bodily movements, and the desire for outward show (in dress, for example). The desire for display, if excessive, clearly would be a sign of *curiositas*.[43] Like thinkers before him, Aquinas then formally separates the two basic kinds of curiosity: desire for intellective knowledge and desire for sensitive knowledge. Unless ruled by temperate studiousness, the pursuit of intellective knowledge, as Paul said, tends to puff men up (1 Corinthians 8:1). More specifically, according to Aquinas, the search for knowledge is sinful if the knowledge desired has any attendant evil (as, for instance, when one studies only to take pride in the knowledge gained) or if the appetite for study is excessive. Such excess occurs whenever a less profitable study distracts a man from more profitable work; when he studies a subject that is itself illicit, like divination or magic; when he seeks knowledge of creatures without directing that knowledge to its ultimate end, God; or when he tries to study anything that lies beyond human understanding.

A man also may be culpable in acquiring knowledge through his senses—mainly the eye and ear. This kind of curiosity, as Augustine first pointed out, is as fearful a sin as intellectual inquiry. Taking private pleasure in observing nature can have wider repercussions; it leads to the itch for sightseeing (which many moralists knew could, in turn, cause more sins of the flesh) and searching out and gossiping about a neighbor's faults. *Curiositas* is a pestilence, wrote Hugh of St. Victor, which manifests itself in backbiting, anger, and the habit of faulting other men.[44] Josef Peiper has called this effect of *curiositas* "the sign of complete rootlessness"[45]—an effect which, if evidenced in certain religious, would signal the violation of *stabilitas*. Aquinas invokes Bede's counsels against this uncharitable, antisocial consequence of curiosity, and other moralists uttered similar warnings.[46] Chaucer's tale-telling pilgrims, in the aggregate, betray their curiosity through an inability to avoid these antisocial, un-Christian effects of the vice.

Aquinas's discussion of *curiositas* is important not because what he said added much to existing ideas but because it provides a convenient restatement and condensation of inherited, orthodox opinion on the subject. Moreover, his juxtaposition of different spheres of human operation (the spiritual and natural, intellective and sensitive) reflects the continuing tendency to bisect *cusiositas* into vagrant scrutinizing by the senses and intellectual wandering. Yet that balancing of the two concerns also demonstrates the ultimate dependence of each phase on the other. Sight, after all, naturally leads to intellection; the mind feeds on what the eyes see. But above all, Aquinas's contrast of curiosity with temperance (specifically, studiousness) hints at some of the larger perspectives that other moralists adopted in their views of just what intemperate affairs could be termed curious. Some examples of these wider perspectives are worth noticing.

Aspects of moral and epistemological problems, for instance, larger

than those properly associated with *curiositas* often were treated as
signs or outgrowths of the vice. Thus, medieval proponents of anti-
intellectualism, convinced of the impossible gulf between *sapientia*
and *scientia*, abhorred "intellective" curiosity because of the implication that the human mind could acquire any useful knowledge. The
Bible was replete with caveats about shunning worldly knowledge and
accepting only the wisdom dispensed by God. Gregory the Great,
Anselm, and others had reminded all men, especially the learned, that
they ought to become as little children and remember that Christ
himself chose simple, ignorant fishermen as followers.[47] (This argument, however, was vulnerable. Richard de Bury could cite as his
authority for the glory of writing and making books the fact that
Christ inscribed words in the dust; and a fourteenth-century preacher
inverted the idea, defining learned doctors as fishermen of souls.)[48]
Of course, *scientia inflat*, yet there was always a problem in deciding
exactly what kinds of knowledge were helpful to one's spiritual
betterment. But the point here is that while these attacks on *scientia*
occasionally got superimposed on arguments used to condemn *curiositas*, the two attitudes were fundamentally unalike. *Curiositas* connoted many varieties of morally unwarranted and *excessive* investigation—which, as Aquinas said, *studiositas* could thwart—but seldom
did anyone preach against the vice on the radical assumption that all
human impulses to know were in themselves tainted with evil. Medieval (and modern) commentators on *curiositas* have at times confused
it with anti-intellectualism, understandably so, perhaps, since the line
between the desire to learn and the inherent worth of human learning is sometimes hard to find.

Aquinas's compendium of views on *curiositas* also suggests how
some medieval writers could flex definitions of the vice enough to
make it cover all sorts of human endeavor. Scholars who studied
pagan or secular literature often were threatened with the stigma of
curiositas; there were as many warnings from critics like Tertullian,
Ambrose, Aldhelm, and numerous medieval mystics about this as
there were attempts by less puritanical spokesmen to hedge such
ventures round with defensive reasons.[49] The complex question about
the utility of art itself has an ancestry involving more than is relevant
to Aquinas's concern for moderation or Bernard's indictment of
church gargoyles, but some definitions of *curiositas* were elastic

enough to permit stern moralists, early and late in the Middle Ages, to attack arts and crafts (as they attacked scientific explorations in the fourteenth century) for their curiosity. In the thirteenth and fourteenth centuries, as in Augustine's time, performing and attending plays were so characterized;[50] so too were the sculpture and adornment of saints' shrines, image worship, and extravagant late-Gothic construction. Lydgate wondered about the breach of esthetic and moral moderation when he said of contemporary masons: "What may avaylle al your ymagynynges,/Withoute proporciouns of weyghte and iust mesour?"[51] And, finally, the constant moral accentuation of the differing perils of sight and insight—that dual worry Aquinas, Bernard, and Augustine shared about the plentiful trivia of the world and consequent idle thinking on it—resulted, particularly from the twelfth century on, in the application of the term *curiositas* to luxuries like fancy dress among clergy and laity alike, richly decorated homes, and the private ownership of books.[52]

However theologically correct, Aquinas's insistence on temperance as an antidote for all these kinds of curious works and displays may seem bland in comparison with Augustine's more personal remorse over the lures of *curiositas* and Bernard's outraged responses, both of which do more to breathe life into the vice (and very possibly make it more appealing). Of course, we need to remember that in the *Summa*, Aquinas, unlike the other two moralists, treats *curiositas* as only a small part of a huge encyclopedic system. But aside from that, the lack of intensity in his commentary may have other causes. *Curiositas* was always intimately tied to *superbia*; and, as Morton W. Bloomfield has argued, by Aquinas's day pride had lost its preeminent position as the worst of the seven deadly sins, to be replaced by avarice as the sin most commonly preached against by moralists facing the new wealthy mercantile congregations.[53] With money, one can buy more books, travel more, dress more gaudily, and construct more sumptuous homes. Perhaps by the end of Aquinas's lifetime, in the late thirteenth century, *curiositas* was so noticeably ubiquitous that vigorous denunciation may have seemed futile. No one stopped denouncing curiosity in the fourteenth century, but new philosophical and practical attitudes about the visible world were gradually draining *curiositas* of its traditional meanings. Before seeing how these attitudes did change, let us briefly recapitulate the salient elements of curiosity as they were understood in de Bury's, Chaucer's, and Mandeville's lifetimes.

Looking back over their delineations of *curiositas*, we can see that Aquinas, Bernard, and Augustine placed a common emphasis on three central matters. First of all, they saw curiosity as a morally useless exercise. In a sense, all other arguments against curiosity follow from this underlying Christian rejection of thoughts, words, and deeds that contribute nothing to man's progress toward heavenly wisdom. Guided by this simple principle, a man ought to avoid any useless activity. It was never enough, then, to condemn *curiositas* as useless effort, for, more than that, it is positively harmful. Aquinas is not making a pointless distinction when he describes curiosity as a turning *away* from profitable matters and a turning *toward* harmful concerns.[54] In fact, this particular characteristic of the temptation aided some theologians in the arduous business of trying to keep it disentangled from several other branches swaying nearby on the tree of vices. Thus, William of Conches and (with more delicate precision) Richard of St. Victor suggested that curiosity and presumption were distinguishable in that the former involved possible but *useless* pursuits, the latter *useful* but impossible aims.[55]

Secondly, the three agreed that *curiositas* begins in the senses, usually the eye, and ascends to infect the mind. However often the workings of these sensible and intellectual preoccupations were analyzed in isolation, the fundamental links between curiosity of the eye and curiosity of the mind were never dissolved. Bernard suggests the connection between motions of the sense and of the intellect in arguing that Dinah sinned by going out to see and be seen and in saying that wise men sin with increasing gravity by desiring to know, to be known, and to merchandize their knowledge. Both Dinah and the scholars err in neglecting the interior life of grace for outside distractions. Aquinas had quoted Aristotle's dictum (all men by nature desire knowledge), and he surely knew the philosopher had immediately added: "An indication of this is our esteem for the senses; for apart from their use we esteem them for their own sake, and most of all the sense of sight."[56] Intellectual curiosity of even the solitary scholar, his eyes riveted only to the words on the page, stemmed from his contact with the physical book, which was a source, therefore, of both sensible and cerebral inquisitiveness. In all cases, the symptoms of disorder were similar—wandering eyes and a wandering mind; and the similar cures that were prescribed—keeping one's eyes to the ground and studying with temperance—sought both to expunge *curiositas* and to restore *stabilitas.*

As sure as these remedies for curiosity sounded, none could ever be wholly successful, just as no definition of curiosity ever fully captured the elusive nature of this basic human propensity. The endless number of medieval criticisms of the vice testifies to the ineradicability of the urge. And a peculiar frustration (rooted, it would seem, in the very nature of *curiositas*) made those who were busy describing and denouncing it unconsciously preoccupied victims of curious inquiry. Augustine, for example, no sooner finishes confessing to failings through curiosity than he begins perhaps the longest, subtlest metaphysical speculation to be found in the *Confessions*, his essay on time and eternity—in which, at one point, he fervently entreats God not to withhold secrets from him because, as he concedes, "My mind burns with eagerness to gain knowledge of this complicated problem."[57] Bernard's long tirade on profane church art is a classic example of the infection *curiositas* can induce in those who approach to denounce it. Meyer Shapiro has noticed this paradoxical quality of Bernard's invective and detected in the very syntax of his epistle a "chiasmic, antithetic pattern" similar to the very sculpture and design he was censuring.[58] Peter Lombard confessed with chagrin that his own speculations on Adam and Eve's existence before the Fall (Were they then mortal? How would she have borne children?) were brought on by a *curiositas* he could not control.[59] Jean Gerson, author of an angry treatise *contra vanam curiositatem*, was also known to be an avid collector of the smallest scraps of information about such things as the "private lives" of Saint Joseph and John the Baptist.[60] One wonders even if the curious speculation on the "wonder" and "why" of dreams that Chaucer indulged in for some fifty lines at the start of *The House of Fame*, while it certainly had rhetorical justification as *praeteritio*, might have raised the eyebrows of sterner clerics.

Ultimately, though, *curiositas* eluded suggested remedies and strict definitions not because of its amorphous nature or its potentially contagious effect on adversaries but simply because it was an ineluctable human inclination. Men have eyes, the world is oppressively visible, and the mind thinks about what puzzles it. It is possible to say of any sin—pride, especially—that a man cannot avoid giving in to it, but *curiositas*, more than other temptations, makes the world into a magnetic attraction for man. Gluttony, anger, and envy may have been traditionally more fearsome than *curiositas* in the ladder of temptations, but none of them fixed on the entire experiential universe as the object of temptation. So long as the world appears to man as a morally dangerous region, curiosity holds the gravest spiritual risks for him. It is rumination on both good and bad features of the offered fruit, idle wonder about both the pleasure and possible pain it can bring; and this world, like the apple in the Garden, has such power to defeat us that it is better not to permit even the occasion for temptation to arise. Monastic dependence on a protective *stabilitas* as the vigilant guardian against *curiositas* shows most clearly this medieval distrust of the world's lure; so, too, does the cautious scholar's trust in *studiositas*. Overmuch interest in detail and *experientia* can destroy the piety that protects one from curiosity. The world waits to be seen, as Augustine warned, and although turning one's eyes toward the ground was the Benedictine solution, the only foolproof cure for curiosity would be blindness and deafness. In his extremity Origen literally chose emasculation to forestall lusts of the flesh; medieval mystics, like the author of *The Book of Privy Counselling*, could urge brethren to blind themselves spiritually to the world that others curiously investigated through books and travel. De Bury, Mandeville, Chaucer, and their inquisitive university friends would do better to look within rather than let "þe curiouste of here ymaginacion peerce þe planetes, & make an hole in þe firmament to loke in þerate."[61] And in the end "what gude, hopes þou, may come þarof," said Rolle, "if þou lat þi tonge blaber on þe boke, and þi hert ren abowte in sere stedes in þe world?"[62]

Finally, there is a third concern expressed by Augustine, Bernard, Aquinas, and many other moralists which is of major significance for our understanding of the conflict between curiosity and pilgrimage. All of them habitually described *curiositas* as a kind of wandering, and this was thought to manifest a deepset inability to observe an established spiritual and social order. Benedict's *gyrovagus*, Bernard's wide-eyed monk, and an eternally restless Lucifer all exemplified this sort of instability. Restlessness, exhibited in traveling, gossiping, and

tale-telling, was believed to be a symptom of curiosity. Probably the
most striking medieval depiction of the *curiosus* as wanderer was that
of Dante's Ulysses in the *Inferno*. In Canto XXVI Dante and Vergil
pause to hear Ulysses' lengthy explanation of the uncontrollable
urge that has impelled him across the globe, prevented his return home,
and at last defeated him. Nothing, says Ulysses,

> Could check the hunger in my restless mind
> To learn the vice and valour of mankind,
> Nor quench the zeal that burned within my breast
> To probe the unknown world beyond the west.

Driven by this lust to see and know all that the world offered, he led
his ship and crew beyond the confines of the known, inhabitable
world, until a storm in some strange land ended his quest with drown-
ing.[63] According to Gerhart Ladner, Dante's characterization, which
did *not* emphasize Ulysses as the Christian symbol of the virtuous,
spiritually wayfaring man, was a reflection of the widespread sense in
the late Middle Ages that the cosmos was unstable and disordered.
Other critics of the *Inferno* have stressed Ulysses' curiosity, pointing
to the influence on Dante of Augustine's conception of Ulysses as the
archetypal presumptuous philosopher and to the exegetical tradition
linking the verbosity and curiosity that inform Dante's portrait of
the hero.[64] To Dante, Ulysses certainly personified *curiositas*—and
what makes this portrait so compelling is the explicit connection of
the human impulse to investigate the world with actual travel and
exploration.

Indeed, from earliest times it seems to have been understood that
curiositas, as an impulse, a "motiva" in Grosseteste's terminology,[65]
could be described most appropriately in metaphors of spatial movement. Even though great imaginative effort was required to invest
with iconographical life what was a movement of the mind as well as
the body,[66] classical and medieval observations about the workings of
the curious mind were often expressed in such figurative language,
and *curiositas* was frequently embodied in historical and mythical
figures like Eve, Lucifer, Ulysses, or Icarus. Seneca, for instance, in a
passage Roger Bacon repeated, had sharpened Aristotle's maxim by
saying that the mind is ever restless and eager to roam (because it is
a celestial spirit and perpetually moves like the stars)[67] and that it

continually suffers from the impulse to explore and wander.[68] Pointless inquiry accomplishes nothing, Seneca chided in another epistle,
so rather than ask, for example, what regions Ulysses strayed through,
man ought to prevent himself from going astray.[69] "I was obliged to
memorize the wanderings of a hero named Aeneas," Augustine had
written in the *Confessions*, "while in the meantime I failed to remember my own erratic ways" (I, 13). To err, to go erratically, is to be a
curiosus. In original sin many theologians had detected another explanation of man's wandering urges. *Curiositas* was a lasting condition
of man's necessary wandering as a stranger on earth, and it also prompted man to unnecessary wandering and further temptations of curiosity.
Cautioned Augustine, "We have wandered far from God, and if we
wish to return to our Father's home, this world must be used, not
enjoyed. . . ."[70]

Instability, waywardness of any sort, sightseeing, and aimless physical wandering became synonymous with curiosity during the late
Middle Ages. It is a "vagabundus animus" that directs the curious,
wrote Bernard.[71] Men who travel about to examine nature scientifi-
cally show a curious disposition; Innocent III listed a whole series of
such fruitless exercises, from climbing mountains to searching the
oceans.[72] Gerson described the secular studies and curious arguments
of the university scholars in Paris at the end of the fourteenth century
as "scientias peregrinas."[73] Petrarch the *curiosus*, who once admitted
that "to know more was always among the first of my desires," held
that man's curiosity and instability were inescapable properties of his
being. He knew the desire needed restraining, but even while saying
so this most inquisitive fourteenth-century figure displayed his own
curiosity:

> I shan't speak of the celestial origin of souls, according to Virgil, nor shall I
> quote Cicero to the effect that our spirits come to us from the everlasting
> fires that we call stars and heavenly bodies. And Seneca has it that the change-
> ableness of our souls, born from the rapid whirl of the celestial fires, is there-
> by to be excused. But I do say this: that our souls are created by God and by
> him are at once infused into our bodies; that God's throne is in heaven, as
> the Psalmist says; that the movement of the heavens is perpetual, as we see
> with our own eyes; so that it is not surprising that we have some relation of
> likeness with the home of our Creator. Whatever its origin, I know that in
> men's minds, especially in superior minds, resides an innate longing to see new

places, to keep changing one's home. I don't deny that this longing should be
tempered and held in bounds by reason. . . . [74]

By the late Middle Ages, despite the Church's traditional warnings,
an older set of assumptions about the fearful seductiveness of the
visible world was slowly giving way before strong new feelings. The
late medievals, engaged in what Donald R. Howard has described as a
new "search for a common world," [75] were conscious of the older
strictures against curiosity (although the defined areas of curious inquiry were now more frequently prone to change). The world of
physical nature, as much as the world of books and the universities,
was a prominent stimulus to curiosity. The great intellectuals of the
twelfth century and their successors of the next centuries resurrected
a naturalistic, scientific attitude toward the physical world which had
been dead since the early Church Fathers placed a barrier between
wisdom and human knowledge. From the twelfth century on, as M.-D.
Chenu has explained,

> These men were bent upon a search for the causes of things—the most keen
> and arduous as well as the most typical of the activities of reason when, con-
> fronting nature, men discovered both its fecundity and the chains of necessity
> by which it is bound; an activity proper to science, and one which clashed
> violently with religious consciousness, which when it was yet inexperienced
> and immature, was willing to engage in its characteristic activity of looking
> immediately to the Supreme Cause, at the expense of disregarding secondary
> causes. [76]

Nature's secrets were again being exposed to scrutiny, and the world
was filled with curious observers. When Innocent III cautioned men
against the curious urges of mountain climbing and earthly exploration, he was not simply echoing Augustine; his complaint was based
on the fact that now men indeed were scaling mountains, measuring,
probing, and examining a new-found natural world. Gerald of Wales
(whose theories on the location of Ultima Thule would lead Petrarch
and de Bury into conversation at Avignon) was making serious marine
studies, and other Englishmen of his time, including Geoffrey of Mon-
mouth and Walter Map, explored the countryside to examine flora,
fauna, and marvels like Stonehenge, motivated principally by what
one scholar says was "objective curiosity and aesthetic appreciation." [77]

Adelard of Bath traveled through Arabia and Africa to learn, as he said, "the causes of all things and the mysteries of nature."[78] Robert Grosseteste's *De natura locorum* shows a definite fascination with natural phenomena; in it he also remarks that scientists are now indebted to mountaineers' reports for accurate topographical information.[79] If it is true that "for the most part mountainous regions were regarded as places of grimness and horror,"[80] late-medieval travelers were at least more willing to examine these awesome regions carefully. Bernard of Clairvaux (not surprisingly) may have climbed mountains with his eyes focused on the ground, but Francis of Assisi did not hide his eyes when he pacifically blessed La Verna peak.[81] Artists and travelers began memorializing ascents of mountains with more frequency after 1300;[82] Jerusalem-bound pilgrims took to climbing the Egyptian pyramids to determine how far they could see; and some, contemporaries of Mandeville, looked up at mysterious Mount Ararat and made plans to climb it.[83] In 1328 the learned Jean Buridan paused on his way from the University of Paris to Avignon to take meteorological readings in the Cévennes Mountains.[84]

But certainly no medieval account of mountain climbing is more famous or more reflective of the curious new feeling for nature than the epistle of Petrarch's dated April 26, 1336, recording his ascent of Mont Ventoux. Since Burckhardt's day scholars have debated the authenticity of his adventure and the apparent contradictions in the letter between his claim that "nothing but the desire to see its conspicuous height was the reason for this undertaking" and his subsequent realization, as he stood at the peak, that his curiosity was only vanity. The letter does epitomize Petrarch's lifelong vacillation between curiosity and piety, between his love of solitude and love for the world—but however we interpret the account in the letter, we cannot ignore the fact that Petrarch *did* climb the mountain.[85] He gives a convincing eyewitness report of what he saw from the summit:

> The sun was already setting, and the shadow of the mountain was growing longer and longer. Like a man aroused from sleep, I turned back and looked toward the west. The boundary wall between France and Spain, the ridge of the Pyrenees, is not visible from there, though there is no obstacle of which I knew, and nothing but the weakness of the mortal eye is the cause. However, one could see most distinctly the mountains of the province of Lyons to the right and, to the left, the sea near Marseilles as well as the waves that

break against Aigues Mortes, although it takes several days to travel to this
city. The Rhone River was directly under our eyes.[86]

But as he "admired every detail," he thought to turn to that constant
companion of all his days, a copy of Augustine's *Confessions*, and by
chance (he says) his eyes fell on that passage from Book X that must
have haunted so many *curiosi*: "Yet, men go out to admire the mountains' peaks, giant waves in the sea, the broad courses of rivers, the
vast sweep of the ocean, and the circuits of the stars—and they leave
themselves behind!" Chastened—for the day at least—Petrarch descended Mont Ventoux in silence, his eyes on the ground.

Petrarch's writings reveal again and again the tension men of his
time felt between the desire to see the world and store up *experientia*
and the Christian warnings against that desire. In the *Secretum*, his
imaginary dialogue with Augustine, he repeatedly exhibits curiosity,
rebukes himself for it, then succumbs again. In the *De Vita Solitaria*
he confesses to being far too curious about such questions as the
existence of the Fortunate Isles and the customs and landscape of
the newly discovered Canaries.[87] His friend Boccaccio, who in defending poetry argued that poets must "be familiar with the geography of
various lands, of seas, rivers and mountains,"[88] was similarly intrigued
by the Canary Islands and wrote a treatise about them.[89] And since
movement and travel are often the most common signs of curiosity,
exploring the unknown oceans, like climbing mountains to gaze into
the horizon, became an emblem of curious men. The early Scandina-
vian explorer, Ohthere, sailed the Arctic north because "he sæde
þæt he æt sumum cirre wolde fandian hu longe þæt land norþryhte
læge";[90] and the thirteenth-century Norwegian author of the *Speculum
Regale* asserted that a requisite motive for countrymen voyaging to
Greenland and beyond was "curiosity, for it is in man's nature to
wish to see and experience the things he has heard about, and thus to
learn whether the facts are as told or not."[91]

Curiosity *is* part of man's nature, but only at the end of the Middle
Ages did widespread general curiosity and professional scientific study
of the earth and its creatures override older medieval warnings about
the need to suppress *curiositas*. Christian Europeans were—irrevocably—
suffused with the curious impulse, and this impulse was being viewed
less as something reprehensible and more as an attitude to be cultivated.

J. J. Jusserand, R. W. Southern, and Charles Muscatine have broadly
described the late Middle Ages as an era in which men (especially
Englishmen) were intent on enlarging knowledge and unbinding
accepted social orders: a period, unlike earlier ones, typified by constant travel and mobility in everyday life and by the imagery of
journey and movement in art.[92] Dante's Ulysses had numerous living
counterparts. Monks out of their cloister now "heeld after the newe
world the space," shirking *stabilitas*; learned men found *curiositas*,
not *studiositas*, a spur to discovery. Travels undertaken to see other
lands, and above all spiritual journeys, pilgrimages, were commonly
suspected now of being motivated by curiosity. What seems evident
is that the persisting anxiety about *curiositas* and the growing absorp-
tion with curious strivings merely testified to late-medieval man's unavoidable concern with such cultural facts as the making and accumula-
tion of books, new-found authors, countries, and schools, and the
less tangible but devastating spread of ideas and discoveries that so
many data-filled encyclopedias, unending dialectical debates, and
voyages into Asia, Africa, the western ocean, and elsewhere offered
to the eye and mind.

Â Â Â Â *Curiositas* never entirely lost its original condemnatory meanings
for Christians; it simply added new ones.[93] By Chaucer's time, as
various dictionaries show, the English and Latin equivalents for
"curious" and "curiosity" could denote simply clever or exquisite
artistry, or peculiarity of taste. When the chronicler Walsingham, for
instance, refers to Richard II's antiquarian bent as that of a "curiosus"
he seems to be neither rebuking nor praising him.[94] The impulse to
see the world, traditionally one of the earmarks of *curiositas*, was
divorced more and more from the vice and acquired less pejorative
overtones. As we saw in the last chapter, similar changing assumptions
about how to explore the world and why had caused nominalist philosophers to cut away reason from faith and dignify the aims of empirical study. Those who confessed most readily to curious urges
were people like Richard de Bury, Chaucer's Wife of Bath, and Mandeville, who had traveled much, relished what they saw, and wanted to
be known as travelers. More and more these curious travelers were
pilgrims—pilgrims were the largest and fastest growing group of
travelers—and their motives for travel, although in part pious, seem

just as often to have been worldly. Their mixed urges made them in fact not very much different from the avowedly secular ocean explorers of the fifteenth century. Curiosity moved them all. And we know it is a curious world when we notice a contemporary biographer of Henry the Navigator, reciting the prince's reasons for sending expeditions into the Atlantic, list first his "wish to know the land that lay beyond the isles of Canary" and, last, a desire "to make increase in the faith of our Lord."[95]

CHAPTER III. PILGRIMAGE

A man should undertake this voyage solely with the intention of visiting, contemplating and adoring the most Holy Mysteries . . . and not with the intention of seeing the world, or from ambition, or to be able to say "I have been there" or "I have seen that" in order to be exalted by his fellow men.—Santo Brasca, an Italian on pilgrimage to Jerusalem, 1481

Like Jacob, David, and all their fathers before them (Genesis 47:9, Psalm 38), every medieval Christian knew himself to be a *viator in peregrinatione*, knew he was homeless on earth, and knew from Scripture and sermon that, as one fourteenth-century preacher put it, he was "bondon to goye here in þis world and not to reste but to traveyll. . . . for here to stonde is to vs impossible."[1] Christianity defined the unstable, mobile quality of human existence as a choice of alternative directions and goals. Impelled by curiosity, man could make the world his destination; impelled by an awareness of his true homelessness, he would make the otherworld his destination. One authority on medieval pilgrimage has seen in this tension "two levels of restlessness, the worldly tending towards ceaseless adventure and experience of the marvelous, and the spiritual struggling for the perfection of the soul and the union with God."[2] The idea had its most famous expression in Augustine's parable:

Suppose, then, we were wanderers in a strange country, and could not live happily away from our fatherland, and that we felt wretched in our wandering, and wishing to put an end to our misery, determined to return home.

We find, however, that we must make use of some mode of conveyance, either by land or water, in order to reach that fatherland where our enjoyment is to commence. But the beauty of the country through which we pass, and the very pleasure of the motion, charm our hearts, and turning these things which we ought to use into objects of enjoyment, we become unwilling to hasten the end of our journey; and becoming engrossed in a factitious delight, our thoughts are diverted from that home whose delights would make us truly happy. Such is a picture of our condition in this life of mortality. We have wandered far from God; and if we wish to return to our Father's home, this world must be used, not enjoyed, that so the invisible things of God may be clearly seen, being understood by the things that are made—that is, that by means of what is material and temporary we may lay hold upon that which is spiritual and eternal.[3]

Every literal pilgrimage imitated the lifelong pilgrimage of all men, and whether on the road toward Jerusalem, Rome, or Canterbury, the pilgrim risked the temptation to delight curiously in what he ought only to use, risked letting the journey itself and the country charm his heart. We have already seen how frequently curiosity was metaphorically described as a kind of wandering. Now, by examining developments in the growth of the practice of pilgrimage—certainly the characteristic form of medieval travel—and by noticing the way motivations for pilgrimage changed with time, it will become clear how closely the impulses for making a pilgrimage came to be bound up with *curiositas*. Much has been written about the medieval institution of pilgrimage,[4] but here it is necessary to focus only on those aspects of pilgrimage that relate to medieval curiosity about the world—and particularly the fourteenth-century world of enshrined books, pilgrim tales, and curious strange vistas respectively created by de Bury, Chaucer, and Mandeville.

Both the custom of going on pilgrimage and the analogy of life as a pilgrimage predate Christianity, having roots in the nearly universal human belief—Buddhist, Greek, Jewish, Moslem—that certain spots of earth are sacred and that man must endure his passage through this world in order to achieve a better life hereafter.[5] Christian pilgrims found important precedents for the custom in the Bible. The Exodus from Egypt, through the desert and across the Red Sea to the promised land (an event as momentous to the Hebrews as the life of Christ had been to Christians), and the later return to Jerusalem offered a significant perspective on the peregrine nature of life.[6] Of course, in the beginning God had told the sons of Adam that they were strangers in exile from Eden (Genesis 15:13, 17:8, 28:4), and the Israelites came to recognize their lot as that of strangers in a foreign land (Exodus 2:22). Throughout the Psalms, particularly in Psalms 38 and 119, man was described as an exile, and his life as a pilgrimage. Paul's expositions of prefigural Old Testament events repeatedly stressed the pilgrim status of man: his characterization of men as *hospes et peregrini* in search of the heavenly city (Hebrews 11:13-16) along with Peter's similar view (1 Peter 2:11) and other echoes in the Bible became the most frequently cited texts in medieval discussions of pilgrimage and in allegorical or exegetical treatments of man's wayfaring state.[7] Peter Lombard testified to the medieval Christian's common opinion of his spiritual condition: pilgrimage is the necessary lot of man because the *patria* is in the next world, not here.[8]

Pilgrimage and exile were, even apart from exegetical tradition, favorite themes among the early Fathers. Ambrose, for instance, in condensing Biblical history, described our life as a three-stage pilgrimage, involving man's perception of the world as a desert, his determination to wander in search of the garden of the Canticles, and his final acceptance into Paradise by Christ.[9] In various places Augustine elaborated his central vision of life as a journey toward either the city of God or the city of man, Jerusalem or Babylon. He writes, in the *Confessions*, of the human restlessness that only ultimate return to God can assuage; and in his widely read commentary on the Psalms he depicts the heavenly city as a place free from pilgrimage, dissension, and temptation: those burdens that are a part of man's sojourn in the homeless desert.[10] The pilgrimage of life may be full of trepidation; nevertheless, because of the redemptive promise of future bliss, the Christian's status as pilgrim is a privileged one—a level of spiritual progress superior to homelessness and exile. The Christian as pilgrim should be happy with the knowledge that he *has* a goal, and this expectation should alleviate his fear of temptations along the way (but not, of course, his susceptibility to them).[11] Anxiety over the pilgrimage itself and optimism about its destination imbued nearly all formulations of what, in the Middle Ages and after, became a commonplace metaphor for the life of man.[12]

The actual practice of making pilgrimages grew slowly among the early Christians, who were at first more concerned with busily spreading the Gospel. But soon certain sacred locations linked in memory to the life of Christ were marked out for worship.[13] In his lifetime Jesus himself "recapitulated the pilgrimage of Israel as a sign of his role as the suffering servant,"[14] and being both God and man he was, as Aquinas emphasized, at once the goal of all pilgrims and the ideal wayfarer.[15] Medieval pilgrims to Palestine normally thought of Jesus as the first pilgrim; they also popularized the legend that his mother spent her last years making constant pilgrimages to sites associated with him.[16] Christ's own visit to Emmaus after his Resurrection, during which he appeared as a stranger to two disciples (Luke 24:13-35), was interpreted as a pilgrimage; and throughout the Middle Ages the Emmaus incident served as a liturgical, homiletic, and dramatic focus for commentaries on the meaning of pilgrimage.[17] While on pilgrimage in the holy places, Saint Helena purportedly discovered Christ's tomb and cross beneath a pagan temple on Calvary in 325, and her son Constantine built a sanctuary on the spot; these events, together with Saint Jerome's ascetic wandering in Palestine, influenced others to journey there. Various surviving itineraries show, in fact, that by the fourth and fifth centuries pilgrimage to the region had begun in earnest.[18]

Though dependent originally on the cult of Jesus, Christian pilgrimage soon expanded to include veneration of the saints and the Virgin. Pious interest in preserving the corpses of saints or scraps of their clothing dated back to at least the middle of the second century, and an edict of the Second Nicene Council (787) confirmed the practice by prohibiting under threat of excommunication the consecration of churches without relics.[19] The large crowds of pilgrims drawn to shrines, often as much by a desire to see the relics as to seek the intercession of the saint, contributed money and rich gifts, and these contributions in turn increased the fame and splendor of the shrine, thus drawing more and larger crowds. The granting of indulgences to pilgrims, like the presence of relics, gave a further impetus to pilgrimage. And not only might indulgences be available to pilgrims at particular shrines, but papal plenary indulgences, initially given by Urban II in 1095 for the first crusade, were extended to pilgrims willing to make a specific pilgrimage. Members of the Albigensian crusade needed "to serve only forty days to secure all the indulgences granted to participants

in the Holy War" going on over the sea.[20] Backing the redeemable
value of all such indulgences was the Church's Treasury of Merits—
formulated in the thirteenth century and ratified by Clement VI in
1343[21]—that inexhaustible repository of the superfluous merits of
Christ, Mary, and the saints. By the fourteenth century, in other
words, most pilgrims could obtain remission for some or all of the
punishment due them for sins first by making a vow to go on a pilgrimage, then by arriving at the shrine; in addition they might purchase
there other abundant indulgences, items like "a gobet of the seyl / That
Seint Peter hadde" sold by that patron of pilgrims, the pardoner. For
making the great pilgrimage to Rome in the first jubilee year of 1300,
pilgrims were promised enormous indulgences.[22] Indeed, by the fourteenth century the word "pilgrimage" had become synonymous with
indulgence[23]—at about the same time that pilgrimage also had become
a common vehicle for the curious. But with such plentiful helps toward salvation, what Christian could fail to think of his pilgrimage as
not only an exceptionally interesting and even amusing journey but
also a final approach to the heavenly Jerusalem?

Medieval pilgrims went to Palestine (always their preeminent goal)
before, during, and even after Arab occupations, but their posture was
never really the same after the crusades began. Unlike the new crusader-
pilgrim, the *peregrinus* known since early Church days was, as in the
Biblical usage, any stranger or traveler. The Roman Empire's legal
view of non-Romans (called *peregrini*) had been adopted gladly by
Christians and given new meaning: the Christian, as despised outcast,
as *peregrinus*, was heartily urged to shun the world.[24] Thus Isidore
defined the pilgrim simply as a man "longe a patria positus, sicut
alienigena."[25] Only in the eleventh century, it seems, did the word
peregrinus come to specifically designate a person on pilgrimage (and,
of course, allegorically, Man on Pilgrimage).[26] But the crusaders, armed
with indulgence and sword, were both pilgrims and soldiers, and medieval chroniclers at first fluctuated in portraying their efforts as holy
wars for Christ or mass pilgrimages conducted to the Holy Land for
the remission of sins.[27] The crusades represented a blending of the
tradition of pilgrimage with that of holy war, and thus for the author
of the *Gesta Francorum*, a witness to the first crusade, the whole venture was more of a *passagium generale*—a crusade—but one composed
entirely of *peregrini*.[28] By the thirteenth century specific terms finally

had come into use to differentiate pilgrims from the newer sort of martial Christians.[29] Although the crusades were, ultimately, a military failure, hope in the eventual liberation of the Christian homeland persisted into the fourteenth century and beyond, producing militant propagandists like Marino Sanuto and knight-pilgrims like John Mandeville and Chaucer's "parfit, gentil" warrior. The crusades also gave rise to the knightly service organizations, the hospitallers and templars, whose really useful work, defending and caring for passing pilgrims, ironically deprived pilgrimage of some of its requisite hazards and thus, indirectly, brought about the demise of pilgrimage as a penitential act.[30]

The combination of the desire to worship with the zeal to conquer for the Lord is but one illustration of the truth, best stated by Donald J. Hall, that pilgrimage "was more than a religious exercise, a custom, a habit, an escape, an entertainment or an act of profound faith. Simply because it contained all these qualities in varying degrees it cannot be viewed in isolation."[31] And yet to see better those features that set pilgrimage apart from other forms of medieval travel, we might contrast it with one other kind of pious Christian wayfaring: that practiced by monks from the beginning of the Christian era. Like the crusaders, they were in some senses *peregrini*, but their motivations revealed how decidedly different they were from all other pilgrims.

Eastern monastic groups of the early Church, mindful of scriptural injunctions to live as strangers in exile, fled from civilization to the desert and lived a homeless, mostly peripatetic existence, bound to no predetermined itinerary or goal. In a monograph describing the cultural significance of *heimatlosigkeit*, a guiding principle of early monasticism, Hans von Campenhausen made the perceptive observation that the gradual shifts from original monachism (single monks living alone in a cell) to cenobitism (solitary cells clustered together), and from cenobitism to monasticism (communal life in the monastery) reflected the compromises that monastic ideals were obliged to make with the demands of social order and responsibility.[32] Western monasticism at first adopted the idea of homelessness, with its emphasis on the abandonment of family and society, on solitude and extreme penance. However, it was soon discarded out of a need for more constructive wandering—travel undertaken, for example, to obtain necessary information on the habits and organization of kindred monastic communities. *Heimatlosigkeit* was at bottom alien to the Western mind, and from Augustine's day to Langland's all such bands of directionless monks and their counterparts among the *gyrovagi* were strongly damned for their unstable style of life.[33] Then, too, the Western custom of going on pilgrimage to Palestine—which meant a round-trip voyage—stressed both the journey to a fixed destination and a return home. Irish monasticism, in particular, by way of reaction to aimless wandering, sought to diminish the obvious dangers of traveling in the world by urging the homelessness of voluntary exile to remote islands, but by binding monks permanently to the rule of *stabilitas* once they reached their lonely outposts.[34] Like the solitary monks in the Egyptian deserts, the Irish put ascetic aims before preaching and evangelism, and it remained for English monasticism to blend Eastern and Irish practices with the more typical Western penchant for making pilgrimages and carrying out vast missionary activities. Concluding his study, Campenhausen argued that it is one thing to leave home, family, and possessions to pursue the ascetic life, but quite another to labor altruistically for the conversion of men to the Word of God.

The pilgrim and the homeless monk were alike in their belief that this world is a place of exile in which no man has a home, but the two figures were dissimilar in almost every other respect. Religious and lay pilgrims who left cloister and family for specific destinations but ultimately returned home did so with a sense of responsibility different from the professed spiritual recklessness of wandering exiles. Disposed to excess in penance and open to the grievous temptations of *acedia* and *tristitia*, the hermit furthermore accepted risks that the pilgrim (however tempted he may have been by *curiositas*) could avoid in part by eventually returning to society. Pilgrimage, then, the form of travel endemic to the Middle Ages, ideally differed from both the essentially worldly crusades and the aimless meanderings of lone exiles in its attempt to embody the best personal and social aims of both. While it flourished, pilgrimage provided all men, whether they set out for Palestine or other sacred sites, with the satisfaction of participating in the grand return from captivity to the Old Jerusalem and in the ascent with the blessed to the heavenly city of the Apocalypse. Whatever the motives of their members, pilgrimages ideally were expected to be occasions for worship and, indeed, like the hermit's seclusion or a modern day spiritual retreat for laymen, a chance to escape the noise and distractions of normal daily routine. In theory, medieval pilgrimage joined ascetic withdrawal from the world—a vocation more easily followed by the monk than by the layman—with the practical need to live and travel in the world. Leaving home offered pilgrims the chance to realize the spiritual value of forsaking the familiar world for an alien environment; but the act of pilgrimage also presumed a return home to the familiar world where each Christian must live and work. It presumed, in short, as Chaucer seems to have understood, the restoration of stability and order. Upon arriving home pilgrims were received back into the safe, known surroundings by friends' good wishes and religious ceremonies of thanksgiving.[35]

But in the later Middle Ages, as the pilgrimage became more of a boisterous social event for groups of traveling citizenry, the opportunity for inner and outer quiet lessened. On Chaucer's Canterbury pilgrimage, silence comes only near the end, when the Host calls for quiet and the Parson preaches to the company, and later, when Chaucer whispers his literary sins. The earliest pilgrims had been monks, but as pilgrimages became morally doubtful enterprises, religious orders and in fact all clergy were discouraged from joining them.[36] Monasticism in time abjured pilgrimage for its proximity to the world just as it had previously rejected eremetic homelessness as an unproductive withdrawal from the world. During the twelfth century, as Jean Leclercq has explained, monastic *peregrinatio*—which before that had served as a means of seeking *stabilitas* in an unstable, imperfect world—was gradually supplanted by a stricter emphasis on residence within the monastery. Against the older search for *stabilitas in peregrinatione* was set a belief in *peregrinatio in stabilitate*.[37] Pilgrims now and then might wish to describe themselves contentedly as Hebrews seeking their Promised Land, as Abrahams leaving some new Chaldee, or as troubled Jobs outlasting storms and enemies;[38] but as the sardonic Walter Map observed, the monastic orders preferred to consider themselves the chosen people and the rest of society the Egyptians.[39]

Notwithstanding the importance of Rome as the political center of the Church or of later renowned places like Compostela and Canterbury,

Jerusalem always held the greatest attraction for pilgrims. It was the center or navel of the *orbis terrarum* for Christians. All holy spots were touched by God, but Christ's native home above all; and many of the other famous pilgrimage shrines, including Canterbury, made a point of underscoring any possible christological associations. Historically prominent in the Old and New testaments, Jerusalem naturally came to be seen as much more than a geographical location. For medieval mystics from Augustine to Hilton and à Kempis it epitomized the spiritual life.[40] Exegetes found in it an apt illustration of the fourfold method of scriptural interpretation. (Rabanus Maurus's gloss on Jerusalem repeated the standard formula that had been a cliché in Cassian's time—Jerusalem was literally the "civitas Judaeorum," "secundum allegoriam Ecclesia Christi," "secundum tropologiam anima hominis," and "secundum anagogen civitas Dei, illa coelestis, quae est mater omnium nostrum.")[41] And, as Norman Cohn has remarked, "in the minds of simple folk the idea of the earthly Jerusalem became so confused with and transfused by that of the Heavenly Jerusalem that the Palestinian city seemed itself a miraculous realm, abounding both in spiritual and material blessings."[42] Like Jerusalem, the Christian pilgrimage had symbolic as well as literal meaning. Pilgrims went on actual journeys to particular sites and came back home; they also saw themselves (and were so imagined by poets and moralists) as moving allegorically in a one-way journey through life to truth and heavenly bliss. Mandeville's *Travels* includes a literal pilgrimage to the Holy Land, but in places it is also allegorically suggestive. Exactly in what sense the *Canterbury Tales* pilgrimage is an actual or allegorical trip—or both—is a question many readers of the work have tried to resolve, among them one fifteenth-century reader of the *Tales* who, in his *Tale of Beryn*, "completed" the pilgrimage by leading Chaucer's pilgrims into Canterbury and then setting them on their way back to London.[43]

Since every medieval pilgrimage ended at Jerusalem, at least spiritually, and since the indulgence-laden act released sinners from purgatorial punishment, pilgrims inevitably looked upon the journey as a preview of their own wished-for final passage after death into the heavenly city. To die en route or at the pilgrimage shrine usually was thought to ensure immediate joyful translation to beatitude.[44] This symbolic quality of pilgrimage was underscored most noticeably in the church ceremonies that most pilgrims, at least all those going to Jerusalem, attended before leaving home.[45] The "Ordo ad Seruitium Peregrinorum" required first that the pilgrims go to confession. Following that they were to prostrate themselves at the altar in prayer, receive their emblematic staff and scrip (the "habitum peregrinationis"), which the priest had blessed, and recite appropriate psalms asking God's guidance and recalling ancient holy journeys like the Lord's entry into Sion.[46] Pilgrims bound for Jerusalem then were invested with a special garment marked by a cross on the shoulder. In the Mass that followed, the Ordinary echoed earlier pleas for deliverance; the *lectio* (Genesis 24:7) repeated Abraham's words to his servant on God's guardianship of wayfarers; and the Gospel (Matthew 10:7-15) recalled Christ's command to his apostles that they preach, heal, and go forth into the world without possessions or money. At the end of the ceremony, the pilgrims took leave of spouse and family [47] (as Bunyan's Christian initially left his wife and children behind) and, armed with staff and scrip, began their journey. Confession had now purified them, and the indulgences available to them on their pilgrimage seemed virtually to guarantee the accomplishment of their holiest intentions. The Lord would be their shepherd in the dark valley (Psalm 23) though lurking knaves and the torments of nature might waylay them. On the road they sang hymns (unless tale-telling curiously diverted them) meant to remind them of their likeness to the homeless Israelites of old.[48] And, as Chaucer may have known, it was not unusual for pilgrims, especially Jerusalem-bound travelers, to hear a sermon as they landed at Jaffa or first entered the Holy Sepulchre.[49] But what the Service for Pilgrims did not mention was the ever present, subtle temptations of *curiositas* that pilgrims faced in facing the world. Pilgrims, like any travelers, were too often distracted by the sights of that unfamiliar world, as moralists unendingly warned they would be. By the fourteenth and fifteenth centuries the increasingly numerous opponents of pilgrimage asserted that it had become an exercise in curiosity. Exactly how much the otherworldly ideals of pilgrimage were tainted by *curiositas* can best be seen by abstracting the pious from the curious motives and examining each.

The true pilgrim directed his steps to a specific goal, a particular shrine, and began and ended his trip with invocations of divine aid. The curious man, wandering in mind or body, very often sought no definite goal but roamed busily from one discovery to another, unguided except by his own serendipity. Pilgrims knew their objectives were divinely authorized or at least approved by the opinion of religious men. Inquisitive men, whether trying to fly like King Bladud and the notorious early English monk Eilmer[50] or spending their days investigating earthly mysteries, acted on purely human impulses, allowing reason and not faith to control their perspective on the natural world.

Genuine humility moved the pious pilgrim to undertake his quest. Men visited holy places to do penance, to ask certain favors of Christ, his mother, or a saint, to obtain a desirable indulgence, or to fulfill a vow made earlier to go on pilgrimage in return for the granting of some special request. Joinville sailing home from the crusades, Aeneas Sylvius (later Pius II) adrift in the North Sea, Columbus and Magellan enduring sea tempests were only a few of the crusaders, pilgrims, and curious ocean adventurers who promised to seek out a shrine if the Lord spared them.[51] All these motives suggested a humble view of man's relationship to higher powers. Hall's conviction that the search for "an intermediary was the real essence of mediaeval pilgrimage"[52] is another way of saying that in recognizing his dependency on divine help, the Christian pilgrim exhibited a deference not unlike that felt by the medieval Christian poet who willingly deferred to a Solomon, Seneca, or Lollius.

Unlike the pilgrim, the *curiosus* renounced humility and chose instead to climb the steps of pride, presumptuously roaming the globe like Ulysses, searching the heavens like Icarus. *Curiositas* was most naturally described as wandering and most often symbolized by the journey, so it is to be expected that curious men would find pilgrimage suited to their own desires—they need to scurry about (*percurrere*), said Bernard.[53] Curiosity focused a man's attention on himself, other people, or the exterior world of things; the good pilgrim worked for the salvation of his soul and looked beyond this world for supernatural assistance. Moreover—and this was most important—the pilgrim's quest, like his daily life, embraced communal concerns, and he traveled most like a member of the Church Militant when he traveled harmoniously in company with other pilgrims. Most curious men, like many of the Canterbury pilgrims, were by contrast solitary figures, unstable threats to the body social and its corporate obligations. They aspired in isolation and, as Gerson noted, the outward sign of their inner curiosity was *singularitas*.[54]

Historically, however, the pilgrim and the *curiosus* were not always separable in this antonymous fashion. Pilgrims were men, and *curiosi* were men; both wandered the earth, in fact or in imagination. And the same attributes so commonly used to define *curiositas*—its aimlessness, its instability, its uselessness and moral irrelevance—came more and more to be applied to pilgrimage in the late Middle Ages. Pilgrims might endure hardship and physical dangers, but their journey could be as often a vacation as a penance, and, like any traveling vacationers, they saw new lands and peoples, heard strange tales, experienced different ways of thinking and living. Too frequently the pilgrim garb of the late Middle Ages was but a mask for the *curiosus* (as well as a common disguise for lovers, criminals, and refugees).[55] According to a contemporary biographer, "secret longings" moved the eighth-century Englishman Willibald in his youth "to travel the pilgrimage roads (which were unknown to him) and to explore and approach the far ends of the earth as well as to track the immense plains of the sea." It is less interesting to read his Holy Land itinerary than to learn that he visited the island Vulcano on his way home because he "was very curious to see what was inside the inferno, and would have climbed to the mountain top above it; but he could not."[56] On the road the pilgrim's vulnerability to the temptations of curiosity was, if anything, greater than it might have been at home, for of necessity he put himself in the occasion of sin. He was undeniably in a strange world, and the tendency to enjoy what he saw there would be unavoidable.

That pilgrims were as curious about the experience of their journey as they were devoutly intent on arriving at the shrine is an observation any student of human nature might agree with even if no evidence linking pilgrimage with *curiositas* survived. But in view of the sorts of attacks made against the medieval institution it would seem that critics at the end of the period never credited pilgrimage with being much more than a religiously sanctioned way of curiously exploring the world. Even in explaining that he had traveled to Palestine in order to observe, touch, and fully experience the land of the Lord, Willibald was unconsciously admitting how precarious was the balance that pilgrims strove to maintain between immersion in this world and dedication to the one signified by the shrine.[57] The sea of this world that we all must cross makes us, as Alain de Lille said, "inquietus per

curiositatem."[58] Honorius of Autun pointedly inveighed against those
who "propter curiositatem vel laudem humanam ad sacra loca dis-
currunt."[59] In the *Roman de la Rose*, itself a study in the multitude
of curious distractions awaiting the mind and eye of the not-so-spiritual-
pilgrim, Jean de Meun contrasted pilgrimage (and allied forms of travel
made for pleasure and gain) with the simple, stable life of men in the
Golden Age.[60] Gregory of Nyssa long before had cautioned his congregation against needlessly traveling to Jerusalem to find God when He
could be found everywhere; and other early warnings against the risks
of pilgrimaging, like Jerome's maxim—not to have traveled to Jerusalem
but to have lived a good life there gains merit—anticipated these later
criticisms.[61] A French preacher of Jean de Meun's time told pilgrims
rushing to Compostela that the real Saint James was in heaven, not
in Spain, and that they could obtain as much grace and forgiveness
by going into their own churches to honor God at Mass.[62] Aquinas's
depiction of the curious man as a sightseer, especially in view of his
reminder that curiosity appealed to all the senses, suggests the great
range of evils pilgrimage was beginning to embrace in the later Middle
Ages, nearly all of them related to *curiositas*. In addition to harmful
gossip and sexual promiscuity, almost all forms of sensual indulgence
tempted the pilgrim. Excessive eating and drinking, the flaunting of
fancy dress, the abuse of indulgences, the curiosity about the riches
and gems at the shrines, and above all, the tale telling—what the
fourteenth-century English preacher John Bromyard called the pilgrims' habitual delight "in nociuis et detractoriis . . . narrationibus"[63]
—these diversions had turned pilgrimage into the medieval equivalent
of a businessmen's convention, the difference being of course that
pilgrimage was intended for worship, not revel.

Curiosity tempted each member of a pilgrimage individually, but a
broader manifestation of the vice—instability—inhered in the body of
pilgrims; for any entourage of travelers, regardless of the motives that
drove them, threatened by their very movement the stability of society.
Late-medieval groups of pilgrims were denounced by the upholders of
social order for this additional reason, the same reason that the bands
of monastic *vagi* were ostracized in an earlier age. To Benedict, even
the pilgrim-monk, who had more of a legitimate excuse for traveling
than the wayward *vagus*, was suspect: *monachi peregrini* forsook
stabilitas, and while they and all pilgrims were welcomed as visitors
in monasteries, they had to take the vow of stability and demonstrate

that quality before they could join the monastery permanently.[64] In the eighth (or ninth) century the *Regula Magistri* reiterated the older view that clerical pilgrims were only unstable tramps.[65] A decree of Charlemagne's forbade perpetual pilgrimage because it created vagrants,[66] and in later centuries (as Richard II's and Charles VI's statutes on vagrants and pilgrims, and various Lollard tracts make clear[67]) both the occasional pilgrim and the universally satirized professional pilgrim, the palmer, continued to be seen as irritants to social and economic order. Much-traveled pilgrims like itinerant friars, Chaucer's Pardoner and Wife of Bath, or Erasmus's roving Ogygius (who more than once visited Canterbury and Walsingham "out of curiosity"[68]) found satisfaction in continual travel that not only contributed to a general social instability but also must have reflected a more personal instability. The indefatigable Felix Fabri, who twice took ship to Palestine in the 1480s, candidly noted in his diary that he refrained from telling brethren at home of his desire to make the second trip for fear they would think he was restlessly "impatient of the quiet of the cloister" or else "guilty of the sin of idle curiosity."[69] Chaloner's translation of *The Praise of Folly*, done in the days when Henry VIII was dissolving monasteries and pilgrimage shrines, restated what previous critics of pilgrimage had been saying for two hundred years about instability and curiosity:

> This man loketh for a new worlde. That man compasseth some depe drifte in his head. Some one hath an especiall devocion to goe to Ierusalem, to Rome, or to sainct Iames in Galice, leuyng his wife and children succourlesse in the meane while at home.[70]

By the fourteenth century the proliferation of relics and the relentless search for new shrines and points of worship had almost obscured a key doctrine in the rubrics of Christian pilgrimage: the primacy of Jerusalem, the holy city of the Lord, which He had set in the center of the earth (Ezechiel 5:5). Jerusalem never ceased to be the most popular pilgrimage site, but gradually the fame of Canterbury and a host of other spots, together with the availability of indulgences at shrines of even lesser reputation, shattered the original focus of pilgrimage and encouraged endless curious wayfaring in all directions. The widespread late-medieval denunciations of pilgrimage, which in England reached a peak about 1400, claimed that the custom had not only upset social stability and fostered a pursuit of the curious but

also subverted the Christian idea that God's presence could be felt
everywhere, not simply in an accumulating number of select spots.
John Wyclif's numerous objections to pilgrimage typified late-medieval
antagonism to the abuses of the institution. He particularly objected
to pilgrimage because it condoned the belief that Christ was more
accessible in some places than in others, because it was spiritually
redundant (since pilgrims began their journey cleansed by confession),
and because it encouraged men to pray to an assortment of statues,
not directly to God or the saints.[71] Wyclif's disciples, among them
the "Lollardi" that Thomas Walsingham reported to be preaching
against pilgrimages before the door of Saint Paul's in 1389,[72] continued to stress the connection between pilgrimage and image-venera-
tion. In the first place, the religious statuary so prevalent at the
shrines was derided as morally distracting, for much the same reasons
Bernard had given in reviling artwork in the cloisters. It was the product of curious interests and served to lure the curious eye.[73] The
Wyclif-inspired Twelve Conclusions of 1395, nailed to the doors of
Westminster Abbey, attacked both image worship and pilgrimage
(along with gold-working) as practices that "did nothing but generate
curiosity and sin."[74] Secondly, such sculpture invited more attention
than the holy person it was intended to bring to mind (although this
argument was usually rebutted with the assertion that pictures and
images were books for the illiterate). These critics of pilgrimage rejected the idea that God or his saints could be objectified in stone for
the same reasons they disputed the notion that supernatural presences
could be localized, or that indulgences could be quantified and dispensed in exchange for money. There also must have been a continuing disgust with the habit of vowing to go on pilgrimage, then not
fulfilling that promise. England's Henry IV was but one of many
offenders. As the carefree son of Gaunt he found plenty of time to
joust and maraud on European crusades in the 1390s, yet he never
successfully mounted the Holy Land pilgrimage he repeatedly pledged
to make as ruler. All he could manage to do was die there—vicariously,
in a Westminster bedchamber called "Jerusalem"[75]—and rest entombed
at Canterbury Cathedral.

Closely bound up with the idea that God was omnipresent—and in
a sense implied in it—was the argument that God's true residence is
within oneself, and that the perfect pilgrimage is an interior journey

of the quiet soul. Christian mystical thought had long stressed this spiritual interpretation of pilgrimage, and as Evelyn Underhill has said, the mystic's craving for the heavenly country most often expressed itself in the metaphor of pilgrimage.[76] While it was a traditional view, the preoccupation of many late-medieval mystics with the contemplative pilgrimage to Jerusalem and their resistance to actual pilgrimage practice—noisy, distracting, worldly journeys—reflected the many other contemporary reactions to the abuse of pilgrimage. Moreover, there recur throughout mystical writings, most notably in Hilton's *Scale of Perfection* and Thomas à Kempis's *Imitatio Christi*, significant oppositions between the curiosity of bookish meditation, intellectual study, or presumptuous world-bound knowledge and the unsubtle humility of quiet, solitary contemplation. Men do better to search for God along the *itinerarium mentis* than on the road to Rome. Walter Ralegh, though hardly a mystic, still knew the silence true pilgrims demanded when he wrote "Give me my scallop-shell of quiet." The boastful palmer in *Piers Plowman*, although he has traveled far, cannot direct other men to the revivifying shrine of Saint Truth; in fact he has never even heard of it:

> 'Nay, so me god helpe!' seide the gome thanne,
> 'I seygh neuere palmere with pike ne with scrippe
> Axen after hym er til now in this place.'

Pilgrimage routes do not always coincide with the highway to heaven, Langland warned, and both wayward pilgrims and men curious about "alle the sciences vnder sonne" could claim the inquisitive Lucifer as their model.[77] Thomas à Kempis stated directly what most critics of pilgrimage—orthodox clergy, wary court officials, Wycliffites, mystics —all implied:

> Many run to sundry places to visit the shrines of the Saints. They wonder to hear of their deeds and gaze upon the spacious buildings of their churches; and they behold and kiss their bones, all wrapped in silks and gold.
>
> And lo! Thou Thyself are here present to me on the altar, my God, the Saint of Saints, the Creator of men, and the Lord of Angels.
>
> Often such pilgrims as these are moved by human curiosity and the quest for novelty, and carry home with them small fruit of amendment; especially when they run so gaily from place to place without true contrition.[78]

But questing for novelty was, by the fourteenth century, an openly

expressed aim of many men who called themselves pilgrims. Their
travels, as curious as they were pious in motivation, may have taken
them to Jerusalem, but now they searched ostentatiously for more
than shrines and relics. The fall of Acre in 1291 and the Turkish victory
at Nicopolis in 1396 made pilgrimaging to the Holy Land more difficult than before and ended the crusading era; brief pilgrimages now
more common to local shrines were no longer arduous trips but, as
Chaucer knew, enjoyable ones. Those pilgrims unable or unwilling to
go even short distances could discharge pilgrimage vows by kneeling
on labyrinthine church-floor designs, symbolically journeying to
Jerusalem. And indeed, it seems quite possible that some late medievals might have found the new popularity of the stations of the cross,
a "counterfeit devotional pilgrimage,"[79] or the saying of the rosary,
itself a miniature pilgrimage,[80] even easier vicarious forms of legitimate
holy voyaging. Jerusalem could still be reached by the more courage-
ous pilgrim; but the cartographers who kept moving Jerusalem farther
away from its ancient spiritual midpoint on the new world maps, together with the one-time Jerusalem-centered crusaders who now had
become merchants, missionaries, and explorers traveling in other
directions were redefining the objectives of Christian journeying.[81] An
early-medieval Christian tracing the steps of Jesus through Palestine
was a pilgrim, but what would one call the Italian goldsmith who
collected pictures, mementos, and writings of Petrarch, and made
personal homage to the revered humanist as one might to a saint?[82]

De Bury on his pilgrimages to books, Mandeville on his actual and
vicarious search for novelties, and Chaucer's pilgrims in their mixed
urges for travel are witnesses to the late-medieval relinquishment of
the ideal of pilgrimage and the espousal of curiosity. These travelers
were pivotal figures in an unstable, inquisitive new age, one well described by Margaret Aston as an era of travel and questioning:

> Much travel will no more make a philosopher than much reading. But the
> exploration of places, like the exploration of books, can act as a powerful
> stimulus to the philosophically inclined, and in the fifteenth century increased
> travel and increased reading were both leading to new questioning. 'The fur-
> ther you go, the more you shall see and know,' as a travel treatise of the period
> put it. Curiosity breeds criticism and, then as now, travel could help to pro-
> mote empirical inquiry. . . . To travel well is to question well and, as both

the writing and reading of books (travel-books and others) shows, the fifteenth century became increasingly appreciative of the virtues of the good traveller. More people were undertaking more travel of various sorts, and their explorations, intellectual and geographical, made an important contribution to the outlook of the age.[83]

What Aston says of the fifteenth century is true of the previous one. And that curiosity about books, new places, and travel suffuses the outlook of the three fourteenth-century English figures we shall examine. Let us turn first to Richard de Bury.

CHAPTER IV. THE BIBLIOPHILE AS CURIOUS PILGRIM: RICHARD DE BURY'S *PHILOBIBLON*

For they search busily among his works,
but are distracted by what they see, because
the things seen are fair.—Wisdom 13:7

While the *Canterbury Tales* portrays the ways in which curiosity subverts the piety of pilgrimage, and Mandeville's *Travels* the ways late-medieval pilgrims inevitably become curious explorers, Richard de Bury's *Philobiblon* is an attempt to show that certain kinds of worldly quests are in themselves commendable and in fact require *curiositas* as a stimulus. The *Philobiblon* is about a search for books, a search ultimately described as if it were a pilgrimage. In 1333, years before Chaucer's imaginary pilgrims rode on their noisy way to Canterbury, Richard Aungerville de Bury (1287-1345)—civil servant, bishop, traveler, and book-collector—made one of his numerous trips to the Continent, this time as a royal ambassador to the pope at Avignon. He had been at Avignon in 1330, but the second mission was to be about more than politics, for on this occasion he met and talked with another famous book-lover, Petrarch. The setting itself was significant; during the Avignonese papacy the city offered men like these two "a uniquely cosmopolitan community and atmosphere, one which fostered scholarship and book-collecting" and attracted an enormous variety of authors and scholars.[1] De Bury left us no record of his encounter with the younger Italian, but Petrarch later remembered it well. In their conversations he found the Englishman to be eager-minded, knowledgeable about literature, and from his youth exceedingly curious about secret lore ("viro ardentis ingenii nec literarum inscio, et qui, ut in Britannia genitus atque educatus abditarum rerum ab adolescentia supra fidem curiosus"). Such an interest in recondite and esoteric matters appealed to Petrarch, who frequently admitted his own curious temperament, and he joined de Bury in scrutinizing all sorts of interesting minutiae ("talibus presertim questiunculis enodandis"). There was no more typically curious topic of speculation than the one they took up before parting—the existence and location of the legendary Ultima Thule, a subject that intrigued Petrarch in much of his reading and writing—and de Bury promised to investigate the matter when he returned home and send Petrarch some books about it.[2] Brief as it was, Richard de Bury's encounter with the "worthy clerk" of Vaucluse was, as Beryl Smalley has said, symbolic.[3] Two late-medieval *curiosi*, in one of those rare historical moments, had met and taken each other's measure. Toward the end of his life de Bury wrote the *Philobiblon*, which, while it began as a rebuttal to contemporary accusations of *curiositas*, concluded as a testament to that very quality of mind Petrarch had detected. Like Petrarch himself in the *Secretum*, de Bury would confess his sins only to defend them.

It has been customary for critics to mention that de Bury never did send Petrarch the books he promised and never replied to Petrarch's many letters.[4] Any number of excuses could be made for de Bury's failure to reply, but a partial explanation for his silence surely would be that the ambitious cleric and courtier was suddenly encumbered by new duties and high offices. While at Avignon the pope had honored him with a position as papal chaplain, and in the next year (1334) King Edward III, his former pupil, designated him successively Lord Treasurer, Bishop of Durham, and finally Lord Chancellor of England.[5] These responsibilities prevented him, moreover, from taking off three years for university study, although John XXII had given him permission for such a sabbatical,[6] and until his death he was engaged in filling a series of ecclesiastical and diplomatic appointments.

Richard de Bury was an influential political figure in early and mid-fourteenth-century England,[7] but his historical importance lies as much, maybe more, in the one literary work he composed and in what Petrarch and his friends and biographers remembered him for, his bibliophilia and learning.[8] Edward III said his friend and one-time tutor was "litterarum scientia praeditum."[9] The philosopher Walter Burley, who with Holcot, Bradwardine, Fitzralph, Maudit, and others formed the circle of university scholars befriended by de Bury,[10] translated Aristotle's *Ethics* and *Politics* at the bishop's request and described his patron as being "sufficienter" knowledgeable in Greek and "augmentacionis scientie ferventissimus zelator."[11] Similarly, William de Chambre, writing about 1380, said de Bury was at least "sufficientis literaturae."[12] Adam Murimuth, another contemporary, did not think much of de Bury as a scholar and recorded with obvious satisfaction that the worldly bishop died in poverty.[13] Murimuth, however, was an office-seeking rival as well as a lawyer (in the *Philobiblon* de Bury had made plain his distaste for lawyers); and so while natural antagonism may account for Murimuth's opinion of de Bury, it is also instructive to know that Petrarch was unimpressed with Murimuth and judged him to be only "mediocriter literatus."[14]

None of these observers describes exactly what kind of scholar de Bury was—Hans Baron has called him simply a "polyhistor"[15]— but they are unanimous in remarking on his passion for book-collecting. Murimuth said de Bury possessed an "infinite number of books"; at least there were so many that five large wagons could not have held them all.[16] De Chambre claimed that the man owned more books than did all the rest of the English bishops, that they filled the libraries in each of his several residences, and that some rooms in his quarters were so stuffed with books as to be impassable.[17] Petrarch, himself an inveterate book-collector, was impressed with de Bury's reputed private holdings. Richard de Bury was, in fact, the first great English bibliophile; according to one modern scholar, next to his library of perhaps fifteen hundred volumes the holdings of "all other fourteenth-century book-collectors appear rather dim and colourless."[18] Indeed, in its size and catholicity, de Bury's library may have surpassed the later collections of Richard II and the renowned book-lover duc de Berry,[19] and it may even have outstripped the famed libraries of fifteenth-century English scholars and patrons like John Tiptoft and Duke Humphrey of Gloucester,[20] who would have found it easier than de Bury did to request and obtain books. Among the few books that have survived from de Bury's libraries is the one he wrote, a Latin work he titled *Philobiblon*. He felt obliged to write the treatise: it

was an apologia for his all-consuming avocation as much as a vigorous
hymn of praise for what should drive men to bibliomania. The magni-
tude of his love for books and the fact that he wrote a whole book
answering his accusers set him off from any lesser book-lovers of previous and following centuries; in George K. Anderson's view, the
Philobiblon "was the most eloquent of such encomia until the appear-
ance of Milton's *Areopagitica*" and "the enthusiasm of [the] *Philobiblon* is worthy of the Renaissance."[21] Like his library, the source
and exact nature of the accusations directed against de Bury have not
come down to us, and they must be inferred from the *Philobiblon*
itself. The chief indictment, however, was *curiositas*; yet while the
book-lover responds to that charge, the narrative of his lifelong travels
in search of books turns out to be one mighty piece of evidence that
curiosity was the mainspring of his intellectual life.

Our first inkling of the reasons that led de Bury to write the work
comes at the end of the Prologue.[22] By that point he has taken us
step by step through the various considerations that long before
prompted him to bolster the Church by supporting its scholars with
books. Now, ill and near death,[23] he has decided to will his books to
the Church; the terms of the will together with his plans for having
a building erected to house the volumes at Oxford are set forth in
chapter XIX. (One scholar has observed that his bequest, "given as a
perpetual almsdeed for his own soul and the souls of Edward III and
Philippa, was in substance the plan of a circulating library.")[24] De
Bury admits that an "ecstatic love has carried us away so power-
fully that we have resigned all thoughts of other earthly things,
and have given ourselves up to a passion for acquiring books" (11);
and he senses the need to exonerate his *amor librorum* from certain charges of excess. He says he writes for posterity as well as for
his own generation, and his immediate strategy is to silence the
"perverse tongues of gossipers" who have accused him. The very
title of his treatise is a taunt hurled in their faces: "we have chosen
after the fashion of the ancient Romans fondly to name it by a
Greek word, *Philobiblon*" (13). In the twenty chapters that follow,
de Bury argues that books are to be loved because they alone hold
and conserve wisdom, allows the books themselves to complain
about various maltreatments, and describes the benefits of book-

collecting and the proper ways to handle and care for books.

Through all of this we wait for the accused to repeat the explicit charges brought against him. Finally, near the end of the book, come the words,

> . . . nunc de curiositate superflua, nunc de cupiditate in illa dumtaxat materia, nunc de vanitatis apparentia, nunc de voluptatis intemperentia circa litteras notabamur. . . . (230)

The last three moral failings in the series result from the motivation *curiositas* supplies; moreover, they are almost synonymous with it. De Bury's unnamed antagonists—probably rivals like Murimuth, other bishops envious of his political connections,[25] and stern moralists in general—have censured him for the unseen motions of his appetite and for the visible fruits: his covetousness (and avarice) in buying books, his vanity in possessing and displaying them (here perhaps is the echo of some annoyed cleric's grumblings, uttered while picking his way through the bishop's book-strewn study), and his excessive delight in secular literature. The bishop loved books as things and he loved them as repositories "abditarum rerum"; his offense against moderation matched the *desmesure* other curious men might exhibit for ornate buildings and vestments, and his eagerness to delve into the contents of his treasures manifested intellectual curiosity.

De Bury was an administrator more than he was a deeply trained scholar, and, as Moriz Sondheim has said, learning, like book-collecting, was a form of recreation for him.[26] Professional scholars knew *curiositas* as an occupational hazard, but a zealous amateur like de Bury was even more open to such temptations. As the conversations with Petrarch show, he apparently made no secret of his curious interests; this forthrightness, combined with his reputation as an overseer of wide-ranging round-table discussions (130-31), would have made his eager book-collecting a natural target for moralists. In the thirteenth century, John of Wales found it necessary to rebuke scholars of his day for too great a passion in acquiring books (although by a reasoning curious in itself he explained that reliance on books inhibited the discovery of things on one's own).[27] Within monastic culture such tensions between the love of learning and the desire for God were never quite resolved, as Jean Leclercq has explained, and the reading and making of books was always pursued in the cloisters with some anxiety.[28] De Bury was aware of this dilemma and of the more general arguments of Christian anti-intellectuals, whose voices were again being raised with new force in the early fourteenth century. He knew that many moralists, in and out of religious orders, still remembered the prediction of Saint Francis as recorded by Bonaventure:

> "My brethren who are led by desire for learning [*scientiae curiositate*] shall find their hands empty in the day of tribulation. . . . For a time of tribulation is to come, when books shall be useful for nothing, and shall be thrown in windows and cupboards." (This he did not say, for that the reading of Holy Scriptures displeased him, but that he might draw back all from overmuch care of learning. For he wished them rather to be good by charity than smatterers through the desire of knowledge [*quam scientiae curiositate sciolos*].) [29]

The bishop's rebuttal, of course, would not silence his opponents. By drawing such a convincing self-portrait of the book-loving *curiosus* he only incited them to further mutterings against clerks whom Sebastian Brant would find "besy bokes assemblynge":

> Say worthy doctours and Clerks curious:
> What moueth you of Bokes to haue such nomber.
> Syns dyuers doctrines throughe way contrarious
> Doth mannys mynde distract and sore encomber.[30]

These, then, were the kinds of charges de Bury faced; and his defense, which in the end only substantiated the charges of *curiositas*, took two basic forms: denial and retort. Meeting the charges head on, he first argues syllogistically that since all men by nature desire knowledge (14), and since books contain all desirable knowledge (ch. I), a man therefore should naturally desire books. The opening sentence of Aristotle's *Metaphysics* provided the major premise, and de Bury avoids any allusion to the use that, as we saw, Aquinas made of the assumption in his discussion of *curiositas*. Aquinas treated curiosity as an offense against temperance (thus the allegation that de Bury suffered from "intemperentia circa litteras"), and he cited Aristotle's dictum to emphasize the need for *studiositas* and restraint in learned inquiry. De Bury, too, begins with Aristotle, but he bends the argument in a different way, urging not caution but devotion to learning and love for the books that sustain it. This emphasis on the human desire to have the treasure "sapientiae et scientiae," felt as an "instinctum naturae," comes at the beginning and near the end of the *Philo-*

biblon (14, 179), and it is the cornerstone of de Bury's defense.

To combat the unfavorable opinion of book-collecting, de Bury repeatedly maintains that books are the armor of the Church's defense[31] and that he assembled books for the use of scholars in protecting the Church. Such an answer was unassailable, for it had been a traditional argument of Christian intellectuals; even in monastic circles, the Church Militant was thought to be dependent on books as weapons and armor.[32] Furthermore, de Bury implies that if he has been amiss in gathering books, then the mendicant orders have been so too, because they served as brokers and rummaged through libraries all over Europe for him (90). Like them and like the book-lovers who influenced him in his youth (117), he put together his library with the purest of motives. Just when he made the plan to donate it to Oxford we cannot tell, but he would like us to believe that this always had been his intention. Regardless of when the decision was made, it at least preceded Petrarch's wish, first expressed in 1361, to give his books to the city of Venice (and Petrarch wondered why no one before him had had the idea of passing on a library in this fashion).[33]

De Bury's fierce love for books will not permit him to remain on the defensive very long. In fact, his patient appeals to common experience (all men desire knowledge) and to tradition (faithful Christians know the usefulness of books) occupy only a small portion of his defense. His strategy throughout is to turn the charges back on his accusers and divert our attention from that word hanging over his head, *curiositas*. Confronting the malicious gossipers directly, he accuses them of imputing motives to him that they could not possibly prove. God alone knows "the aim and purpose of our inmost will," and, since honesty of intention determines the rightness of an action (231), who can find fault with "the sincere love of study and zeal" undertaken "for the strengthening of the orthodox faith" (233)? Indeed, if his enemies want to disparage him as a *curiosus*, he can (and does) as easily point to a related moral infection in their own ranks: by prying into other men's business, spreading gossip, searching for motives that only God can discern, and discussing "hidden things that are not revealed to the eyes of men" (235), these detractors have proved themselves to be culpably inquisitive, victims of what Plutarch would have called *mala curiositas*. Moreover, his enemies are not untainted by the love of worldly things. Frivolous monks, he complains, no longer care for books or observe Augustine's command to read books daily (80-81). The friars ignore their vows of poverty and take pleasure in food, dress, and crenelated dwellings; they read only to garner tales of heresies and "apocrypha deliramenta" with which they regale congregations from the pulpit (87-88). University students study not to learn but to earn money (148-49). And lawyers, by trivializing the powers of reason, encourage rather than extinguish the greedy contentiousness of man (168). Chaucer presents us with monks, friars, scholars, and lawyers guilty of these very violations.

Yet at no point does de Bury describe any one of these failings as offenses against *curiositas* (although most of them are), for affixing to his enemies the label they gave him would not eradicate their charges. In a debate centering around the proper use and enjoyment of worldly things, it presumably seemed wiser to him not to cloud matters by pressing the same charge too heavily on his opponents. What he can at least imply, however, is that *curiositas* may manifest itself in various ways. And he can even divest the loaded word of some of its pejorative connotations. With forensic tact, then, he makes a point of using the word *curiositas* only twice in the *Philobiblon*, both times in connection with activities unrelated to the vice of which he has been accused. He describes shepherds' proper attention to their flocks as *curiositas* (75), and in another place he terms the careful labor of his household scribes and commentators *curiositas* (176). Inasmuch as both sorts of work are laudable and require a certain dedication, it may be we are expected to believe that curiosity in book-collecting is no more a misdemeanor than sheepherding and book-making. Of course, *curiositas* always did have the separate, morally neutral meaning of "care" or "right attention to duty"; yet perhaps de Bury has gone further and subtly made *curiositas* not just a thing indifferent but a minor virtue. If so, we can see in this an event of some importance in the word's semantic history.

However, all these defenses and counter-charges, so carefully mustered with "rhetoric . . . logic . . . [and] examples from history" (40), are finally dropped in the last chapter. There the bishop humbly admits that he will not "venture entirely to justify the zealous love which we have so long had for books, or to deny that it may perchance sometimes have been the occasion of some venial negligence, albeit the object of our love is honourable and our intention upright" (245). He asks the Lord to pardon "the lapses of our feebleness" and to teach him how to deplore his "past most vain elations" and "most insane delectations" (248). Still, this is no capitulation to the indictment of his peers. De Bury here is addressing God and us—posterity— not his contemporary critics, whose views were already dismissed as irrelevant; and to this one true Judge he makes his confession. Even now he thinks of his negligence as only venial, and any admission of curiosity goes unuttered to the end. The kind of praiseworthy or at least noncommittal verdict Petrarch had given in calling de Bury a *curiosus* would have satisfied the bishop immensely, for he congratulated himself on being an inquisitive man (like John Mandeville) and an acquisitive one. His refusal to repeat the word his antagonists wished to bury him with is only one indication of his belief about the worth of curiosity. The *Philobiblon* itself provides all the evidence we could want.

Richard de Bury died just a few months after completing the *Philobiblon*, probably too soon to learn what impact his defense and glorification of books had on the anonymous gossipers. Whether or not they were swayed by his protestations of upright intention, they clearly were not appeased by the scoldings he gave them for their own worldliness. And most galling must have been the bishop's exhibition of all those characteristics of the *curiosus* that he was at the same time supposed to be denying. For de Bury's treatise begins, continues, and ends with flourishes and ornaments that betray a curious bent. His vocabulary, syntax, tropes, and methods of argument—as well as his overt expressions of zealous affection for books—all attest to an abidingly curious outlook. While the ornate qualities of his work, especially his dependence on figures like apostrophe and personification, would have been understood by anyone familiar with rhetorical principles, de Bury's literary style is nevertheless definitely *curiosus* in its complexity and diffusion. His exaltation of books as desirable things, then as companions and friends, and finally as the constant goals of his special pilgrimage must have aggravated his critics beyond even their worst expectations. For, in addition to denying that his curiosity was a vice, he also has secularized pilgrimage.

The bishop opens and closes the *Philobiblon* with sober claims that books are worth collecting because they preserve knowledge, which in turn helps preserve the Church. Such asseverations, however, are less conspicuous than his imagery and rhetoric of passionate love and religious devotion. The Holy Spirit's "illuminating fire" (3) may have inspired the idea to donate his library; but his "amor ecstaticus" (11) was the declared motive that led him to gather the books in the first place, and throughout the work de Bury unconsciously represents his curiosity for books as lust of the flesh as well as lust of the eyes. Friends and book-donors everywhere are aware that he burns with desire for their gifts (119). Like a Petrarchan lover, the bishop alternately burns and thirsts in his passion. His own unquenchable thirst (124) is matched by the parched desires of those youthful clerks who, having tasted knowledge, are then prevented from drinking deeper because of a scarcity of books (7). Using an image he later applied to the labors of restoring old books, de Bury complains that these students, "so fruitful in the cultivated field of youth, not being watered by the rain that they require, are forced to wither away" (5). Men both hunger and thirst for knowledge's sake, for the nourishment books provide (14-17). We can think of books, he says, as wells of living waters, corn, grain, food in abundance, manna, honey, and the milk of life (27-29), "if we choose to speak in figures." The Biblical imagery he has been echoing, and exaggerating, also underlies his reference to the quadrivium as the students' route of access to "the three loaves of the Knowledge of the Trinity" (47). Books are the unleavened loaves that feed hungry minds (76); the books this collector gathered up from mendicants' libraries become, as it were, table scraps. "We discovered in their fardels and baskets not only crumbs falling from the masters' table for the dogs, but the shewbread without leaven and the bread of angels having in it all that is delicious; and indeed the garners of Joseph full of corn" (135).

The degree of de Bury's lust for books can be measured by the seriousness with which he pursues this metaphor of books as nourishment. *Curiositas*, not *studiositas*, is the desideratum for those who hunger to learn. Eat books, he urges the studious clerk, so that "the belly of your memory may be sweetened" (57). What Alain de Lille once confessed about his own extended comparison between grammatical and sexual relationships—that it may have been "too strained

a metaphor"[34]—could as well describe de Bury's equation between
books and victuals, reading and eating. Those freewheeling discussions
he presided over at home customarily took place around the dinner
table,[35] and it is characteristic that he remembers them each as "a
rich and well-varied intellectual feast" (130). To a wealthy collector,
books, like fine foods, are commodities to be bought; to the *curiosus*,
books are items to be collected, their contents, nutriment to be di-
gested.

His opponents would have received such metaphoric expressions
of his love for books as proof of that "superfluous curiosity" (230)
they had tarred him with. So too they might have pointed to the ex-
uberant use of words, phrases, and conceits symptomatic of a curious
mind. De Bury styles himself as a zealot for books, upbraids members
of the mendicant orders (particularly the Dominicans) for not being
"zelotypi" (85)—Saint Francis surely would have taken that criticism
as praise—and he commends those of his agents among the orders who
were "zelatores" in procuring books (133). An "amor hereos" for
books has possessed him since youth, he writes, "quorum zelo languere
vice voluptatis accepimus" (170). Elsewhere he speaks of yearning
"cupiditate" (119) and "voluptuose" (121), and in closing he characterizes both the acquisitive and inquisitive sides of his nature as "ela-
tiones vanissimas . . . ac delectationes insanissimas" (248). His eyes (a
key feature in the physiognomy of every *curiosus*) guide him to the
forgotten chests of books and enable him to appraise their value (119).
Sight, which generally "reveals to us more of the qualities of things"
(24), surpasses the faculties of hearing and touch where books are
concerned. With stylistic elaboration he adds that "the written truth
of books, not transient but permanent, plainly offers itself to be observed, and by means of the pervious spherules of the eyes, passing
through the vestibule of perception and the courts of imagination,
enters the chamber of intellect, taking its place in the couch of memory, where it engenders the eternal truth of the mind" (25). Love—
but sin, too, as de Bury's critics would be quick to add—strikes men
through the eyes, and curiosity is lust of the eyes.

It is in connection with his curious attachment to books and his
insatiable delight in the variety of his library's holdings that we must
consider de Bury's twin affections for Christian and pagan literature.
By the fourteenth century English scholars were beginning to read

the classics more in a manner we associate with the later humanists and to retreat from earlier moralized interpretations. Men like Thomas Waleys, John Ridevall, and de Bury's friend Robert Holcot (to whom some manuscripts ascribed the authorship of the *Philobiblon*[36]) were reading the classics as attentively as Scripture and religious writings, and more importantly, they often mixed Christian and pagan authorities in their writings.[37] One's reason for turning to the classics was always a problem, of course, especially if a curious desire for information or for discovering the unknown figured in the reading; conservative theologians of the day kept warning scholars that they risked sinning by a too-avid concern with the broad range of secular studies, particularly natural philosophy. And remarks scattered throughout the *Philobiblon* suggest that de Bury read the classics with just this kind of approbation and curiosity.

For example, in proving the inestimable value of books, he instances the prophetic Sibylline books of the Romans and thinks of them in the way Christians thought of the Scriptures: as sources of *sapientia*, as "sacri libri" (43). At Paris, a "paradise" of libraries and bookstores, de Bury sees all about him replicas of Academe, Athens, and Parnassus; the famous inhabitants of this bookish community are nearly all pagans—except for Paul, whom de Bury, without any qualms, mentally situates on a shelf between Ptolemy and Dionysius (126-28). During the after-dinner sessions at de Bury's home, his learned friends offered him an assorted menu of curious, mixed topics, all of which he enjoyed: logic, physics, theology, and *moralitates* (130). In defending the worth of eloquence, he eclectically cites as authorities the god Mercury, the ancients Cicero and Livy, and the Old Testament figures Moses and Jeremiah (191); and on a different question he recalls with equanimity, and in this order, the arguments of Plato, Jerome, Xeocrates, and Origen (193).

Another reflection of de Bury's syncretic interests is his ambivalent sense of the exact relationship between secular and divine learning, *scientia* and *sapientia*. In the opening sentence of chapter I, both realms of knowledge are subjoined under the one rubric, "thesaurus sapientiae" (14). Elsewhere the *libraria sapientiae* is said to include both divine and human studies (38). Following common Christian authority, de Bury can argue (as did Petrarch and Boccaccio)[38] that ancient literature, especially pagan poetry, is useful for study of the

Bible and Fathers (183-84); but merely by emphasizing the equal
relevance of secular and spiritual writings he is risking overstatement.
He was aware of contemporary complaints that preachers and
theologians were succumbing to *curiositas* in using non-Biblical or
profane materials, and in what was perhaps an attempt to soften
charges against himself de Bury does appeal for more intensive study
of Scripture. But, ironically, the reason he gives is that this study
will supply preachers "the freshest novelty" (*recentissima novitate*)
and "the most delightful savours" (*sapidissima suavitate*) with which
to please their audiences (89). Similarly, in the dispute over the rela-
tive worth of ancient and modern writers he sides with the ancients;
yet with the breadth of taste typical of a *curiosus*, he also embraces
the *moderni*—mainly because they create "novitas" and contribute
opinions "subtiliter" as well as "utiliter" (145).

   If Richard de Bury was more a name-dropper than a learned scholar
when it came to books, perhaps his critics were right. People who
collect books are apt to value them as material objects more than as
receptacles of knowledge, and a lack of discrimination can lead them
near that dangerous zone of negative capability that medieval humanists like Holcot might reach only after a longer, more thoughtful experience with books. But de Bury really seems not to have been a
dilettante. He was a connoisseur. Almost all books pleased him because almost all varieties of learned inquiry interested him: *scientia*
and *sapientia*, the ingenious together with the morally useful. *Curiositas* knows no limitations; indeed, it brooks none. "Out of olde
bokes," as Chaucer the humanist could say, comes "al this newe science
that men lere."[39] And nowhere in the *Philobiblon* is de Bury's love
for old books, forgotten lore, and curiosity for new knowledge so
ardently expressed as in his long elegy on the destruction of the
Alexandrian library, a tragedy as epochal for bibliophiles as the dis-
solution of the monasteries would be for modern medieval scholars.
De Bury recites us the litany of disaster:

> The secrets of the heavens, which Jonithus learnt not from man or through
> man but received by divine inspiration; what his brother Zoroaster, the servant
> of unclean spirits, taught the Bactrians; what holy Enoch, the prefect of Para-
> dise, prophesied before he was taken from the world, and finally, what the
> first Adam taught his children of the things to come, which he had seen when
> caught up in an ecstasy in the book of eternity, are believed to have perished

in those horrid flames. The religion of the Egyptians, which the book of the Perfect Word so commends; the excellent polity of the older Athens, which preceded by nine thousand years the Athens of Greece; the charms of the Chaldeans; the observations of the Arabs and Indians; the ceremonies of the Jews; the architecture of the Babylonians; the agriculture of Noah; the magic arts of Moses; the geometry of Joshua; the enigmas of Samson; the problems of Solomon from the cedar of Lebanon to the hyssop; the antidotes of Aesculapius; the grammar of Cadmus; the poems of Parnassus; the oracles of Apollo; the argonautics of Jason; the strategems of Palamedes, and infinite other secrets of science are believed to have perished at the time of this conflagration (109-10).

Such nostalgia and regret are natural for one so infatuated with books. But, infatuation aside, there is evidence in the *Philobiblon* that de Bury *was* discriminating and learned enough to bear the label Beryl Smalley has applied to the classicizing friars and thinkers who surrounded the bishop. They were, in her phrase, "proto-humanists." W. A. Pantin has described the outlook of these Englishmen, especially de Bury and Trivet, as "pre-humanist."[40] R. R. Bolgar finds de Bury's love of the ancients a characteristic that links him with contemporaries like Petrarch and Salutati.[41] James Westfall Thompson has suggested that de Bury's own book is important "because it marks a transition toward humanism, in its enriched vocabulary and attention to style, and most of all in the personal tone which pervades the entire work."[42] Yet the *Philobiblon* shows that de Bury was more than a proto- or pre-humanist. In an essay as important as Southern's and Smalley's studies of humanism, Paul Oskar Kristeller has cautiously but precisely delineated several essential marks of Renaissance humanism, and three "medieval antecedents" of it;[43] and the characteristics he cites fit de Bury (whom he does not mention) so closely that they compel us to consider the *Philobiblon* and its author's predilections as definitely humanistic. In the fourteenth and fifteenth centuries, a humanist was one who professed the *studia humanitatis*, which, as Kristeller explains it, comprised five subjects: grammar, rhetoric, poetry, history, and moral philosophy. Grammar meant the study of Latin, the language of scholarship, the Church, and international correspondence; de Bury the cleric, lord-chancellor, diplomat, and book-buyer was obviously proficient in it. Poetry, for the humanists, was the study and imitation of the Latin classics as models (the *Philobiblon* and de Bury's *Liber Epistolaris* or collection of letter models show he tended, like his friends, to approach the classics in this fashion); studying poetry also meant writing treatises defending poetry (the *Philobiblon* includes such a defense). Rhetoric encouraged the art of letter-writing and oratory (and de Bury, as chancellor, must have been accomplished in both). It is difficult to know for sure if de Bury viewed history the same way the rest did, that is, as the study of ancient historians and ancient texts. But the final branch of the *studia humanitatis* (and, according to Kristeller, the most important), moral philosophy, was certainly a subject de Bury understood in the new sense. "When the humanists were prompted by the attacks of narrow-minded theologians to defend their studies," writes Kristeller, "they insisted upon their concern with moral and human problems, and claimed to provide a moral as well as an intellectual training for the young, a claim that is also expressed in the ambitious term *studia humanitatis*." The *Philobiblon* throughout is a *humanista*'s response to just that very problem. And the literary elegance and concern for erudition, which Kristeller sees as typical of these humanist treatises, are everywhere apparent in the bishop's book. Finally, were one to read the *Philobiblon* only with Kristeller's three medieval antecedents of Renaissance humanism in mind—the *ars dictaminis* tradition (especially of Italy), the study of grammar and poetry (in France), and classical studies (in Byzantine Greece)—the case for de Bury's humanism would be strengthened even more. His acquaintance with the *ars dictaminis* is evident;[44] so too is his awareness of the varied uses of grammar and poetry, his advocacy of Greek (and indeed Hebrew) study in the universities, and his familiarity with the Greek language, a familiarity some think was superior to Petrarch's.[45]

Surprisingly, this curious early-fourteenth-century English book-collector thought, wrote, and acted in ways most scholars normally would associate with fifteenth-century Italians. Continuing inquiry into the writings and activities of de Bury's Oxford colleagues, their varied ties to Avignon and Italy, and their direct influence on later fourteenth-century countrymen like Chaucer will no doubt reduce such surprise and skepticism about the nature of late-medieval English humanism.[46] But the *Philobiblon* itself seems the product of a humanist, one whose solicitude for decaying books elicited the pledge to revitalize them—a pledge filled with the imagery of renascence:

Amongst the mass of these things we found some greatly meriting to be restored [*renovari*], which when skilfully cleansed and freed from the disfigur-
ing rust of age, deserved to be renovated [*reformari*] into comeliness of aspect.
And applying in full measure the necessary means, as a type of the resurrection
[*resurrectionis*] to come, we resuscitated [*resuscitata*] them and restored them
again to new life and health [*redivivae reddidimus sospitati*] (142). [47]

De Bury's *amor librorum* was indeed an excess, although in his
own eyes a joyous one, a devotion worthy of its object. Of course the
word *amor*, so often repeated in his work, suggests the depth of his
passion. But perhaps his enemies' irritation over it is made more understandable in that startling moment when we notice him cleverly
substitute the term "caritatem librorum" for *amor* (124). It was a
bold semantic maneuver. In no way does the context of this passage
require a shift to the spiritual term; de Bury is still speaking of his
mundane love for books—that love he had earlier distinguished from
other kinds of worldly attachment (11). It is one thing for him to
describe his desire as *amor*, quite another to brazenly identify it as
a spiritual love, especially since he was accused of *cupiditas* and more
especially since he himself agreed that his preoccupation was *cupiditas*
(119). What we have to conclude is that the opposition between
caritas and *cupiditas*, which orthodox moralists would have appealed
to in contrasting virtuous love and book-love, was basically unper-
suasive to de Bury. Only by overlooking this attitude can a modern
exegete like Hans Schnyder say that de Bury urged reading only for
knowledge and "not for the pleasure of it." [48] On the contrary, the
bishop's offhanded use of *cupiditas* and then *caritas* as synonyms for
his love of books is part of his determination to vindicate curiosity.

The source of his critics' unease and the focus of de Bury's *curiositas* was, of course, all those books. To recapture some sense of the
annoyance his pastime provoked in others we must look closely at
the roles he cast for books in his work. His foes may not have considered his personification of books to have been in itself exceptional;
rhetorical authority, classical and medieval, lay behind his use of the
figures of *prosopopeia* and *apostrophatio*. [49] But it is the zeal and
exaggeration with which de Bury develops this trope that would have
drawn fire from his enemies, for his books emote, speak, argue, and

are spoken to.[50] Here, in the wake of their complaints about his curiosity, this book-lover confronts critics with more of that *elegantia*, the fantasy of books living and speaking. De Bury perceives books in three distinct ways: as objects (and also repositories of knowledge), as living things, and most striking of all, as the goal of a bibliophile's pilgrimage.

To begin with, he time and again stresses the basic worth of books as possessions, as objects felicitous to the sight and touch (23). No price is too high to pay for them (ch. III); as property having value apart from the knowledge they contain (32), they are superior to horses and money (123). He writes excitedly about his book-buying trips and scavenging missions to old libraries, and he explains in detail how the library he will establish later ought to be operated (ch. XIX). Chaucer's poor clerk—who, unlike de Bury, was not "so worldly for to have office"—shared with the bishop not only a regard for Petrarch but a preference for books over other possessions:

> . . . al that he myghte of his freendes hente,
> On bookes and on lernynge he it spente,
> And bisily gan for the soules preye
> Of hem that yaf hym wherwith to scoleye. [51]

Whether or not de Bury always showed gratitude with prayers,[52] he liked cluttering his house with books. He prized them as works of art, as belongings, as furniture. As Curtius has reminded us, throughout the Middle Ages, materially as well as artistically "the written book had a value which we can no longer feel."[53] Once he obtained a book, de Bury took care to restore it, if necessary, and to preserve it, maintaining a private scriptorium of scholars and scribes "who devoted themselves with unwearied zeal to the correction, exposition, tabulation and compilation of various volumes" (138, 143). But books are also for reading and study, and so for the collector who is also a patron of learning they have another value at least equal to their physical beauty. The *Philobiblon* testifies to what de Bury's unkindest critics may have wished to deny, that he did read what he owned. He was a student before he was a wealthy book-buyer,[54] and to exchange curiosities with Petrarch or participate in round-table talk with Merton fellows he would have had to do more than fondle the books' bindings. The bishop was no scholar, only the servant and patron of

scholars, and his treatise was intended to glorify books and study
rather than show off his own learning. But nevertheless the treatise
does show him to have been a learned, imaginative, and well-read man.

Second, and more striking, de Bury treats books literally as living
creatures. Saintsbury and J. W. H. Atkins have commented on his
sympathy for books as animate things, and Smalley has claimed that
the extended personification of books, a tour de force that lasts for
four chapters (IV–VII), was original with de Bury.[55] Books, in fact,
are seen to have vegetal as well as sensible life. In the same way that
de Bury envisioned the youthful generation of clerks as a flowering
field needing his husbandry, he conceives of old refound books as
"sweet-smelling flowers." He finds these forgotten beauties in the
"little plots and gardens" of small schools, miniature copies of the
paradisiacal garden that is the libraries of Paris. Once found they are
given a new home and rejuvenated for the use of the next generation
of scholars. Those things that provide nourishment for students must
themselves be given nourishment.

Ultimately, de Bury elevates his books to the status of rational
creatures and lets them, as embodied friends, voice their own defense.
In his survey of various late-medieval uses of books as symbols, Curtius noted examples of an author addressing his book and a writer
calling the human mind a book,[56] but here the sustained complaint of
books against war and against the abusive treatment given them by
priests, monks, and friars (44–115)[57] presupposes a more intense sort
of imaginative identity between an author and his work. The *Philobiblon* is a book about books, and it is in keeping not only with de
Bury's loving acceptance of them as friends but with his rhetorical
design to have them speak out as, in a sense, his alter ego. So human-
ized, there is no limit to the role-playing books can indulge in. As
teachers, they neither angrily reprove students nor laugh at the ignorant (26). As parents, they nurture clerks and confer on the clergy
any distinctions they attain (44–46). Chief among them is the Bible,
ordained for man by God, who is the Book of Life (17). This one
book safeguards clerks when they need to claim benefit of clergy;
and for this redemptive power alone, observes the bishop, it "deserves
to be called the book of life!" (55) Books are also fragile and suffering creatures. They fret about being "altogether exiled" from the

homes of clergy by jealous women (one thinks of the Wife of Bath and that book of Jankyn's she "made hym brenne"), their coverings are torn off, their "native whiteness that was clear with light" turns yellow as if "diseased with jaundice," and they undergo the corruption of Lazarus (60-64). Worthless compilers bastardize the creatures by attributing to them the wrong authors (68). Careless copyists (like Chaucer's Adam scrivener) ruin books (71), stupid translators mutilate them (71), and illiterates mar them with too much gold-leaf (72). Despite these ravages, and although they were slain like helpless innocents in the fires of Alexander (107), books revive and become whole again, serve as ambassadors between friends, and if properly cared for, endlessly beget new progeny (207).

De Bury's extravagant imagination is responsible for another series of ideas, which, like his personification of books, suggests the range and excess of his appetite for the written word. As we have already seen, he thinks of the proper desire for books as a thirst and hunger and links it to the "feast" of intellectual discussion held round the dining table. Associations between books, authors, and his scholarly companions become equivalences; he talks of books as comforters in misfortune (197) and of his learned friends as helpmates (131). Books —his friends—and human friends are his companions at meals, and books themselves are to be eaten. De Bury's contemporary, de Chambre, used exactly the right verb to explain that the bishop delighted ("delectabatur") both in his books and in his scholarly acquaintances.[58] In similar fashion, de Bury employs synecdoche to blend together writers and their works. Describing how war dissipates libraries, he visualizes Aristotle being borne off in chains (103). In one of their soliloquies books complain that they once were dispersed abroad by Theodoric "while Boethius was in exile" (113), and when he finds Ptolemy measuring the heavens in Paris de Bury almost seems to believe literally what he presents as a figure of speech (127).

His portrayal of books leads him to unexpected, novel, and audacious conclusions at several other points in the work. While arguing the principle that books are to be loved above the world and wealth, he quotes a line from Jerome—"The same man cannot love both gold and books"—and supports that sentiment with some verses from John of Salisbury. Then, aware that he has nearly invoked the thought in Matthew 6:24, he decides to quote it (or almost quote it): "No man, therefore, can serve both books and Mammon" (194). There is no escaping the implied identity. Gold is to Mammon what books are to God. So what his accusers had equated with sinful curiosity the bishop here identifies with divinity. Soon after, while speaking of the journeys men's minds can take by means of books, de Bury mentions that terrestrial spot, the antarctic pole, just opposite on the globe from Ultima Thule; but he describes it with the words used in the Old and New testaments (Isaiah 64:4, 1 Corinthians 2:9) to depict the Promised Land—that "which eye hath not seen, nor ear heard" (199). Being a *curiosus* who sees book-hunting ultimately as a devout pilgrimage, Richard de Bury is naturally as eager to see and hear about such remote regions (the new worlds Mandeville evoked) as he is to search for books in Paris, the place he considers to be another kind of promised land.

A more surprising example of de Bury's manipulation of Biblical language for his own ends occurs at the beginning of his argument that restoring old volumes should be a pleasurable habit for book-lovers. It is necessary, he says, to replace old books (and to write new ones) because the Bible tells us that "Of making many books there is no end" [Ecclesiastes 12:12](206). Now the bishop knew very well that the other half of the verse read "and in much study there is weariness for the flesh." Medieval commentators generally understood the *sentence* as a warning against intellectual pursuits and a too-deep immersion in books. Hugh of St. Victor, for instance, told those "who wish to read everything" that "the number of books is infinite; don't pursue infinity! Where no end is in sight, there can be no rest."[59] Roger Bacon cited Seneca's counsel that too many books burden rather than instruct the student and that the loss of forty thousand books at Alexandria (or one hundred thousand by de Bury's affectionate calculation) symbolized the fate held out for any excessive undertaking.[60] By inverting the words of Ecclesiastes, words directed against *curiosi* like himself, the bishop openly draws attention to the questionable nature of his avocation. Vincent of Beauvais well knew the relevance these words had for enthusiasts like de Bury: "Indeed of making many books there is no end, and neither is the eye of the curious reader satisfied, nor the ear of the auditor."[61]

These instances of de Bury's conceptual and stylistic extravagances —books speaking through ventriloquism, the Bible surrendering to unusual meanings—are literary manifestations of the intemperance, zeal, and love of novelty that characterize him as a curious book-collector and humanist. Apart from the fact that rhetoric manuals countenanced such expression, it could not but reinforce the view of de Bury's critics that his was a curious mind. His colleague Holcot once judged Alain de Lille's *De Planctu Naturae* to be a work written in a "curiose" stylistic manner,[62] and de Bury shared with Alain an enjoyment of the strange conceit, the elaborately raveled metaphor. The number of newly coined or strange Latin words in the *Philobiblon* offered another kind of testimony to de Bury's curious disposition. One fifteenth-century scribe, in fact, thought it necessary to add in an appendix to the *Philobiblon* a special glossary of 244 uncommon and exotic terms the reader would not have been expected to recognize.[63]

Implicit in medieval treatments of *curiositas* had always been the emphasis on avoiding excess, elaboration, and ornamentation; very often, in fact, denunciations of the vice took into account esthetic as well as moral matters. Bernard of Clairvaux's discussion of the vice was but one of many in which moral and esthetic norms seemed to merge. In Aquinas's and the Parson's rejections of curiously elaborate dress,[64] in Saint Francis's contrast between simplicity of soul and the curiosity of book-learning, this blurring of criteria is just below the surface. Nicholas Love praised the Holy Family, "pilgrymes and straungeres, pore and nedy," for going without fancy clothes and other luxuries during their flight into Egypt. Their poverty, he said, should be a lesson to men who indulge in any kind of curious activity, including proud and subtle workmanship or artistry which deflects them from simpler, plainer labors and turns their unstable hearts from God.[65] Attacking miracle plays, a fourteenth-century preacher could interweave moral and artistic judgments: plays are evil recreation, they snare men's eyes with vanities. Unlike paintings, which (if they are not too "curious") can be excused since they serve as books for illiterates, plays "ben made more to deliten men bodily" and "thei ben quike bookis to schrewidenesse more than to godenesse."[66] At the start of his treatise on the astrolabe Chaucer vows to shun "superfluite of wordes" and "curious endityng" in order to compose a straightforward exposition for his son.[67] This is a stylistic comment, but it seems to derive from a moral distinction between the values of simplicity and complexity. In showing how the curious style and content of sermons came to infect contemporary church music, Beryl Smalley quotes a fourteenth-century moralist whose criticism of novelty and complexity focuses on the old rhetorical distinction between the aims of instruction and delight.

> It is the same with sermons today as it is with motets. In the old days chant was simple and plain. Then the tune and words and everything could be understood, because they could be distinguished. But now there are discants in the motets, so that only the tune can be followed. It charms the ear and has no other use. Similarly in the old days sermons were such as to profit the people. But now they have rhymes and curious comparisons, and philosophical subtleties are mixed with them; so many sermons do no good; they only please the hearers as oratory.[68]

In the previous century Saint Edmund of Canterbury argued that in dignity and conciseness the Pater Noster was superior to all other prayers; it was short, it had no "curyous rennynge wordes," and it did not abet through "curyous speche" the showy devotion preferred by men who luxuriated in "the multyplycacyon of prayers."[69] It is the prolixity of prayers, like de Bury's multiplication of books, that is curious; it is the exaggerated and complicated style, present in the *Philobiblon* but missing in the Pater Noster, that reveals curiosity.

The *Philobiblon* clearly has just this diffuse quality, and perhaps the Latin prose rhythms of the work dictated by the artificial *cursus* style de Bury employed contribute to the elegant complexity of the book.[70] The ornateness of the style—it is almost never simple and plain—is truly meant to please the ear, but there are moments when the style nearly obliterates the sense. Notice, for instance, what happens in a passage where the bishop is describing the progressive downfall of a clerk who takes up with thieves (52 ff.). He pictures the clerk committing crimes, then being confined by the law. As the man awaits execution he suddenly turns into an imprisoned Christ— "Peter swears that he knows not the man: the people cry to the judge: *Crucify, crucify him! if thou let this man go, thou art not Caesar's friend.*" Just as abruptly, the clerk is again depicted as an ordinary man, standing before the judge, ready to be hanged. Pleading privilege of clergy, he is given the Bible and saved in the nick of time. At the end of all this the clerk metamorphoses into still another figure, the prodigal son. De Bury's exuberance and unintegrated allusiveness can destroy coherent meaning. At times like this he shows himself to be as much the overreacher in curiosity of expression as the supernumerary of books.

As if to account for both his *amor librorum* and his elaborate style, he tells us late in the treatise that he lives under the influence of Mercury (234), the planet that supervises writing, writers, eloquent speakers, and seekers of profound knowledge.[71] John Gower seems to have gotten closer to the point when he explained that Mercury's nature is such

> That under him that bore is,
> In boke he schal be studious
> And in wrytinge curious. . . . [72]

Curious travelers like Mandeville were moved to wander by Mercury; so too were men of labyrinthine stylistic complexity and vicarious loves like de Bury. But de Bury would not be a complete *curiosus* unless his urges led him to physically wander, to journey restlessly in order to gratify his needs. His many trips made to locate books are, of course, journeys, but he does not disappoint us in his characterization of those journeys: they are finally, for him, pilgrimages. This attitude is the most amazing and prominent of all his curious literary conceits: the idea that the book-lover is a pilgrim and that the approach to books constitutes a pilgrimage. For him, books are the equipment of the *curiosus*; but while he sees them as inquisitive men's guides to knowledge, he also considers them goals in themselves. He has equated books with curiosity (they both whet and fulfill curious appetites) and to suggest the high value man ought to place on books and to counter arguments that they obstruct Christians rather than propel them toward wisdom, he connects the experiences of bibliophiles and pilgrims. These connections are less obvious in the *Philobiblon* than in, say, Mandeville's *Travels*; but then the curiosity of a scholarly mind is at times less vividly proclaimed than that of the restless explorer.

It is true that de Bury does speak quite legitimately of the heavenly goal to which all book-learning should be directed. All knowledge comes ultimately from God above, the Book of Life, who established books as the "tabernacle" of knowledge (17). Truth is the "via sine devio" we travel to achieve wisdom (22). Through books men may

gain knowledge of the heavenly Trinity even while *viatores* on earth
(47). The latent imagery of pilgrimage in remarks like these is more
or less reflexive, an almost unconscious iteration of a favorite Christian theme.

But since all books are homologues of the Book of Life, every book
is a destination for the reader-pilgrim. Some of the "many thousand"
of Biblical types which de Bury makes into equivalents for books,
including the rivers of Paradise, the ark of Noah, and the ladder of
Jacob (27-29), are also the sort of places and attractions one might
find on the agenda of pilgrims going to the Holy Land. As it is the
duty of Christian *viatores* to daily make or write books (210), so it is
the delight of book-worshippers like de Bury to exhume and revere
old relics, old books. He rejoices in the ancient *translatio librorum*
from Persia to Athens (114) as devout Christians might exult in the
translation of a saint's body to a new shrine. Pilgrims went eastward
in imitation of inner spiritual quests for Jerusalem, the *visio pacis*, or
in expectation of the final journey to heavenly paradise, but this
worldly pilgrim's real moment of ecstasy occurs when he enters Paris,
the earthly paradise of book-lovers (126 ff.). Then too, the claim that
de Bury paid less attention to the Bible than to other books and preferred matters *nova* and *curiosa* is not unlike late-medieval complaints
that pilgrims cared less about visiting Christ's homeland than about
local saints' shrines. And perhaps de Bury's attachment to books as
physical objects enjoyable in themselves is somewhat comparable to
the unfocused preoccupation one notices in pilgrims who were more
interested in the journey itself than in their sacred destinations. Augustine's reminder to inquisitive pilgrims to beware of being charmed
by the journey echoed a much older stricture: "For they search busily
among his works, but are distracted by what they see, because the
things seen are fair. . . . For if they so far succeeded in knowledge that
they could speculate about the world, how did they not more quickly
find its Lord?" (Wisdom 13:7, 9). Books are distractingly fair in the
bishop's eyes, and his every search was a pilgrimage to a shrine.

De Bury draws out the explicit pilgrimage metaphor only so far,
however, because his expressed motives for collecting books obviously
would have seemed too worldly to permit such associations. And it is
true he terms each of his book-buying journeys an *iter* (131). But in
the passage where he summarizes the importance of all these political-

recreational trips it is significant, I think, that he refers to them generally as *peregrinationes*, travels made through the "perplexas intricationes" and "labyrinthos" of worldly affairs (125). There is for him little difference between the *peregrinatio* and the *iter*: each is finally a pilgrimage to books. Only in his special understanding of the term are they religious pilgrimages. As de Bury must have realized, in his time pilgrims were apt to be *curiosi*, and *curiosi* pilgrims. The bishop would have appreciated Paracelsus's conception of the "whole earth as a book or library 'in which the pages are turned with our feet,' which must be used 'pilgrimly.'"[73] For, once rediscovered, books present to men the "truest likeness of the beatitude to come" (196); but in a much more worldly way books of all kinds enable us to have "the reward of our beatitude, while we are yet sojourners below" (200).

The other metaphors of movement and travel that de Bury employs to illustrate his restless passion correspond loosely to his notion of a pilgrimage to books, but actually they amount to a different language altogether. This humanist book-collector lives in a world of motion: he knows the fame of his love for books has "winged abroad everywhere" (119); his friars go searching for books throughout Europe ("perlustrantes" and "perscrutantes"), along the way collecting for him gossip, news, and the latest tales about "novis causis" (133-34); and all through the *Philobiblon* eager students are to be observed flying ever upward on the wings of knowledge (18, 47, 152). Books, like those who quest for them, are the most kinetic features on the landscape. The bishop seeks them out, "ubilibet visitandi" (117), searching "ad mundi diversa dominia" (124) because they have been strewn by time "in diversa mundi climata" (113). But no more passive than he, they too travel. They come as gifts, in a "multitudinous flight," he says (144). "While resting they yet move," for, once fixed in the minds of readers, they can then journey everywhere. "What an infinite host of books lie at Paris or Athens, and at the same time resound in Britain and in Rome!" (58) Passed by means of books through the hands of successive scholars, knowledge is continually purified and expanded (158, 161-63). The legacy of the world's learning, through the books which preserve it, has survived by unending movement. De Bury describes this ongoing *translatio studii*:

> We see that [Minerva] has already visited the Indians, the Babylonians, the
> Egyptians and Greeks, the Arabs and the Romans. Now she has passed by

Paris, and now has happily come to Britain, the most noble of islands, nay, rather a microcosm in itself, that she may show herself a debtor both to the Greeks and to the Barbarians (157).

Through books, knowledge sweeps across the world with the aid of book-collectors like de Bury who accelerate the process by gathering and conserving the past for the future.

At some point, however, perhaps as he sits reading a book amid the trunks and stacks in one of his libraries, the bibliophile realizes that, like Minerva, he too can travel with books. They will show him "things that are past, and even prophesy as to the future" (202), but to the greater delight of the *curiosus* they will transport him spatially, as he rests in his room. This admission of vicarious enjoyment is one badge of the *curiosus*, and de Bury proudly displays it:

> In books we climb mountains and scan the deepest gulfs of the abyss; in books we behold the finny tribes that may not exist outside their native waters, distinguish the properties of streams and springs and of various lands; from books we dig out gems and metals and the materials of every kind of mineral, and learn the virtues of herbs and trees and plants, and survey at will the whole progeny of Neptune, Ceres, and Pluto (198).

And surveying the earth is not enough; the eyes of the curious always stray higher:

> But if we please to visit the heavenly inhabitants, Taurus, Caucasus, and Olympus are at hand, from which we pass beyond the realms of Juno and mark out the territories of the seven planets by lines and circles. And finally we traverse the loftiest firmament of all, adorned with signs, degrees, and figures in the utmost variety. There we inspect the antarctic pole, which eye hath not seen, nor ear heard; we admire the luminous Milky way and the Zodiac, marvellously and delightfully pictured with celestial animals (199).

One can imagine Bernard grimacing and Pope Innocent clucking at such raptures. No poor devout pilgrim this—head bent in prayer, eyes fixed on spire or relics; the curious bibliophile is booked for travel on a very different, unreligious pilgrimage.

Not so paradoxically, de Bury's feverish *curiositas* is soothed by quiet moments spent with a book, by returning to his library where the longest, sometimes the best journeys can begin. Like that other public figure and traveler, Geoffrey Chaucer, he seemed to find the world within books at least as wide as the world of affairs. For the curious bookman and humanist like the bishop of Durham, home is as important as any remote land. There is the library and its silence, a place less permanent than the heavenly home but more satisfying than the demanding world outside. Home is the place meant to house the books once exiled "ad patrias peregrinas" (112) and to hold de Bury's gift to Oxford later on. It is the resting place living books long for, the rooms where "inscriptions of gold and ivory are designed for the several compartments, to which the volumes themselves are reverently brought and pleasantly arranged, so that no one hinders the entrance of another or injures its brother by excessive crowding" (114). Here the books in turn offer a refuge to all the prodigal sons who desire a retreat to the house of studies and the *vita solitaria*. And here we find the lover of books, drawn back centripetally to the shrine of his passion, safe for a time from the clamorous accusations of his enemies, sedentary, *mens absentia cogitans*[74]–but prepared like Mandeville and the eagle's friend, "Geffrey," to journey again, as Petrarch did, "back in memory and to range in imagination through all ages and all lands."[75]

CHAPTER V. CURIOSITY
AND THE INSTABILITY
OF PILGRIMAGE: CHAUCER'S
CANTERBURY TALES

*As long as the talkative fellow, Talebearer, dwells
in the city, he utters many slanders in abuse of
people. For a talkative man harms other people like a second plague, and he often
strikes as suddenly as a whirlwind. And since an evil tongue inflicts every sort of
wickedness upon the world, I intend to speak of what its grievous powers are. A
tongue sets quarrels in motion, a quarrel sets people in motion, people set swords
in motion, swords set schisms in motion, and schism brings ruin. A tongue up-
roots rulers from their kingdoms, sends estates up in flames, and pillages homes.
A tongue loosens marriage bonds, and makes into two what God has declared to
be one. Slandered wives shun their husbands, and husbands shun their wives, and
they talk incessantly about the evils being done to them. . . . Where the tongue
of a chatterer rules is not a place of peace, and he who does not have peace does
not have God.—John Gower,* Vox Clamantis

By the time they have finished the *General Prologue*, readers of the
Canterbury Tales sense that most of the talkative pilgrims who are
journeying to Becket's shrine, ostensibly to thank or beseech the saint
for favors, are deficient in the piety appropriate to a pilgrimage. The
narrator claims to have set out "with ful devout corage," and among
the fellowship at least the Knight, Parson, Clerk, and Plowman seem
to be so motivated; but the majority of the tale-telling travelers are
clearly on a holiday outing. Their guide, Harry Bailly of the tavern,
has tempted them all with a rationalization for mutual entertainment
—why ride "doumb as a stoon"?—and as a whole they are quite ready

to engage in storytelling. And, after all, why not? Pilgrimage by this
time had become largely an outlet for *curiositas*, no longer a strictly
solemn spiritual exercise. In the *Tales* we will learn that the Wife of
Bath views it as an opportunity for *daliaunce* (III, 556ff.),[1] that the
merchant in the *Shipman's Tale* looks upon pilgrimage as one convenient way of eluding creditors (VII, 233-34), and that the Friar
thinks the pilgrims, as they "ryde by the weye" here, "nedeth nat to
speken but of game" (III, 1274-75). Even a contemporary archbishop
of Canterbury condoned the mirth and festivity of pilgrimages (which
the Lollards objected to) as permissible diversions for weary travelers.[2]
Along with the *recchelees* Monk, who has abandoned the rules of his
order to freely wander about following after "the newe world the
space," Chaucer's pilgrims accept the innkeeper's second offering of
a menu, a feast of talking they might have expected anyway, the
chance "to talen and to pleye."

At the very beginning of the *General Prologue* the pilgrims exude
an air of *felaweshipe* (26, 32), and the narrator, who senses it too,
tells us he and the rest made a *forward* to rise early on the next morning and depart. Then, to further emphasize the fellowship of this
group of pilgrims, Chaucer has the Host propose a contest of tales, a
game, the rules of which Harry must explain at some length. A more
spiritual motivation for pilgrimage would have generated a true Christian fellowship among the pilgrims, but the Host has provided them
with a game as a distraction from piety, and then suggested a pact far
removed in aim and purpose from a pilgrimage. The contest of tales
which ensues, always shifting from *earnest* to *game*, full of rancor and
sweetness, will test the viability of each pilgrim's sense of fellowship;
it will also point to the central hollowness of the corporate pilgrimage
and, in the end, the directions the talebearers should have had in mind
at the time they launched their game. I want to emphasize the pilgrims' willingness to make a game and contest out of the pilgrimage
and to pursue it according to the rules of a *forward* or pact because
I think Chaucer's own emphasis is on this issue—he in fact devotes
the last one hundred lines of the *General Prologue* to it. It helps us see,
first, some general underlying relationships between the idea of pilgrimage and the tales which follow, and, in addition, special thematic
relationships among the several large groups of linked tales. In light
of this emphasis, I would like to propose some new reasons for

Chaucer's setting the *Tales* within the pilgrimage framework by re-directing our attention to certain institutional and social aspects of pilgrimage.

Some critics of late have treated the pilgrimage of the *Canterbury Tales* as an exclusively allegorical journey—John V. Fleming asserts the work is one of "the best known of the longer allegories of the fourteenth century"[3]—and some, following suggestions of Ralph Baldwin and D. W. Robertson, Jr., have sought to discover the force of this allegory at work in individual tales.[4] Even allowing for the apparent critical uncertainty about how to recognize polysemy in the *Tales*,[5] problems such as the exact ordering of the tales and the identity of the tale-tellers make the work resistant to any full allegorical gloss. Moreover, as Judson B. Allen has lately demonstrated, "Chaucer's poetry reveals a fundamentally ironic attitude toward spiritual sense allegories."[6] Most recent discussions of the *Tales* have acknowledged this problem. Paul G. Ruggiers's treatment of the mixture of themes in the "great middle" of the work (that Baldwin perforce leapt over) and Robert M. Jordan's theory about the inorganic nature of the work's structure, which he too sees as having a shifting middle, have forsaken the hunt for allegory.[7] My own view of pilgrimage as an institution and custom with a particular social relevance to the tales within the frame owes much to these two critics—and also to a study like John G. Demaray's on Dante, which shows that the poet "drew upon the oral and written materials of the Holy Land pilgrimage tradition in creating *Purgatorio* and infusing this part of the *Commedia* with a body of 'real' experience recognizable to readers of his period."[8]

The *Canterbury Tales* not only defies wholesale allegorical interpretations; it also obstructs critical attempts to discover (or invent) any one ironclad meaning for the total work, to claim that in this incomplete and disjointed collection of tales there lies a single unifying theme. The *Canterbury Tales* is "about" many things; its author is not a simple moralist but a complex one; and every sensible reader's response to the work is bound to change with each rereading. No one can read or teach the *Tales* as if it were a doctrinal treatise, monolithic in its moral vision, so full of serious *sentence* that the humor, farce, irony, and variegated points of view in it must be explained away or overlooked. Nevertheless, as Robert O. Payne has remarked, the work invites continuing analysis, and it *is* impossible to read it without thinking clusters of tales are thematically connected.[9] I agree with Payne and believe that large segments of the *Tales* are interconnected, even dependent on each other, because of their direct or indirect relationship to pilgrimaging. I readily admit that pilgrimage does not "explain" the *Canterbury Tales* (any more perhaps than an understanding of principles of gothic architecture does), and I neither can nor will try to account for all of the tales in my argument. But in their own way, it seems to me, Chaucer's pilgrims and their tales reflect the culturally energizing tension between curiosity and pilgrimage that de Bury and Mandeville likewise reflect in their own ways. And Theodore Silverstein's reminder that the pilgrimage of the *Canterbury Tales* "is a device, not a plot or an argument," and his question— "What other principles than dramatic human accident really determine the order and relevance of the actual *Tales*?"[10]—go to the heart of my discussion. My own sense of the reasons Chaucer chose pilgrimage derives from a belief that he had a mixture of esthetic, social, and moral motives for using the institution to bind the tales together, and that the curiosity by his day associated with pilgrimage permitted him to thread the collection—mainly its large unified segments—with ideas that mirror his conservative attitude toward both the remembered ideals of pilgrimage and its contemporary decline.

The ideals of pilgrimage as a devout communal practice seem best expressed in the Knight's, Clerk's, and Parson's tales, and in Chaucer's own *Tale of Melibee*. But the pilgrimage to Canterbury begins with a contest suggested by the Host and codified as a pact; the contest leads to noisy rivalry, disputes, and reciprocal hostility; and the disorder visible among the tales and their tellers (which is foreshadowed in the *General Prologue*) creates, by the end of the work, a portrait of the social instability that curiosity has engendered all along the way. Nevertheless, while the behavior, dress, motives for travel, and taletelling all betray curiosity, Chaucer has also embedded in the work the norms of pious pilgrimage. Opposed to noise and disorder are the values of silence and order, qualities thought to be essential for fruitful pilgrimaging. Chaucer sensed the conflict between order and instability and enunciated it by focusing on the curiosity of pilgrimage because that conflict was an inescapable fact of life in late-fourteenth-century England. Chaucer lived, wrote, and worked in an era and for a government riven by political, economic, and religious chaos. Plague,

labor unrest, popular civil and parliamentary dissensions, national and
European ecclesiastical decay and controversy, turbulence and divisiveness within Richard II's court, wasteful military adventures like John
of Gaunt's escapades in Spain and Despenser's "crusade" in Flanders[11]
—all these catastrophes justify Muscatine's description of Chaucer's
environment as one of crisis and Froissart's bleak view that (in 1381,
but likewise true for the last twenty years of Chaucer's life) "never
was any land or realm in such great danger as England at that time."[12]
The *Canterbury Tales* comes out of this period of noise and instability.
Pilgrimage was one of many venerable institutions losing their vitality;
and by selecting *it* as the vehicle for his own *commedia* and peopling
it with representative citizens, Chaucer was able to reflect the anxieties
of the age in a form easily recognizable as a social and spiritual act
that had traditionally symbolized Christian order but by his time had
evolved into a worldly—a curious—exercise.

These are the reasons I believe Chaucer seized on pilgrimage as an
organizing principle for the *Canterbury Tales*, and my argument can
be simply summarized here as follows:

(1) Chaucer valued pilgrimage, as a framing device, more for its
applicability to certain broad social concerns than for its allegorical
implications. There is a large gap between the pilgrims' playful attitude
toward the journey and the attitude they ought to have had as peni-
tent Christians, riding in brotherly accord; Chaucer underscores this
spiritual indifference to pilgrimage by binding the pilgrims to a pact
that requires them to tell tales and be judged for and by them. The
pilgrimage thus becomes, indirectly, a gathering of people indeed bound
to a common purpose, but not the purpose spiritual authority and
contemporary critics approved of. Pride, contempt, social prestige,
and other urges move these pilgrims, but the real purpose of their
temporary bond eventually turns out to be the antagonizing and over-
coming of one's neighbors—because of the contest at the heart of the
pact.

(2) The tension between the unity required by the pact (not, ironically, by piety) and the desire to better other contestants underlies
thematic relationships between the large blocks of tales which I will
focus on, particularly Fragment I, the so-called Marriage Group, and
the final sequence leading up to and including the *Parson's Tale*. This
pilgrimage made to tell tales surely falls short of "thilke parfit glorious

pilgrymage/That highte Jerusalem celestial," which it (and any earthly pilgrimage) was meant to have symbolized; but an understanding of the allegorical nature of pilgrimage is, finally, of remote importance. Like Troilus's elevated perspective from the eighth sphere, the ideal is invoked only at the end of the work. Admittedly, this trip to Canterbury has slight spiritual worth judged against the pilgrimage all Christians make to Celestial Jerusalem. Yet in the *Tales* Chaucer dwells on another, more immediate contrast: the disparity between that peaceful, devout company the pilgrims would have been expected to form and the noisy, disputatious, unstable assembly they all too quickly become as a result of the motivations supplied by the very pact they make to "talen and to pleye." Chaucer knew pilgrimage was a curiosity-ridden institution, and the Canterbury pilgrimage he shapes his tales around is an example of the disintegrating ideal. Most of the members on the pilgrimage corroborate this; throughout the work, curiosity undermines pilgrimage.

General Prologue

Taken together, the opening lines of the *General Prologue* and the montage of pilgrim portraits that follow show how the ideal motivations for Christian pilgrimage have been compromised. The blurred religious motive for pilgrimage is underscored by the imagery of natural regeneration; and the not-so-religious longing is further attenuated by the casual mention of the inveterate pilgrimage-goers, the palmers, who lust "for to seken straunge strondes,/To ferne halwes, kowthe in sondry londes" (13–14). Partly because of its position near the end of the opening sentence, this comment on the impetus for curious traveling strengthens our sense of the worldly urges back of *this* pilgrimage.[13] The implication of the long initial sentence of the *Tales* is that curiosity at least as much as piety draws these pilgrims away from home. Even before we meet the pilgrims we might suspect that most of them are too much "perced to the roote" by April and other forces to be able to focus clearly on Becket's shrine at the horizon. Already Chaucer has highlighted the disorientation that, in our own time, Thomas Merton warned against: "The geographical pilgrimage is the symbolic acting out of an inner journey. The inner journey is the intrapolation of the meanings and signs of the outer pilgrimage. One can have one without the other. It is best to have both."[14]

Before he has the Host propose the pact of tale-telling, Chaucer describes the entourage of Canterbury-bound pilgrims. In different ways these portraits suggest the conflict between the worldly and spiritual motivations of the pilgrims, all of whom have formed a *compaignye* and consider themselves joined in *felaweshipe*. For nearly all of them are characterized by their attitudes toward travel and wandering, many are portrayed as having less than amiable relations with their neighbors, and a number of them are described in one way or another as "takers" rather than "givers." This combination of traits points to both the questionable motivations of certain individuals and the probability that the body of pilgrims will degenerate into a "route" before it becomes a "faire compaignye." What Chaucer exposes in the *General Prologue* and what they will reveal in so many of their tales is that tale-telling, a curious activity on pilgrimage to begin with, leads to discord, enmity, and the breaking of bonds of friendship and Christian harmony; so also, within the tales these issues of broken friendships, marriages, social and governmental pacts become oppressively obvious. The opening segment of the work and the Marriage Group dwell on order and disorder among neighbors and spouses; this is followed by a middle group of tales that stresses the social damage of tale-telling; and the work ends with tales and a non-tale that put an end to tale-telling.

The Knight is the first pilgrim portrayed, and as an ideal representative of his class, his precedence in the series of portraits symbolizes the receding ideal of pilgrimage. For he is one of the Church Militant, a lifelong Christian crusader—and therefore a *peregrinus*—now just returned from another *passagium generale*. He no doubt is making this pilgrimage to Canterbury to give thanks for his success or survival on that recent "viage" (77). In the long list of his travels "As wel in cristendom as in hethenesse" (49) there is no hint that he ever wandered out of motives other than dutiful love for church and country.[15]

If we can infer the Knight's piety on this pilgrimage from what we know of his previous journeys and moral worth, we can also estimate the impiety of some other pilgrims on the basis of *their* predilections for travel. The Monk abuses his position as an outrider to wander curiously beyond the cloister, flouting that basic Benedictine precept, *stabilitas*. His *acedia* has led to roaming and that in turn to verbosity and chattering;[16] like the *gyrovagi* Benedict disdained to speak of, and

like any restless man unwillingly bound to an exacting *ordo*, this
monk finds in the "newe world" enough reason to play the vagrant.
By profession, the Knight is a traveler; by his own choice, the Monk
is a wanderer. One pursues infidels, the other rabbits.[17] Two more
ecclesiastical figures, the Friar and Summoner, travel about practicing
specialized brands of deception, and like the Monk they abuse their
licenses for travel. These two infringe upon the authority of the local
parson and despoil the community of Christians whom the Knight
seeks to protect while fighting enemies in foreign lands. But most
ruinous to the Church and its members is the Pardoner, who has joined this pilgrimage hoping to sell his relics and indulgences. As the pilgrims later find out, he lives by his tongue. His tale-telling lures, de-
ceives, and causes disorder among men; he does in miniature what the
Canterbury Tales shows the tale-telling group does as a whole. The
Pardoner is freer from supervision than the Friar and the Summoner
(his riding companion here) and perhaps thus bolder and more corrupt-
ing. It would be one thing if these assorted religious and ecclesiastics
were making the pilgrimage to atone for their separate failings, but
evidence for this is lacking. In contrast to the highest-ranking member
of the laity present, these figures are all wanderers by nature, stricken
by restlessness, moving aimlessly through the world, either oblivious
to the duty of their calling or intent on exploiting the Christian society. They are extraterritorial vagrants, morally *exorbitans*, emblems
of curiosity.

Exactly how many of the others present are stimulated to pilgrimage chiefly by the love of travel we cannot know for sure, but certainly
the Wife of Bath is driven by *curiositas*. Expert at "wandrynge by the
weye" (467) and a veteran of many pilgrimages (including an extra-
ordinary and improbable three voyages to Jerusalem[18]), Alice is the
typical curious pilgrim. Full admission of her curiosity will come in
the prologue to her tale, but the *General Prologue* portrait reveals her
natural errancy. Her fondness for gay clothing—which we learn more
of later—belies a different but related kind of *curiositas*. Yet the
Wife, as seen here, is not as notable for curious display of dress as
many other pilgrims are.[19] A glance at the Ellesmere drawings, for
instance, shows that our eye is supposed to be caught, as Chaucer
the narrator's was, by the Monk's "ful curious pyn" (196), the Friar's
"double worstede" (262), the Prioress's "Ful fetys" cloak and beads

(157, 159), and the fashionable attire of the Squire. This "superfluytee of clothyng," as the Parson will call it, is a mark of *curiositas* at any time, but here on pilgrimage it is especially out of place, for laity as well as religious. The correspondence between outward show and inner motivation is apparent: those pilgrims more interested in traveling to *see* than to worship are the ones dressed to be seen. On the other hand, the sartorial poverty of those pilgrims like the Knight, who still wears his "bismotered" tunic, the "thredbare" Clerk (whose studying has made him lean, as the Monk's avoidance of books has helped make him a fat gourmand),[20] the "povre" Parson (of whose dress we hear nothing at all), and his poorer brother of the soil testify to a more spiritual sense of the traditional meaning of pilgrimage.

All these signs of the divergent tendencies toward piety and curiosity are part of a yet larger pattern of oppositions Chaucer developed in order to stress the basic instability of this social group. Arthur Hoffman has investigated this pattern in his analysis of the twin destinations of the Canterbury journey: the shrines of Becket and Venus.[21] Ruth Nevo's suggestion, however, that the *General Prologue* amounts to a description of social rank in terms of economic behavior—and that the poorer, humbler pilgrims adhere to the ideal of pilgrimage while the richer, worldly ones do not—is, to my mind, an observation more responsive to the social nature of the issues that will grow out of the *Prologue*. Most of the pilgrims are seen and see themselves wrapped in a mutual economic struggle that pits the selfless against the assertive.[22] The exhibition of riches and a concern for money and goods was of course inappropriate on pilgrimage. The Scriptures counseled all wayfaring Christians to leave worldly goods behind them, and the Gospel of the Mass for Pilgrims repeated the advice. Wyclif's belief that pilgrims should be poor in things of the world[23] lay back of contemporary complaints (not all Lollard) about the general economic ambience of pilgrimages—the fact that pilgrims spent money for travel which ought to have gone for alms, that the benefits of pilgrimage could be had vicariously by hiring professional pilgrims, that the money given to shrines was used to make more statues, and that indulgences were obtained for a price.[24] Undoubtedly, the "pilgrims going to Canterbury with rich offerings" whom Falstaff, Hal, and Poins planned to ambush were little different from Chaucer's five pouch-carrying guildsmen. And, indeed, this discrepancy between rich

and poor pilgrims presages the later discord among the pilgrim story-
tellers and accounts in great measure for the connected themes of
mercantile chicanery, deception, and vengeance in a number of tales.

Chaucer depicts too many of the pilgrims as charitable "givers" or
selfish "takers" for us to overlook the fact that their fellowship is a
fragile thing. The Knight risks his life for God and king; the Clerk
humbly learns and teaches others and gratefully prays for his benefactors. The Parson daily, continually serves his flock by preaching
and teaching, walking pilgrim-like with staff in hand to safeguard the
"ferreste in his parisshe" (494-95)—just as no man traveled "ferre" in
defense of Christianity than the Knight—and the Parson's brother
serves God by giving tithes and working for his neighbors without
payment. But on all sides of these fellow-serving figures cluster others
who serve themselves by neglecting duty and using people for personal
gain. The Monk's hypocritical and ambiguous attitude as reported by
the narrator is "How shal the world be served?" (187). Like him, the
Prioress has left the confines of her proper society (for she was not
supposed to be riding out on pilgrimage), and the ambiguous love
motto on her rosary is only a little less audacious than the venereal
outrider's "love-knotte." [25] The Monk is as self-blind about the question "How shal the world be served?" as his companion the Prioress
is about the meaning of *Amor vincit omnia*; the dogs she keeps show
her carelessness about the Benedictine Rule[26] and the coral of her
rosary as much as the "crowned A" is cause for wonderment about
the sort of love she thinks she professes.[27] Three other pilgrims, the
Friar, Summoner, and Pardoner, claim to be in the service of the
Church, but these vagrants extract money from folk for penance, for
blackmail, and for indulgences. The Shipman has no "nyce conscience"
about liquidating his enemies at sea, the doctor and his druggists maintain a "frendshipe" to bilk clients and enrich their own coffers, and
in general disregard for neighbors Alice of Bath and the burgesses'
wives always go "bifore" all others at church services. Finally, the
Miller, Reeve, and Manciple—all servants—cheat both overlords and
clientele.

Now these related considerations—the travelers' mixed intentions
for making the pilgrimage, their attitudes toward worldly possessions,
and their customary relations with fellow Christians—suggest the basic
divisions that, from the start, preclude the kind of harmony these

citizens ought to have found in true pilgrim *felaweshipe*. Even the juxtaposition of certain portraits points to the fundamental disunity of the pilgrims. Contrasted with the Knight, his son, and his yeoman, who form one unit from one household, there are the Miller and Reeve, who out of animosity ride first and last in the cavalcade. Unlike those true brothers, the Parson and Plowman, there is that pair of false brothers, the Summoner and Pardoner. Unlike the complementary positioning of the Knight and Parson at the two ends of the tales, here in the *Prologue* whatever stability and order the Knight represents is challenged by the presence of the last-named pilgrim, every parson's bane, the disruptive Pardoner.[28]

This inherent disorderliness of the group of pilgrims thus makes the contest and pact suggested by Harry Bailly seem almost necessary. For, if in their normal daily lives and in their motives for going on pilgrimage most of these Christians exhibit instability and a lack of true fellowship, then perhaps only a game and contest like that offered by their ebullient Host of the tavern can harness all their various urges. But the pact to tell tales is unsuccessful as a stabilizing influence, too. The failure was predictable before the contest even began; what these people—as pilgrims—generally lack at their departure from the Tabard is what moralists specially urged them to cultivate: friendship, harmony, and order. A popular exemplum of the day encouraged wayfarers always to be charitable by reminding them of twenty-eight pilgrims en route to Compostela who nullified their pilgrimage when none of them gave aid to another of their party who fell sick along the way.[29] All pious Christian pilgrims must avoid quarrels, said Bernard,[30] and as one could read in the *Ayenbite of Inwit*, they should travel in good company[31]—not the kind of company for instance, that in *Piers Plowman* is too ready to refuse laboring in the search for Saint Truth, not the band of friends that deserts Everyman during his final pilgrimage. Above all, this warning to travel in friendship and peace would have been still echoing in the pilgrims' ears had they recently attended the service and Mass held specifically for pilgrims. The Psalms they would have sung emphasized the nature of the pact they bound themselves to: by going to worship God and his saints they could expect Him to protect them—but their uncharitable treatment of fellow pilgrims would violate that agreement.[32] In the Gospel of the Pilgrim Mass, Christ's instructions to the apostles were repeated for them all, especially the pointed command, "Freely you have received, freely give."[33] And finally they were advised to seek out only worthy companionship and lodging.[34] But for the bulk of Chaucer's pilgrims, all this sound counsel (which is but an expansion of the two great commandments) goes unheeded, so it is left up to the tourguide on this non-pilgrimage to attempt to bind them together. And the reader cannot help but notice that until the Parson ultimately puts an end to tale-telling, the pilgrims' acceptance of the Host's proposal is the last matter they unanimously agree on.

Harry Bailly, who is fit to be "a marchal in an halle" (752), was not at first a part of the pilgrim fellowship; only as they are paying their bills does he consider joining the group. Like most of them, he has little interest in the devout aims of the journey. He sees his customers as a "myrie" company and, being "a myrie man" himself, suggests a "myrthe" to enliven their trip. The term *pilgrymage*, which has been used already three times by the "ful devout" narrator, is significantly missing from Harry's vocabulary. He can imagine no body of pilgrims traveling in silence, and he unwaveringly thinks of their endeavor as merely a riding by the "weye" (771, 780, 791, 806, 834). Hardly a spiritual guide, the Host behaves more like a dragoman or the captain in charge of a shipload of Jerusalem-bound pilgrims. The *felaweshipe* sensed by the narrator at the beginning of the *General Prologue* appeared more social than religious, more like the Wife of Bath's *felaweshipe* in which "wel koude she laughe and carpe" (474), and the Host's suggestion of a contest now underscores that fact. This pact sealed by oaths—"This thyng was graunted, and oure othes swore" (810)—to tell tales and be judged by the Host has drawn the pilgrims into a tighter though scarcely more devout fellowship. Yet in telling tales as they ride, the pilgrims reflect another aspect of the curiosity and instability that has already begun to impair their corporate undertaking. Pilgrims like John Mandeville proved themselves curious by telling tales upon returning home, with their "scrippes bret-ful of lesinges," as Chaucer says in the *House of Fame* (2123); but so did pilgrims who indulged in the pastime en route. In itself tale-telling on pilgrimage diverted men's thoughts from spiritual matters and only raised the level of distracting noise that the Lollard critic William Thorpe made virtually synonymous with pilgrimages. Speaking before Archbishop Arundel, Thorpe declared:

Also Sir, I knowe well that when diuers men and women will goe thus after their own willes, and finding out one pilgrimage, they will ordaine with them before, to haue with them both men and women that can well sing wanton songes, and some other pilgrimes will haue with them bagge pipes; so that euerie towne that they come through, what with the noise of their singing, and with the sound of their piping, and with the iangling of their Canturburie bels, and with the barking out of dogges after them, that they make more noice, then if the king came there away, with all his clarions, and many other minstrels. And if these men and women be a moneth out in their pilgrimage, many of them shall be an halfe yeare after, great ianglers, tale-tellers, and liers.[35]

Walter Hilton's view of the impropriety of tales applied to pilgrims heading for Celestial Jerusalem *or* Canterbury. "And also if men will tarry thee with tales and feed thee with falsehoods, for to draw thee to mirths and for to leave thy pilgrimage, make deaf ear, and answer not again, and say nought else but that thou wouldest be at Jerusalem."[36]

The Host notices the pilgrims' desire for mirth and encourages it, but the first of his many mistakes is to assume he can govern this unstable band of travelers. He appoints himself judge and begins somewhat humorously to impose his own sort of order: he reminds the pilgrims four times that his "juggement" shall prevail (778, 805, 818, 833), pronounces his "voirdit" after they agree (787), requests their sworn obedience to him, and finally proclaims himself their "governour,/ . . . juge and reportour" (813-14).[37] But Harry has little chance of so ruling this wayward troupe. He has helped debase the purpose of the pilgrimage and in a way substituted himself for Becket, the miracle-worker the pilgrims seek, who was revered for his powers as a mediator of conflicts.[38] It may be only a coincidence (and perhaps unknown to Chaucer), but Harry Bailly is as loud and noisy as the famous large bell that hung in the main tower of Canterbury Cathedral and was called "Bell Harry."[39] Inevitably, the Host, who can speak "as lordly as a kyng" (3900), ends up as a lord of misrule.[40] He is less efficient at restoring that harmony which his own plan for tale-telling disrupts than the Knight, less able to control his own subjects than Duc Theseus in the Knight's tale, hardly effective in quelling disturbances, which as a "marchal" he would have been expected to do.[41] And as he prepares us for the first tale, we might also note that, as secular guide, the Host impinges on the office best filled by that good shepherd, the Parson, when he officiously calls the pilgrims "togidre alle in a flok" (824) on the morning of departure.

Out of these distorted notions of piety, stability, and governance develops a series of connected issues, all related to curiosity, that enfolds the tales which follow. As will become evident, the *Knight's Tale*, Chaucer's *Tale of Melibee*, and the *Parson's Tale*, coming at the beginning, "middle," and end of the work, seem to best present solutions to the large problems of Christian pilgrim instability. And at the heart of these three tales, and in other tales as well, is a concern with exactly what both the Host and Chaucer, for different reasons, would place such value on: order, justice, and harmony among the company of men. In the tales and in the links between, the related themes of social and spiritual stability, noise and disorder opposed to silence and order, justice, and the governing of self, family, and country recur too often for us to ignore their relevance to the ideal of pilgrimage as it has already been abrogated in the *General Prologue* by the curious pilgrims. In fact, insofar as they concern special kinds of fraternal, marital, and social bonds, large segments of the *Tales* stress the importance of pacts, and this metaphoric expression of the debts men owe each other corresponds to the issue of neglected and inappropriate pacts in the *General Prologue*. From the days of the early Church, political theorists often had described the basis of social and governmental order as a contract or pact, a *foedus* or *pactum*.[42] The principle that a mutual contract bound the ruler and the ruled underlay traditional medieval political theory.[43] Likewise, all Christian citizens—as neighbors, not only as subjects—were seen to be joined by contractual obligations; Augustine, Aquinas, and theologians and canon lawyers up through the fourteenth and fifteenth centuries considered the various *pacta* that men formed to be the essential ties that maintained harmony within society.[44] In forgetting the meaning of the pilgrim's badge—that "sign of Christian fellowship and the revered token of international brotherhood"[45]—the pilgrims upset the social order. The Christian fellowship Chaucer speaks of had roots in the idea of *amicitia*, and the sworn brotherhood of friendship carried connotations of the Latin term *societas* or *fides sociis*. As in the *Troilus*, it is this conception of brotherhood that is tested and in general vitiated by Chaucer's pilgrims.[46] The Canterbury pilgrims begin their journey with a spiritually impertinent kind of sworn pact, and thereafter they break more pacts than they make or keep. Curious to tell tales, they agree to a contract, and the incentive to win the contest only makes them more curious and divisive.

Fragment I

Socially, the Knight outranks the other pilgrims, and "aventure, or sort, or cas" aside, he is the one who ought to tell the first tale. His story is a romance of frustrated love and death, of brotherly enmity and affection, of pagan bewilderment over the workings of Fortune and near-Christian acceptance of the divine control over things. Theseus's understanding of worldly disorder lacks the full Christian perspective, yet the tale does suggest, as Joseph Westlund has said, that men must always endure tragedy on earth before they can find relief in the world of the *Parson's Tale*.[47] Critics have found various merits in Chaucer's choice of this tale as the initial utterance of the work, some even arguing that the tale is as comic as it is solemn;[48] but I believe its assertion of order in the face of disorder, so well analyzed by Muscatine and others, acts as a corrective to the instability of pilgrim life that has just been exposed in the *General Prologue*.[49] As a statement on order, the Knight's piece is appropriate and necessary at this point in the *Tales*. Noble Theseus—back of whom stands the devout Knight who has seen "Contek, with blody knyf and sharp manace" (2003)—speaks seriously to Palamon and Arcite about order in much the same words Harry Bailly used addressing the pilgrims about their contest:

> And forthy I yow putte in this degree,
> That ech of yow shal have his destynee
> As hym is shape, and herkneth in what wyse;
> Lo heere youre ende of that I shal devyse. (1841-44)

When he rebukes Palamon and Arcite for fighting "Withouten juge or oother officere" (1712), then proceeds to administer justice with firmness, Theseus proves himself superior to Harry as a judge and mediator. And the sworn brotherhood of the two knights, at first broken but repaired at Arcite's deathbed, is a bond few of the pilgrims can boast of. In fact, as one scholar has argued, the ceremonial bond of friendship that ties together the two warrior/lovers is described not in terms of a feudal agreement but more intimate domestic and familial obligations; in short, Chaucer has in mind a bond between equals, a contract.[50]

Order remains a central concern of the rest of the tales in Fragment I, despite the Miller's sudden introduction of several new perspectives on the Knight's *matere*. The Janus-faced stance adopted by the Miller in his *Prologue* enables us in fact to see the relationship of all these tales to the common theme of social orderliness. The Miller first vows to "quite" the Knight—which can mean repay as well as match—then, in announcing his subject, prepares us for the Reeve's rejoinder and, in turn, the Cook's incomplete tale. In requiting the Knight, the Miller turns the world of the *Knight's Tale* upside down. Whereas marriage came at the end of the first tale as the conclusion of the lover's pursuit and symbolized a reaffirmation of social order, in the *Miller's Tale* it exists at the beginning, and it exists only as part of the mechanism for the disorder that follows. The Knight offered a vision of order that countered the general disharmony portrayed in the *General Prologue*, but the Miller returns us to contemporary England and social disharmony. Theseus the overlord maintained order by fiat; each character in the *Miller's Tale* toils alone in the dark of night to undo himself and others around him. In a further remove, the choleric Reeve ignores the Knight to "quite" the Miller with a tale about quiting.[51] By the end of the Cook's abortive tale, the Knight's perception of order, embodying fraternal, marital, and social harmony, has been ignobly refined to a narrow joke about copulation.

Order, seen in terms of the bonds that link or sunder men, and the justice that preserves it comprise an overriding concern in Fragment I. Three of the four tale-tellers quarrel with one another or with their "juge," the Host, and each aims to revenge himself on another. The feud between the Miller and Reeve, as one critic has observed, parallels the feud between Nicholas and Absolon, and both sets of opponents are parodies of Palamon and Arcite.[52] As the *Knight's Tale* obliquely comments on the ceremony of the contest and pact at the end of the *General Prologue*, so the three following tales feed on the animosities that dominate the intervening links. The pilgrims and the characters in their tales intertwine. Clearly, the "principle of retaliation," to use J. V. Cunningham's term, controls the tales and speakers of this set of tales,[53] but when we recognize the quarreling among these early tale-tellers (as well as among later enemies like the Friar and Summoner and the Manciple and Cook) as an issue thematically tied to the nature of this particular pilgrimage, then it becomes more than a unifying idea within the first Fragment. The theme of order beset by disorder links the pilgrims with their tales and Fragment I with the *General Prologue*. The *Knight's Tale* posits one model of the stable society. Love and chivalry, by themselves potentially disruptive forces, can be properly blended with the right guidance, and "the bond/That highte matrimoigne" (3094-95) is a perfect resolution of both. In succession, the next three tales demean this ideal, substituting for marriage cuckoldry, then a grosser double swyving, and finally blatant promiscuity: in other words, violations of a bond for preservation of the bond. Similarly, the brotherhood Palamon and Arcite represented disappears in the differentiated characters of Nicholas and Absolon; fraternity of a sort is barely restored in the figures of the students Aleyn and John, but then it is simply ignored in the *Cook's Tale*. While the ideal of marriage and the high value placed on brotherly bonds gradually dissipate through Fragment I, there occurs a corresponding descent from high style to low, from romance to fabliau, from high-principled love to unruly lust. There is a spatial contraction as well: from Theseus's mythic voyages to the underworld and the knights' enormous arena to a small village, then a one-room home, and finally a house and bed in which the wife "swyved for hir sustenance." So too, the long years that leisurely define the action of the *Knight's Tale* dwindle to a period of days in the *Miller's Tale* and to a day and night in the *Reeve's Tale*.[54]

This continuous shading of one tale into another, as a narrative technique, can be best thought of as a kind of concatenation. In Fragment I (and, as we shall discover, in other segments of the work) adjacent tales reveal a seeming dependence on one another; they share resemblances. And yet crucial changes, made repeatedly at analogous points in the tales, abruptly reshape familiar confines, allowing a new emphasis to replace an old one. It might have been possible to work endless permutations on the characters and themes of the *Knight's Tale*, but the Miller's and Reeve's tales suffice to make Chaucer's point. They mirror an attitude toward justice, neighbor, and solemn bonds that the devout pilgrims in the company, especially the one who has spoken first, would reject. However, once initiated, themes generate their own variations. The Reeve's idea of justice and vengeance, consciously expressed in legal language[55]—"For leveful is with force force of-showve" (3912)—becomes John's and

Aleyn's justification for vengeance (4179-82), and following the Cook's promise to revenge himself on the Host, the Man of Law showily protests his desire to abide by the law. Now, having presented us with a series of tales about the related concerns of fraternal and social harmony—forms of order subsumed by the bliss of marriage which closes the *Knight's Tale*—Chaucer moves next and naturally toward a large group of tales in which marriage is the central topic.[56] Marriage, more than vows of sworn brotherhood, symbolizes that perfect stability required of true Christian pilgrims linked by the pact of pilgrim fraternity.

Fragments III-V

Ever since Kittredge identified the tales in Fragments III-V as a Marriage Group, the view that this series of tales is thematically unified has been widely adopted. Though the *Friar's Tale* and *Summoner's Tale* usually (and I think incorrectly) have had to be brushed aside as inexplicable interruptions of this discussion of marriage,[57] still the dominant concern here with marriage has provided critics the opportunity they have not easily found elsewhere in the work to speak confidently about "unity" in the *Canterbury Tales*. However, the topic of marriage is really an outgrowth and restatement of the problem of order that Chaucer has already begun exploring in the first group of tales. As an expression of stability, and especially as a sacrament, marriage signifies the perfectibility of Christian relationships on both personal and social levels. It is significant that the Wife of Bath herself, the catalyst of the debate here, stresses the sense in which marriage is a pact, an exchange of debts (although it is surely *she* who formulates the pact and her *husbands* who owe the debt). As "dettour" and "thral" (155), each husband rendered to her his "dette" and "paiement" (130, 131); she "governed hem so wel, after my lawe" (219), and when she and Jankyn were at last "acorded" she obtained the "governance" of his house, land, tongue, and hand (811 ff.). The Wife's emphasis (and that of subsequent pilgrims) thus suggests a yet more specific way in which a concern with bonds, debts, and pacts —in the tales of Fragment I and even in the apparently dislocated tales of the Friar and Summoner—links the topic of the Marriage Group with other approaches in the *Tales* to the problem of social order and spiritual stability.

It is instructive, first, to compare the authoritative postures of the Wife and the Knight, each of whom initiates a string of disputatious tales. In opposition to the Knight, who tells a tale in which justice is administered by a benevolent ruler, the Wife offers us in her *Prologue* an autobiographical tale that demonstrates how perilous the administration of justice can be. The *Knight's Tale* postulated male, supernatural, and rational forces as agents of justice; but Alice opposes them with feminine power, the cunning of empirical knowledge, and sensual experience. And in her tale she "quites" the Knight by having another knight forcibly marry a woman both non-noble and old. Her female universe contradicts his male universe. Duc Theseus conquered the land of Femenye, and Palamon and Arcite both won the passive Emily; but the Wife, Arthur's queen, the ladies of the court, and the old hag who is eventually beautiful and learned dominate a world composed of old men and rash young ones, a seldom-seen Arthur, and a fearful rapist. The Knight's defense of a stable order elicited the Miller's parodic response and, indirectly, the Reeve's attack on the Miller. Alice, a believer in wandering by the way, brings about not only the debate on marriage but also the squabble between the Friar and Summoner (who, like the Miller and Reeve, tell fabliaux).

The Wife's mind is fixed on marriage, but her introduction of the subject has been anticipated by the tales of Fragment I. In particular, her basic desire—to have both "governance" and freedom of movement—echoes the drunken Miller's advice on the dangers of becoming too curious:

> An housbonde shal nat been inquisityf
> Of Goddes pryvetee, nor of his wyf.
> So he may fynde Goddes foyson there,
> Of the remenant nedeth nat enquere. (3163-66)

The difference between meddling with one's spouse and keeping oneself at a distance is the dilemma variously posed by nearly all the tales of Fragments I and III-V. Palamon and Arcite are both initially separated from Emily by prison walls, and Arcite, even after gaining freedom, complains that his comrade has "the sight of hire, and I th' absence" (1239). As the Miller said, "'Alwey the nye slye/Maketh the ferre leeve to be looth'" (3392-93). *Hende* Nicholas (at least for a time) holds both the upper and lower hand while Alisoun's husband sits alone atop the roof; Alice of Bath enjoys herself most when she is on pilgrimage or when her husbands are out of town; compulsive Walter watches Griselda closely but cannot see her virtue; January meddles too intimately with his wife, who later punishes him at close range for his blindness; and, before they disentangle themselves, Arveragus, Dorigen, and Aurelius all must learn in their own ways the rewards and penalties of approaching each other too closely and asking too much.

At its heart, the problem of these marital ties, and particularly the question of sovereignty in marriage, is part of the much broader discussion of social order as it is expressed in terms of pacts and bargains. The pact of brotherhood between Emily's suitors, at first broken but later resworn, is supplanted finally by the bond of marriage. The Miller and Reeve, however, take vengeance on one another; the oaths they originally swore before the Host in accepting the pilgrims' *forward* turn out to be vows of mutual hatred. The two clerks in the *Reeve's Tale* resort to a retribution they call justice: ". . . gif a man in a point be agreved,/That in another he sal be releved" (4181-82). Pacts become excuses for furthering disorder, not preventing it. The Wife of Bath, little accustomed to observing the "statut" of marriage by which she nevertheless expects her husbands to feel bound (198-99), tells a tale remarkable for its emphasis on the pacts the trapped knight has to honor: he must return to court with an answer in order to live, he must grant the hag's wish to find the answer, and he must choose to have his wife either chaste but ugly or youthful but lecherous. When Alice has finished retaliating against husbands, the Friar and Summoner fulfill the vows of reciprocal vengeance they made before the Wife told her tale. Indeed, it would seem that they have been struck by the notion of the pact in the Wife's prologue and tale—one critic has suggested that their tales are "rooted in the Wife of Bath's discourse"[58]—and the climactic points of their tales are constructed around pacts. In the *Friar's Tale* the summoner's desire to be "evere enqueryng upon every thyng" (1409) leads the curious man to make the devil's acquaintance—they are soon "sworne bretheren" (1405)—and then to agree on dividing all spoils equally with his brother, a bargain that results in the summoner's being summoned away. In his angry retort, the Summoner claims that friars never keep their promises to pray for benefactors. And in *his* tale, the flatulent bargain he has the inquisitive friar strike with Thomas is shown to be as airy as the *limitour*'s promises.

I think the importance of pacts in all three of these tales enlarges the implications of the marriage debate. In following the *Wife of Bath's Tale* with the Friar's and Summoner's tales, which devolve on the idea of pacts, Chaucer suggests that both social bonds and verbal agreements are reflections of the continuing concern with order and disorder, stability and curiosity. In the *Clerk's Tale* the necessity for marriage and the problems of marital disharmony are bound up at many points with social demands for the orderly government of a kingdom. Walter's arrangements with his subjects and with his wife, who will crush discord and reinstate the "reste and ese" (434) that he cannot, are couched in the terms of sworn "demandes" he obtains from both. In the next tale, January ignores Justinus's warning about the potential disharmony of a January-May union and, curious to try an experimental marriage, forces his subjects to be "assented fully that he sholde/Be wedded whanne hym liste, and where he wolde" (1575-76). Finally, the Franklin joins the debate about marriage with a tale that raises more questions than it answers. What answers his tale does hold are locked up inside three related bargains: the husband's and wife's delicate "accord," the questionable exchange the wife offers Aurelius, and the squire's pact with a magician—"This bargayn is ful dryve, for we been knyt" (1230).[59]

Perfect marriage and love are metaphors for order. Troilus, wishing to bind his heart with Criseyde's, appeals to "Love, that knetteth lawe of compaignie,/And couples doth in vertu for to dwelle" (III, 1748-49). As Robertson has suggested, in the *Canterbury Tales* Chaucer's interest is with "the proper function of marriage as an ordering principle in the individual and in society,"[60] and as Chaucer will say in the *Melibee*, marriage is ideally a pact between man and woman dependent on a harmony that can bring about general social stability.[61] However, it is disharmony, not harmony, within the home and in the state that has been the conspicuous feature of the tales about marriage in Fragments III-V. But then this is not unexpected, for the imperfection of the marital bonds in these tales, like the broken fraternal and social ties in the earlier tales, is a phenomenon that reflects the disorder and misdirection of this particular band of pilgrims.

There is still another sense in which marriage is a suitable topic for conversation on this pilgrimage. The widespread criticism of pilgrimage in Chaucer's day focused not only on curious pilgrims' instability or their penchant for tale-telling but also on the disastrous effects pilgrimage could have on married life. This criticism took several forms. To begin with, pilgrimages were widely thought to be occasions for sexual promiscuity. In the time of Jesus, said Wyclif, men and women made holy pilgrimages, while nowadays "pilgrimage is mene for to do lecherie."[62] A French knight could warn his daughters that pilgrimages, like tournaments, offered too many temptations against chastity.[63] Margery Kempe and her husband, whose mutual vow of continence was known to all, were still suspected of making many pilgrimages together simply in order to secretly satisfy their lusts.[64] Moreover, it was popularly thought that men and women went alone on pilgrimages to escape the other spouse, to seek out adulterous liaisons, or to look for a new mate.[65] The *Tale of Beryn*, an attempt to "finish" Chaucer's Canterbury story, suggests that pilgrimage was seen as an occasion for sexual adventures as well as tale-telling. Echoing Bernard's opinion about curious and easily tempted females, Lydgate charged that unstable wives go on pilgrimages to see and be seen; they chatter in sanctuaries, show more interest in kissing "lusty yong images" than in worshipping, and search more for acquaintances than for relics.[66] When "spring approaches and the virtues are stirred by the influence of the elements and the planets," wrote the fifteenth-century author of *Les quinze joyes de mariage*, wayward wives itch "to frolic in the fields" and "to go on pilgrimage." They will be trouble for their husbands whether the latter go with them or stay home, and each wife will ever after "wish to travel and be on the highroad now that she has once begun."[67] Their very presence on this journey, then, might make us wonder about the fidelity many of Chaucer's pilgrims feel toward their own marital bonds; and of course it should be remembered that none of the pilgrims, regardless of the reasons, have brought their spouses along to Canterbury.

Some of these pilgrims, as Hoffman has said, are more impelled toward the shrine of Venus than toward the shrine of Becket. The procession is headed up by the Miller playing a bagpipe, that "instrument with which male lovers make melody."[68] The "stif burdoun" that the Summoner bears to the Pardoner—the eunuch who boasts about wedding a wife—hints at phallic as well as melodic accompaniment;[69] and the emblem of one patron of pilgrims, Saint Joce, whom the Wife of Bath invokes against her fourth husband, is the same item: a *burdoun*, which as both phallus and pilgrim's staff suggests the diversity of the Wife's quests.[70] Much of this imagery was probably inspired by the *Roman de la Rose*, to which Chaucer may have been indebted for the literary form of the *General Prologue*[71] and generally for much else in the *Tales*. In the *Roman* the central quest of the lover is overtly sexual, while in the *Tales* the pilgrims' lubricity is only hinted at to characterize their profane motives for making the pilgrimage. Jean de Meun describes the last stages of the lover's sexual progress in terms more suitable to a pilgrim itinerary. We might recall Palamon the lover's "pilgrymage/Unto the blisful Citherea" (2214-15), the Wife of Bath's lusty errancy, and the Host's unholy threat to enshrine the Pardoner's *coillons* (VI, 951-53)[72] as we read:

> I've made a vow to God that I will go
> To make a visit to this holy shrine
> And touch the relics that I have described.
> So soon as I find opportunity,
> If time and place conform to my desire,
> Please God, I'll seek them with my staff and scrip.
> . . . .
> A hundred thousand thanks I offered him
> And promptly, like a pilgrim most devout,
> Precipitate, but fervent and sincere,
> After that sweet permission, made my way
> Like loyal lover toward the loophole fair,
> The end of all my pilgrimage to achieve.
>   With greatest effort I conveyed with me
> My scrip and pilgrim staff so stiff and stout
> That it no ferrule needed to assure
> That it would hold the path and never slip.[73]

Chaucer nowhere uses the metaphor of pilgrimage to so describe the pilgrims' libidinous desires, but he does make it clear that inasmuch as marriage signifies a stable order, ungoverned sexuality signifies its opposite. The Wife of Bath's combined wanderlust and lechery exemplifies this instability.

> For evere yet I loved to be gay,
> And for to walke in March, Averill, and May,
> Fro hous to hous, to heere sondry talys—(545-47)

She is the preeminent Venerian wanderer, curious to tell tales, see and be seen, and make pilgrimages (during Lent, of all times):

> Myn housbonde was at Londoun al that Lente;
> I hadde the bettre leyser for to pleye,
> And for to se, and eek for to be seye
> Of lusty folk. What wiste I wher my grace
> Was shapen for to be, or in what place?
> Therfore I made my visitaciouns
> To vigilies and to processiouns,
> To prechyng eek, and to thise pilgrimages,
> To pleyes of myracles, and to mariages,
> And wered upon my gaye scarlet gytes. (550-59)[74]

Alice goes to others' marriages almost as often as she takes leave of her own, and if her fifth husband were still alive it is just possible that she would not have received his permission to make this short pilgrimage to Canterbury, as the Church required her to do. (To go to distant Jerusalem, as she says she did three times, no such consent of the spouse was needed.)[75] It is fitting, in other words, for the Wife to start the discussion of marriage and marital disorder. The two pilgrims who tell tales after her are as disorderly and meddlesome as she is. The Friar depicts a restless summoner whose curiosity finally damns him.[76] The Summoner responds by telling of a friar who wanders with "scrippe and tipped staf" and makes a habit of curiously nosing into every household along his way; and for groping too deeply after what Thomas has hid "in pryvetee" he is suitably rewarded.

One might even want to argue, therefore, that the *Clerk's Tale*, more than the Friar's and Summoner's tales, is an "interruption" of this sequence of tales about curiosity and disorder. It is a reply to the Wife of Bath, and although Griselda and her unmodern wifely patience are dead, this peasant wife nevertheless possesses what the curious, wayward Wife lacks: the virtuous ability to watch another's marriage procession from the door of her home while busily attending to the "labour which that longeth unto me" (285), to be in no way inquisitive about her departed children, and to remain stable in loving her husband and keeping order in his realm. From the curious Wife of Bath and the quiet, studious Clerk one should not expect anything other than instability and stability. Alice the weaver, whose clothes are meant to attract men's eyes, is garrulous; the Clerk is poorly

dressed and "Noght o word spak he moore than was neede" (I, 304).
Walter—who in Petrarch's version of the tale was "curious and given
to experiments,"[77] much like Cervantes's Anselmo in "The Tale of
Foolish Curiosity"—is ultimately overcome by Griselda's constancy.
The Clerk's tale, no less than the Knight's, as Muscatine and Heninger
have argued, reflects an abiding, stern belief in the necessity of stead-
fastness and order in the face of unexpected and nearly unbearable
threats of disorder. Set beside the *Knight's Tale*, Chaucer's *Melibee*,
and the Parson's treatise, it provides us and perhaps some of the other
pilgrims with one more reaffirmation of the political, spiritual, and
social stability requisite to the medieval Christian. It is directed at the
Wife of Bath, but to all the rest as well; as Heninger says, it amounts
to "more than just another point of view in a Marriage Group."[78]

But in the *Merchant's Tale* we again encounter one of the Wife of
Bath's own kind. January's "Heigh fantasye and curious bisynesse"
(1577), both the cause and effect of his lechery, characterize his blindness to reason. In his enclosed secret garden he is too inquisitive about
his wife's *pryvetee* when he engages in acts "whiche that were nat
doon abedde" (2051). And in the *Franklin's Tale* it is appropriate that
Dorigen's irresponsible offer to Aurelius be made in a garden "curiously"
wrought by the hand of man.[79] Unwilling to accept "a parfit wys God
and a stable" (871) because He tolerates "confusion," she grows inquisitive about God's mysteries and dares Aurelius to alter nature;
wise and stable justice demands that she be repaid and trapped by the
effects of "artes that been curious" (1120).

Thus, the tales of Fragments III-V, like those of the first Fragment,
have as one recurring concern the problem of social stability. Even
the tales of the Friar and the Summoner, seemingly digressions from
the major topic of discussion, actually highlight the essential principle
of both fraternal and spousal relations: vows and pacts. Of course, at
the same time, their tales contribute to the disorder that has rent the
pilgrim fellowship and the pilgrims' approach to most issues since the
Knight stopped speaking. Vengeance has made men enemies, outside
and inside tales; requital has turned neighbors against one another;
sexual errancy and curiosity have been in league to undermine the
stability of marriage. People devoid of proper religious motivation
have (not unexpectedly) weakened the bonds of pilgrim brotherhood
and marriage in the very act of telling tales. In a sense, they have

entered too far into the world of their own tales; except for the
Knight and the Clerk, these pilgrims have mirrored each other in one
another's stories. The Miller, Reeve, Friar, and Summoner have pursued the curious art of tale-telling to harshly fable each other. The
Wife of Bath has been not only heard by the other pilgrims but also
overheard by a character within another tale: in the *Merchant's Tale*
Justinus advises January to remember the tale Alice has so recently
told (1685-87). In talking about one another the pilgrims have almost
exhausted the limits of mutual verbal abuse, and it is now up to others
about to be heard to reassert certain principles of orderly behavior
and to begin questioning the very value of telling tales. In Fragment
VII, which is as mixed an *unbokeled male* as Harry Bailly could wish
for, this restoration and questioning begins.

Fragments VII, VIII, IX-X

Social stability, defined mainly by fraternal and marital relationships, has been the chief topic of discussion in two large linked segments of the *Tales*. Stability, order, and the significance of keeping
pacts are concerns pertinent to this curious company, although many
of the pilgrims, in their relations with one another and in the tales
they choose to tell, thrive on its opposite, discord and enmity. Many
tales remain to be told besides those in Fragment VII,[80] but in the
third and last large block of tales[81] Chaucer recapitulates the themes
of brotherly and marital ties—mainly in the *Shipman's Tale*—simulta-
neously modulating them with an added new emphasis on the doubtful value of tale-telling itself.[82] Tale-telling on pilgrimage was a symptom of *curiositas*, and just as moralists mixed esthetic and moral
norms in denouncing the vice, here in Fragment VII the question of
whether or not to tell tales at all becomes an artistic and then a moral
one. And by the end of the *Canterbury Tales*, when the Manciple and
Parson speak, these two overriding concerns of the work—telling tales
and disorder—will have become conflated. As characteristics of a band
of pilgrims who never reach their goal, tale-telling and instability become synonymous; and, from a final perspective, they are the noisy
and disruptive opposites of the ideal silence and orderliness that ought
to have preoccupied devout pilgrims.

In the *Shipman's Tale*, which begins this group of tales, the two
components of social stability that have informed the *Tales* up to now,

brotherhood and marriage, coalesce. It is the last of those tales (most of which, like the *Shipman's Tale*, have been fabliaux) to dwell on the corruptibility of brotherly and marital bonds. There is, first, the marriage of a rich merchant and his beautiful wife. Then too there is the friendship of the husband and a monk; out of "cosynage"

> Thus been they knyt with eterne alliaunce,
> And ech of hem gan oother for t'assure
> Of bretherhede, whil that hir lyf may dure. (40-42)

The third relationship, the affair of the wife and the monk, severs both these bonds. All three ties have roots in money and gain. To the merchant a wife is a costly possession (just as for January, May is "the fruyt of his tresor"); when he leaves on business, he has to be sure that the wife has enough money and clothing to last through his trip. His cousin the monk, a traveling business agent for his order, endears himself to the merchant's household by bringing food and gifts. Money highlights the fundamental instability of the husband's, monk's, and wife's pacts. All three bonds are built on selfish interests and thus may be canceled. Friendship and marriage, which ought not to be mutually exclusive, become so because the characters prefer getting to giving.

When the "revelous" wife (ironically, accompanied by a child she is supposed to wisely "governe and gye" [96]) accosts the monk in the garden, she willingly reveals to him her marital troubles and offers him her "service" in order to obtain money for clothing. Immediately after they have sworn each other to secrecy, the monk forswears his bond of friendship to her husband (148 ff.). Marriage and friendship are both compromised. As "an officer, out for to ryde" (65)—like the pilgrim Monk—this monk is already suspect in his fidelity to vows. On his travels this busy, mobile man carries a *chilyndre*, a portable sundial (206); it serves to remind him, as it should us, that there is always a time to enter upon affairs and a time to hurriedly leave them. It is a fitting symbol of the instability of his worldly way of life, and perhaps, by extension, of his changeable loyalties. He uses his portable breviary (*porthors*) to say his daily office faithfully, but he and the wife also use it to swear oaths that break faith (131 ff.).[83]

The husband and friend they set out to deceive leads a life no more stable than theirs. From behind a closed counting-house door he

describes his profession in terms reminiscent of the descriptions of
the pilgrim Man of Law ("Nowher so bisy a man as he ther nas" [I,
321]) and the circumspect pilgrim Merchant ("Ther wiste no wight
that he was in dette" [I, 280]). This merchant's life is truly one of
"curious bisynesse" (225); he will not allow his marriage or even the
devout intention for pilgrimage to deflect his anxious pursuit of the
world:

> We may wel make chiere and good visage,
> And dryve forth the world as it may be,
> And kepen oure estaat in pryvetee,
> Till we be deed, or elles that we pleye
> A pilgrymage, or goon out of the weye.
> And therfore have I greet necessitee
> Upon this queynte world t'avyse me;
> For everemoore we moote stonde in drede
> Of hap and fortune in oure chapmanhede. (230-38)

Bidding his wife to be similarly "curious" in governing while he is
gone (hardly the sort of attitude tranquil, stable Griselda showed in
governing on Walter's behalf) and pausing to lend "daun John" money,
the merchant leaves home. While he is away borrowing money to
stabilize his *taillyng*, his debtor the monk is claiming his own debt by
borrowing the wife's body; appropriately, these curious partners
effect their exchange in a "bisy" manner (318), as they requite the
merchant. By the end of the tale, sex and wealth have been equated:
what the wife tells her husband in bed at his homecoming—"by God,
ye have ynough!" (380)—is what she cried out to him earlier as he
was reckoning his *tresor* (219).[84] The interloping monk has gone, and
the now nicely matched husband and wife, he the misfortunate seeker
after wealth, she the well-dressed woman who enjoys being seen, begin literally to repay their marriage debts.

Husbands and wives like these have wandered in and out of the
Tales before, and other comparable doubtful bonds of marriage and
friendship have been torn and raggedly sewn up. The *Shipman's Tale*
revives all this again for us and, by mixing the desires of spouses and
friends, focuses more sharply on the need for the kind of social stability that true fellowship and ideal marriage represent. The jokingly
literal understanding of the payment of the marriage debt here in the
Shipman's Tale puts an end to the growing tendency of tale-tellers to

turn what a few pilgrims have been claiming is an earnest matter into a riotous game. In, for example, *Melibee*, and in the dialogue between Chaunticleer and Pertelote, Chaucer will continue to stress the need for order in the relationships of spouses, friends, and all ranks of society. Yet while the pilgrims go on listening to each other speak about the meaning of order and disorder, they also begin to learn something of the irrelevance of their immediate preoccupation, tale-telling. After the Shipman's tale, the Prioress tells us of a little "clergeon's" innocent faith, his willingness to learn the Alma Redemptoris Mater without understanding its language—in short, without being curious, only childishly pious. More than this one would not expect from the naive child; yet Chaucer (if not Lady Eglentyne) may want us to notice that this holy innocent knows when and when not to speak, knows that prayer and song are the only necessary moral utterances of the most devout Christian. Few pilgrims, including the one who tells his story, could emulate this saintly model of uncurious behavior. But gently passing by the gentle Prioress, one discovers in the last four tales of Fragment VII that the telling of tales is a paramount issue. And it is a question moralists would already have known the answer to: Does tale-telling, especially in view of its attendant evils, have any place on a pilgrimage? This new concern, evident in *Sir Thopas, Melibee,* the *Monk's Tale,* and the *Nun's Priest's Tale,* is with how to tell tales and whether to tell them; and I believe Chaucer raises the artistic issue in order to unfold the moral one. It is notable that Chaucer the artist is consequently more visible at this point in the work than previously; he chooses the occasion to contribute two tales as pilgrim, one more than anyone else. In addition, the tales of this group remind us more and more of what we may have forgotten, that the pilgrims have been engaged in a *contest* of storytelling. As Charles Owen has remarked, "In none of the fragments are so many critical questions raised. Chaucer and the Nun's Priest show a sophisticated concern in their tales for the uses and abuses of style and form, while the Monk reveals what insensitive and literal acceptance of medieval principles can mean."[85]

We may admire the artistic brilliance of the Shipman's and Nun's Priest's tales, but we can be sure Chaucer's first tale and the Monk's tale, both of which were interrupted and cut short, will not win the supper Harry Bailly has ready for the victor. In its burlesque of abused romance conventions *Thopas* is for the poet and us an example of how to tell a burlesque, but for the Host and pilgrims it is a model of how not to tell a tale. The Monk's ineptitude at making a long catalog of tales about tragic falls interesting is not really surprising, since we already know the Monk is by nature an undisciplined, erratic figure, afflicted with monastic *instabilitas* and resultant verbosity. It cannot be argued that Chaucer's wide-wandering pilgrims are always monotonous or verbose (three errant ones, the Pardoner, Wife of Bath, and Canon's Yeoman are certainly chatty, but they are not monotonous). Yet there seems to be an esthetic and moral propriety in the fact that the Monk is no more able to tell a tale well than to abide by the rules of his order. As one critic of monastic failings in his day wrote, men like the Monk are usually found "leding þer lif curiously," and the only way for them to stabilize their lives and minds is to "schak a wey idilnes, vanite, curiosite, and superfluite." [86] His collection of repetitious *ensaumples*, many of them in fact underlining the effects of "misgovernaunce" and disloyalty among families and brothers, obviously suffers by comparison with Chaucer's own collection of tales of which it is a part. Appropriately, it is the Knight, who has told a tragic tale worth listening to, who puts an end to the Monk's proliferating inventory.

In the middle of this series of tales and flanked by the seeming blunders of *Thopas* and the *Monk's Tale* comes Chaucer the pilgrim's second effort, his *Tale of Melibee*. Like the *Parson's Tale* it is in prose; indeed, although its meager narrative line does qualify it as another "tale," its abundant *sentence* reminds us more of the Parson's non-tale than of any other offering in the *Canterbury Tales*. And along with the *Knight's Tale* and the *Parson's Tale*, it constitutes a major restatement in the running debate on order and social stability. Dame Prudence's argument has been that of Chaucer the critic of pilgrimage throughout the *Tales*: marital, fraternal, and spiritual harmony are social necessities. And only through interminable talking can Prudence, Melibee, and their neighbors demonstrate the truth that the wrangling tales in verse have illustrated—that noise is disorder.

Chaucer's prefatory remarks to the tale, according to Robertson, should incline us to "pay attention to the *sentence* of the Melibee because it affords a clue to the *sentence* of all the other tales which

come before it."[87] The single *sentence* Robertson would find in the
Tales, however, is not one I perceive; and, moreover, it can be argued
that *Melibee* reflects as much on the tales that follow as on those that
precede it. *Melibee* explores right and wrong relationships between
spouses, friends, and all members of the community, and to that extent it is a reprise of the whole work's concern with order. The husband-
wife debate over the question of mastery in marriage (and, specifically,
the problem Melibee finds in accepting wifely counsel) introduces debate about other issues in the tale. Only after Prudence has won Melibee's ear can she start restoring his lost wisdom, and bring him into
harmony with his neighbors. But because Prudence continually is
forced to defend the wife's role as counselor, even as she leads Melibee toward reconciliation in other matters, it seems mistaken to over-
emphasize this dispute about mastery (as, for instance, W. W. Lawrence has done[88]) in order to link this tale with the Marriage Group.
Harmony in marriage is but one factor of the larger desideratum; the
overlapping concern with different human relationships in *Melibee*
reflects in miniature this complex issue of social order in the *Tales*.

Prudence begins guiding Melibee toward conciliation with God and
neighbors even before she has to confront his doubts about her ability
to advise him. Like other pilgrims and like characters in other tales,
this unwise man's first desire is for quick vengeance, but Prudence
urges him to avoid both haste and anger (1122ff.). He comes to recognize that those who have suggested vengeance are not truly friends
and that the enemies he wants to destroy can be forgiven. The patience
of Griselda (and quick-wittedness of Alice of Bath) sustain Prudence
as she conducts Melibee through the catechism of virtues. At times
she reminds us, as she may have reminded Chaucer, of Lady Philosophy consoling Boethius. The longer she speaks, the calmer Melibee
becomes, and one effect of this uninterrupted prose discourse is to
hush the noisy bickering that has so far characterized the pilgrimage
of tale-telling. Prudence's first consideration, however, is the noise
and dissension that envelop Melibee. Immediately after Melibee's legal
advisers have urged cautious deliberation, some of the youths and
"the mooste partie of that compaignye" begin "to make noyse" and
press for a war of vengeance (1035). When a wise elder tries to quiet
their outcry, they all rise at once "for to breken his tale" (1043) and
finally shout him down. This cacophony, Prudence tells Melibee,

inevitably results from depending for advice not on a few trusted friends but on the "greet multitude of folk ther every man crieth and clatereth what that hym liketh" (1069). Chaucer's tale-telling, tale-interrupting pilgrims are just such a multitude of nosy and noisy folk. Prudence's warning of the risks involved in riding with groups of strangers could have been as usefully uttered back in Southwark while the Host was cementing the pilgrims in their pact:

> And after this thanne shul ye kepe yow fro alle straunge folk, and fro lyeres, and have alway in suspect hire compaignye. For Piers Alfonce seith, 'Ne taak no compaignye by the weye of a straunge man, but if so be that thou have knowe hym of a lenger tyme. And if so be that he falle into thy compaignye paraventure, withouten thyn assent, enquere thanne as subtilly as thou mayst of his conversacion, and of his lyf bifore, and feyne thy wey. . . .' (1308-11)

So, too, her appeal to her husband for peace and silence is equally applicable to the Canterbury pilgrims:

> For Salomon seith, 'It is a greet worshipe to a man to kepen hym fro noyse and stryf.' . . . studie and bisye thee rather to stille the same grevaunce than for to venge thee. . . . And the same Salomon seith, 'The angry and wrathful man maketh noyses, and the pacient man atempreth hem and stilleth. . . .' (1485-87, 1514)

The not-so-Christian fellowship of pilgrims, riven by curiosity and the discord of story-telling, might also meditate on the further words of Solomon:

> For the lawe seith that 'he is coupable that entremetteth hym or medleth with swych thyng as aperteneth nat unto hym.' And Salomon seith that 'he that entremetteth hym of the noyse or strif of another man is lyk to hym that taketh an hound by the eris.' For right as he that taketh a straunge hound by the eris is outherwhile biten with the hound, right in the same wise is it resoun that he have harm that by his inpacience medleth hym of the noyse of another man, wheras it aperteneth nat unto hym. . . . (1541-44)

The order imposed upon human affairs by Theseus is once more affirmed here, and it will be reasserted from the Parson's Christian perspective at the end of the *Tales*. All three of these tales conclude with a restoration of harmony: there is a marriage of "blisse" to end the first tale, reconciliation with enemies and "blisse that nevere hath ende" in *Melibee* (1888), and the promise of "endeless blisse of hevene" in the *Parson's Tale*. Whereas spouses exact unwise promises at the beginning of the Merchant's, Clerk's, and Franklin's tales, in *Melibee* they reach an accord after a rational exchange of viewpoints. And the final bargain of the tale—Melibee's challenge to his foes to place themselves at his and Prudence's mercy—results in social harmony. Dissension and wrangling are silenced. *Melibee* is truly an important link between the beginning and end of the *Canterbury Tales*; it may well be, as Donald R. Howard has suggested, Chaucer's direct address to the contentious court of Richard II,[89] and as an open plea for political stability its emphasis on the wise choice of counselors might reflect specific political worries within the turbulent English government.[90] The metaphorical embrace of the tale is wide (one critic has read it as an allegory embodying Walter Hilton's expression of the Christian pilgrim's journey to heavenly Jerusalem[91]) but Prudence's appeal for order, friendship, unity, and quietude seems intended for Chaucer's company of pilgrims as well. *Melibee* is a restatement of the conflict between order and disorder, silence and noise, that has been a major concern in large portions of the *Tales*. Moreover, by equating noise with disorder, Chaucer the tale-teller has transmuted the theme of social stability into a question that dominates the remainder of the *Tales*: the inadvisability of talking too much and talking out of place. Loquacity is dangerous any time; talking and tale-telling on the road to Becket's shrine is, morally, a greater danger.

The Monk has shown how not to tell a tale; his iterative list of tragedies offends the listeners, as he has often offended against his monastic rule. At the end of the noise and chaos in the *Nun's Priest's Tale*, the sly fox, speaking for Chaunticleer and for himself, admits that misfortune is due anyone "That is so undiscreet of governaunce/ That jangleth whan he sholde holde his pees" (3434-35). There may be several morals Chaucer wishes us to draw from the priest's fable, but certainly one of them is that a sense of time and place ought to control the urge to speak. The Nun's Priest's animals talk too much and at the wrong times.[92] And then, that figure who is appropriately a blend of the cock and fox, the Pardoner, a wondrous tale-teller, finally undoes himself with his own words. This wandering huckster's astonishing candor—he preaches about *coveityse* because he pursues it—and his open scorn for his audiences ("For lewed peple loven tales olde;/ Swiche thynges kan they wel reporte and holde" [437-38]) are turned back against him by the Host. The Pardoner's tales and sermons contribute nothing to spiritual order; instead of serving others, his "entente is nat but for to wynne" (403), and it is his custom in the pulpit to tell a "hundred false japes" and sting critics with his "tonge smerte."

In the *Pardoner's Tale* itself, a superbly told parable of all-devouring concupiscence, the Pardoner presents us with refractions of his own hateful loves. His story is about disorder and curiosity. The three young "riotoures," drunk, sinful, and given to incivility, earn their easy damnation through a mutually destructive quest for the curious man's most forbidden goal: not treasure, but the death that comes for those whose inquiry takes them too near to the tree of hidden knowledge. The "olde cherl" and the bushels of gold by the oak tree are rich symbols, but whatever other meanings we and the Pardoner extract from them, we cannot avoid realizing that the Old Man has knowledge no one should so curiously tap, and the "faire and brighte" gold hides secrets no one should so curiously investigate. The Pardoner is as engaging and fascinating to watch and listen to as the Wife of Bath, but his tale does in microcosm what most of the Canterbury tales do; it shatters the piety of pilgrimage with the lure and effects of curiosity. For this scourge of pilgrimages who likes to "quyte" others, tale-telling merits a special sort of condemnation. Harry cuts him out of the "felaweshipe" which he eagerly joined (938), and although the Knight intervenes as peacemaker, the telling of a tale has once more caused disharmony. If the Pardoner had remembered the verses from 1 Timothy 6 that immediately precede the text he lives by ("*Radix malorum est Cupiditas*"), he at least might not have made the flagrant error at the end of his tale that led to his own entrapment and the ensuing discord. The false teacher, wrote Paul, "is proud, knowing nothing, but doting about controversies and disputes of words. From these arise envies, quarrels, blasphemies, base suspicions, the wranglings of men corrupt in mind and bereft of truth, supposing godliness to be gain."

The Second Nun and the Canon's Yeoman, whose tales make up Fragment VIII, prove that certain tales are worth telling, that there is a proper time to talk and a proper time to stay silent. Like Griselda (and Virginia of the *Physican's Tale*) the Prioress's attendant considers her tale the product of "leveful bisynesse" and not a symptom of what "men clepe in Englissh ydelnesse" (5, 2). Unlike the Wife of

Bath, whose busy vagrancy led her on curious searches for sex, riches, and gossip, this woman announces that she will do "feithful bisynesse" (24) to tell a pious tale of holy martyrdom. The newly arrived canon's yeoman hardly pauses to catch his wind before he begins repenting a life of deceit. Critics have noted the appropriateness of the yeoman's "confession" at this stage of the pilgrimage;[93] the Pardoner has made a false confession, Melibee has asked forgiveness of his wife and granted it to his enemies, and shortly the Parson will draw his audience toward Penitence. As the vagabond alchemist, ever eager to "bisye hym this art for to seche" (1442), flees from the pilgrimage he never actually joined, his assistant righteously exposes the *pryvetee* of their frenetic pastime. Inquisitive alchemical pursuits of the *pryvetee* of Nature lead men literally and symbolically away from the pilgrimage road and into the labyrinthine byways of curiosity. Unfortunately, the yeoman's "confession" entails a vilification of the canon, and his awkward blend of sorrow, humility, and anger reflects the tension that the latter end of the *Tales* tries to resolve—not simply whether tales should be told, but, more importantly, why.

The *Manciple's Tale* finally stifles the tendency to tell recriminatory tales and strongly emphasizes a *sentence* the Parson will corroborate.[94] "Hold your tongue" has been one theme variously expressed in the Wife's, Pardoner's, and Franklin's tales, but the point is made more explicitly in the Manciple's tale. Remembering his dame's advice (itself windy and repetitious), the Manciple says:

> Lordynges, by this ensample I yow preye,
> Beth war, and taketh kep what that ye seye: . . .
> Daun Salomon, as wise clerkes seyn,
> Techeth a man to kepen his tonge weel. . . .
> My sone, thy tonge sholdestow restreyne
> At alle tymes, but whan thou doost thy peyne
> To speke of God, in honour and preyere. (309-10, 314-15, 329-31)

The pilgrims ought to realize by now something Gower also said about the effects of misguided talking:

> Right as a swerd forkutteth and forkerveth
> An arm a-two, my deere sone, right so
> A tonge kutteth freendshipe al a-two.
> A jangler is to God abhomynable. (340-43)

The curious avocation of the pilgrims has, like the noise of Phebus's crow, sundered both silence and fellowship. As the Manciple says, the damage done by tale-telling can be irreparable:

> Thyng that is seyd is seyd, and forth it gooth,
> Though hym repente, or be hym never so looth.
> He is his thral to whom that he hath sayd
> A tale of which he is now yvele apayd.
> My sone, be war, and be noon auctour newe
> Of tidynges, wheither they been false or trewe.
> Whereso thou come, amonges hye or lowe,
> Kepe wel thy tonge, and thenk upon the crowe. (355-62)[95]

By the conclusion of the *Tales*, the practice of tale-telling, like the broken pacts of friendship and marriage strewn along the route, comes to signify disorder. It would have been too much to expect a pilgrim like the engaging Wife of Bath, who is curious, wayward, and talkative, to sympathize with this point of view. She of course found it desirable once to silence a talkative tongue, her husband Jankyn's; she tore up his book and put an end to his irksome tales in order to reimpose her own kind of order. But noise, disputation, and tale-telling mean something different to Alice than they do to the last speaker, the Parson. To focus on the *Parson's Tale* as a "gloss for many of Chaucer's best poetic writings," as E. Talbot Donaldson warns, is to miss the poetry and wrongly create stark moral contrasts in a work whose author is anything but a simple moralist. "After all," says Donaldson, "what Chaucer was good at was not the formulation of doctrine on sin but the revelation of the marvellous variety of life in a world which, however sinful, is the only world we've got, and one that can mingle much delight with its inevitable corruption."[96] Only an insensitive reader would refuse to endorse this sensible, Pelagian attitude toward the whole work and toward the *Parson's Tale*. Yet I believe it is still arguable that certain parts of the *Parson's Tale* and the overall tone of his prologue and treatise can be fruitfully juxtaposed to earlier parts of the *Tales*. Chaucer may be more distant from the rigid dogmatism of the Parson than he is from, say, the Knight, the Clerk, or the pilgrim Chaucer's *Melibee*, but much of the closing treatise does pertain to the cluster of social and political concerns so many tales and pilgrims have raised. I believe that in the Parson's voice, to some degree, we can hear Chaucer's, and it is his closing observation on the "inevitable corruption" of a medieval institution now irrevocably changed by *curiositas*. The *Parson's Tale*, standing at the end of all the rest, constitutes the final comment on the noise generated by many of the pilgrims' tales and, from a viewpoint consonant with the *Knight's Tale* and *Melibee*, offers a straightforward remedy for the problem of disorder that has distracted the curious pilgrims from the beginning. This reestablishment of silence and harmony is accomplished by the Parson in three ways.

First, while he agrees to knit up this great "mateere" or "feeste" (28, 47), he refuses to "sowen draf" by telling a fable as the Host has suggested. Fables like those the other priest in the company told (or tales of any sort) are reprehensible to the Parson. Paul Strohm has convincingly shown that the Parson's rebuff to the Host indicates not only his antagonism to moralized animal stories and any narratives with fictitious plots but finally his "refusal to deal with any kind of plot on any terms" and even (*pace* Tupper and Baldwin) the allegorical method.[97] He will tell no fiction, offer nothing to divert the pilgrims any longer on their journey, nothing that might exacerbate divisiveness. Like the pilgrim Chaucer, he will talk in prose and stress "sentence." He intends to restore that concord between *viage* and *pilgrymage* (49-50) which his riding companions generally have ignored ever since Chaucer last linked those two words in rhyme in the *General Prologue* (1723-24). The Parson knows his wayward congregation's misconception of pilgrimage, and thus perhaps his incomplete epigraphic citation of Jeremiah 6:16 is intentional. For not only did the prophet say

> Stondeth upon the weyes, and seeth and axeth of olde pathes (that is to seyn, of olde sentences) which is the goode wey, and walketh in that wey, and ye shal fynde refresshynge for youre soules, etc.

but he also reported the people's response: "And they said: We will not walk." It is up to the Parson at this late hour to tell the pilgrims how to make the pilgrimage, and only he has the spiritual, intellectual, and moral authority to do it.

Secondly, the Parson's brief allusion to every Christian's ultimate destination, "thilke parfit glorious pilgrymage/That highte Jerusalem celestial" (50-51), carries an implied comment on the pervasive noise and dissension of this literal, imperfect, earthly pilgrimage.[98] In traditional Christian thought, the life of every man was conceived of as a pilgrimage, and thus earthly pilgrimage, a symbol of the *vita activa*,[99] denoted a time of labor and confusion. Augustine spoke of heaven as the far country that lay at the end of pilgrimage, dissension, and temptation, and Alain de Lille defined this world as the time and place of the unquiet active life.[100] Consequently, in this world which old Egeus in the *Knight's Tale* described as nothing "but a thurghfare ful of wo," the affliction of noise and confusion is great enough already without the dissent that the pilgrims have added by telling tales, especially tales designed to gibe at each other. It is noise, the *discordia* of musical instruments, bells, barking dogs, songs, and tales which the Lollard Thorpe complained of in criticizing the false pilgrimages that no "true pilgrimes trauelling towarde the blisse of heauen" ought to be part of.[101] As "a lerned man, a clerk" (I, 480), the Parson surely knew that Jerusalem had long been etymologized as *visio pacis*; the celestial city was a place of peace and harmony, traditionally opposed to both the city of Babylon and the tower of Babel, so called "because there the Lord confused the speech of all the earth" (Genesis 11: 9).[102] Jerusalem symbolized the universal peace that, according to Dante, is the goal toward which all human endeavor is directed. "Concord is a harmonious movement of several wills. This definition shows that the unity of wills connoted by 'harmonious movement' is the root of concord or is itself concord." Tale-telling, the babble of voices, gossip, mutterings against neighbors, personal insults, and challenges of true authority—all this noise violates the quietude or tranquillity of peace (*quiete sive tranquillitate pacis*) that, as Dante says, must be man's destination.[103] If his brother pilgrims cannot find peace and silence on the way to Canterbury, the Parson can at least point them to a superior city where, in the words of à Kempis, "the hidden things of darkness shall be brought to light, and the arguments of tongues shall be silent."[104]

Lastly, having dismissed tale-telling as an obstacle to a more perfect journey, the Parson begins preaching to his flock on a topic exactly suited for them: reconciliation. His discourse on Penitence offers all Christians, but particularly these pilgrims, the chance to recapture inner stability by humbly showing contrition, by speaking of what should concern them, their sins, and by doing satisfaction—for example, going piously "naked in pilgrimages, or barefoot" (105).[105] And in his analysis of sin and repentance this overlord who has "kepte wel his folde" (I, 512) talks specifically about social disorder.

To instill the desire for true contrition he describes for them the region of hell, where there is no friendship, only cursing and hatred. What men should strive for and what heaven offers is impossible in that place; for in hell there is "noon ordre of rule. And al be it so that God hath creat alle thynges in right ordre, and no thyng withouten ordre, but alle thynges been ordeyned and nombred; yet, nathelees, they that been dampned been nothyng in ordre, ne holden noon ordre" (217-18). Sin, which brings men to hell, is disorder:

> And ye shul understonde that in mannes synne is every manere of ordre or ordinaunce turned up-so-doun. For it is sooth that God, and resoun, and sensualitee, and the body of man been so ordeyned that everich of thise foure thynges sholde have lordshipe over that oother; as thus: God sholde have lord-shipe over resoun, and resoun over sensualitee, and sensualitee over the body of man. But soothly, whan man synneth, al this ordre or ordinaunce is turned up-so-doun. (260-63)

Nearly all the deadly sins can be shown to contribute to disorder among spouses, friends, and neighbors. Because of pride, a man rebels against God and "hath desdeyn of his neighebor, that is to seyn, of his evene-Cristene" (395). The proud man will have neither "maister ne felawe" (400), will "speketh to muche biforn folk" (406), and in his love for superfluity of dress, food, and possessions will deprive the poor and offend Christ. Out of envy a man will curse his neigh-bor's good fortune, indulge in "bakbityng or detraccion" (493ff.), and cause "discord, that unbyndeth alle manere of freendshipe" (511). Avarice accounts for deceit and theft and leads a man to "reneiynge of God, and hate of his neighebores" (793). The "stynkynge synne of Lecherie" sunders the holy bond between man and woman, the sacrament that "bitokneth the knyttynge togidre of Crist and of hooly chirche" (843).[106]

However, of all the deadly sins, anger is the one most detrimental to the stability of Christian society, and it is the one most aptly ana-lyzed at length for the horseback pilgrims. Because of all he has heard and seen since leaving the Tabard, the Parson treats this evil at greater length than he treats any of the others; the pilgrims have often enough demonstrated anger in their "wikked wil to been avenged by word or by dede" (535). Rhyme and reason support the analogy between fire, which "is moore mighty to destroyen erthely thynges than any oother element," and ire, which destroys social harmony and thus "alle spiritueel thynges" (547). In part, anger arises from envy and pride (533-34) and in its manifestations overlaps other deadly sins. Anger produces strife, wrangling, hatred, discord, war, backbiting, "and every manere of wrong that man dooth to his neighebor, in body or in catel" (563). (There is also, of course, such a thing as righteous anger, and the Parson exhibits it when he scolds his own parishoners.) Angry men lie by telling false stories—"they wol forge a long tale, and peynten it with alle circumstaunces, where al the ground of the tale is fals" (610). By chiding and reproaching others, they "unsowen the semes of freendshipe in mannes herte" (622); and, interestingly, the Parson mentions disputes between husband and wife as the most grievous kind of argument (631 ff.). Evil counsel, idle talk, and foolish joking all issue from anger; the social effects of anger are manifold, and they disrupt the stable community of man. Touching on just one of anger's effects the Parson has them all in mind:

> Now comth the synne of hem that sowen and maken discord amonges folk, which is a synne that Crist hateth outrely. And no wonder is; for he deyde for to make concord. And moore shame do they to Crist, than dide they that hym crucifiede; for God loveth bettre that freendshipe be amonges folk, than he dide his owene body, the which that he yaf for unitee. Therfore been they likned to the devel, that evere is aboute to maken discord. (642-43)

Discord, jangling, the foolish meddling of men: those have been the irrelevantly unifying forces among pilgrims and tales. This paradox is but a corollary of the central discrepancy between pilgrimage as it ought to have been and the journey as it was curiously performed. Ultimately, in its emphasis on these matters the Parson's treatise complements the tales of the Knight and Chaucer in the *Melibee*. The world of the *Knight's Tale* is populated by the nobility, and its prevailing point of view is masculine. A tale of friendship and rivalry, it develops the theme of brotherhood by stressing pacts and obedience to higher justice. Its concern is the battle between order and disorder, in love and in war; and the judgments of Theseus, especially at the end, assert (but do not assure) order. Long after the Knight's premises for order have been denied and the pilgrims have made their debate on marriage a sign of their corporate dissension, Chaucer presents a view of the harmony possible within marriage and outside it. Primed with *sentence*, the *Melibee* anticipates the later prose tale of the Parson as much as it recalls the Knight's. As in the *Knight's Tale*, order, while threatened, is preserved. The characters in *Melibee*, however, belong to the wealthy bourgeois class rather than to the aristocracy, and the ruling voice is feminine. Prudence pursues justice with all the wisdom she must have had to bear a daughter named Sophia; she possesses what her husband lacks, the patience of Constance, the sanctity of Saint Cecelia, and a more clerkly erudition than the Wife of Bath. Theseus's governance of the nation included his arbitration of the private war between two knights and their armies, and Prudence's domain extends nearly as far—she begins by counseling her husband at home and goes on to mediate between enemies and prevent war. Although different in emphasis, the *Knight's Tale* and *Melibee* speak to the need for social harmony. Justice must underlie the pact between brothers and spouses; reciprocal trust between husband and wife prepares for the trust between neighbors. As the Franklin pointedly said of both married couples and friends, " . . . freendes everych oother moot obeye,/If they wol longe holden compaignye" (V, 762-63).

But now the Christian conception of order promulgated by the Parson supersedes the perspectives of Theseus and Prudence. To the Parson, the humble but demanding shepherd of his flock, social stability depends on each person's fidelity to virtue and the commandments; a spokesman for the divine, he views human behavior from a vantage point above reason. The community he sees is not an assortment of knights, monks, story-tellers, spouses, and brothers—but simply Christians. And the bonds between members of the community have meaning only if they reflect each man's pact with the Redeemer. Every sinful Christian can repair the broken bond with God and with neighbor by taking the "ful noble wey and a ful convenable," penitence. And going to confession is better than wandering by the way, for it requires a sincerity that some forms of speech lack: "Thow shalt nat eek renne to the preest sodeynly to tellen hym lightly thy synne, as whoso telleth a jape or a tale, but avysely and with greet devocioun' (1024).

It would be clear from his preaching alone that the Parson bodies forth in his own life the appreciation of quietude, stability of purpose, and neighborly love that the curious Canterbury pilgrims, in the aggregate, have disregarded. Only he can be expected to assume that role of judge and arbiter which the Host, however facetiously, usurped in the beginning. His heavy emphasis has been on those issues that the talkative, wrangling pilgrims have made central to their contest; and here, in the end, by their unanimous consent to hear the Parson speak, they become more truly a Christian "flok" than they were when the Host first so described them. This priest has reminded them of his own role as shepherd in warning against evil governors who let their flocks run to the wolves (720-21); against lords who, like wolves, plunder Holy Church (768-69, 775); and against corrupt churchmen who sell souls to the devil-wolf and so deny themselves entry to "the pasture of lambes, that is the blisse of hevene" (792).

Home is every true pilgrim's proper bastion. It is where the Parson probably would prefer to be, where his parishioners await his stern guidance. And it is that dwelling place where these garrulous, argumentative pilgrims would have been spiritually better off staying. In Erasmus's dialogue, *A Pilgrimage for Religion's Sake*, the sedentary Menedemus explains to a palmer that a man has enough to do at home without wasting time going on pilgrimage. I wander about at home, not at Rome, he says;

> I go into the living room and see that my daughter's chastity is safe. Coming out of there into my shop, I watch what my servants, male and female, are doing. Then to the kitchen, to see if any instruction is needed. From here to one place and another, observing what my children and my wife are doing, careful that everything be in order. These are my Roman stations. [107]

Unlike Menedemus, many of Chaucer's pilgrims, and the majority of the ecclesiastics, know no home. Restless as palmers, these *curiosi* find in their travels a succession of changing destinations. Gap-toothed urgency has led the Wife of Bath away from home to Cologne, Compostela, and Jerusalem; back in England she roams with her *gossibs* "fro hous to hous" and from pilgrimages to miracle plays. The Pardoner, fresh from Rome, has intersected this pilgrimage but shortly will be gone, off in search of other victims for his tales and false relics. The unscrupulous Shipman travels along the coasts "from Hulle to Cartage," at the fringes of society as well as of the land. The Friar and Summoner wander the communal fields and parishes cared for by plowmen and parsons, slipping in and out of the town taverns, pausing only to snoop and threaten. The Monk sumptuously and aimlessly rides out into the new world beyond his monastery; and the sweating canon and his yeoman scurry down London alleys, escaping from one outrageous deception but, in their addiction, preparing for another. Now, for a short while, these errant Christians have traveled together, but their unison was mostly physical. What they have said to and about one another, like the effects of their individual occupations, has largely worked against the social order. Perhaps the reason the sculptor at Chartres depicted *Curiositas* slaying *Justitia* is not so enigmatic after all.[108] Curiosity thwarts stability, and if men's private worlds lack silence and order, the world they mix with on the road to Canterbury will mirror the same discord.

The saint whose shrine they seek was thought to stand for exactly those virtues the Parson exemplifies and talks of: stability in government and pastoral love for the fold of Christian Englishmen.[109] These pilgrims may or may not find this "hooly blisful martir" who died defending clergy and humbled kings with his death. Their success could depend on how well they have understood the pleas for social stability uttered first by the king's man, then by the king's poet, and finally by the highest King's priest. Another priest, one of Chaucer's neighbors in Kent, Bishop Thomas Brinton, saw in the yearly celebration of Becket's translation a reminder that all virtuous men would eventually be taken out of the noisy pilgrimage of this life into the serenity of heaven, "de peregrinacione ad quietacionem."[110] It is in this world, however, that pilgrimage and curiosity exist, and it is here that men must endure the one and avoid the other. In the process, perhaps through Becket but assuredly through penitence for their individual and corporate curiosity, they can discover the path to

the endeless blisse of hevene, ther joye hath no contrarioustee of wo ne grevaunce; ther alle harmes been passed of this present lyf; ther as is the sikernesse fro the peyne of helle; ther as is the blisful compaignye that rejoysen hem everemo, everich of otheres joye.... (1076-77)

CHAPTER VI. THE PILGRIM
AS CURIOUS TRAVELER:
MANDEVILLE'S *TRAVELS*

For the things of the world cannot be known except through a knowledge of the places in which they are contained. For place is the beginning of the generation of things, as Porphyry says: because in accordance with the diversity of places is the diversity of things; and not only is this true in the things of nature, but in those of morals and of the sciences, as we see in the case of men that they have different manners according to the diversity of regions and busy themselves in different arts and sciences.—Roger Bacon, Opus Majus

Mandeville's *Travels* was internationally popular in the fourteenth and fifteenth centuries (over 250 manuscript versions of it survive): it influenced contemporary writers like Chaucer and the *Gawain*-poet,[1] and Columbus, among other explorers, turned to it for advice before making his ocean voyages.[2] In our time, however, it is largely unread and seldom discussed by medievalists. There may be some excuse for this neglect. The complicated manuscript tradition of the *Travels* has long demanded most of the attention scholars have given the work (there are, for example, three modern editions of the Cotton MS English version alone, which dates from about 1400[3]). Debate about the provenance of the book has led to a concentration on the date of composition, the author's still-uncertain identity and nationality, and his reading and sources.[4] New discoveries about these matters will surely be made, but more attention should begin to be given to the *Travels* as imaginative literature and to its contribution toward modern understanding of certain intellectual concerns of its time. Except for an

occasional remark in commentaries to editions and in some portions
of two book-length studies of the work, there has been little discussion of the literary worth of the *Travels*.[5] Readers have long been
fascinated by its revelations about Asia, but the book—a "romance
of travel," in Josephine Bennett's view[6]—ought to interest us also because of its peculiar attitude toward pilgrimage and exploration, its intricate structure, and its sophisticated point of view. And what should
intrigue us above all is the insistent presence of a narrator who interests us in him and his travel book because *he himself* is so curiously
interested in the world. The mind of its author is at once naive, inquisitive, ironic, self-deprecating, and serious; it is a mind that intel-
ligently speculates about the differing mores and values of late medieval Christian and pagan cultures. Approaching the book with this in
mind at least would enable us to shunt aside what seems an irrelevant
issue: the longstanding assertion of historians, geographers, and textual
scholars that the work is an unoriginal mixture of half-truths mostly
borrowed from other sources, a fraud, a hoax.[7] These, in substance,
are the opinions Mandeville's readers have untiringly rendered—and
the application of a term like "fraud" to both the identity claimed
by the author and the veracity of what he reports has accounted for
confusion and harshness and misunderstanding in many of these
judgments.

Mandeville's *Travels* is in part the record of a pilgrimage to the Holy
Land, but it is in greater measure the account of a curious man's exploration of the earth. And the book is not simply a diary-like summary of
successive experiences, composed seriatim (as, for example, Marco Polo's),
but a consciously arranged sequence of adventures. Structurally, the
book breaks into two parts, and these reflect the differing motivations
of the traveler.[8] The first part recounts the pilgrimage routes through the
known world from Europe to Palestine; the second and slightly longer
part describes the marvels of the unknown world that stretches beyond
Jerusalem to the lands of Prester John, the Great Chan of China, and the
Terrestrial Paradise. The changing nature of Mandeville's itinerary corresponds to (and indeed demonstrates) the author's actual motives for traveling. In the linear narrative of the book, the devout pilgrim metamorphoses into the wide-eyed curious wanderer. But at the same time, in a
number of other ways Mandeville shows himself to us, from the moment
of departure from "the west syde of the world," as an incorrigible

curiosus, made so in part by the thirty-four years he spent "longe tyme ouer the see." Furthermore, Mandeville's book reveals that for him, as for humanists like de Bury, *curiositas* was rather a happy condition of mind than a moral fault. Unlike the Chaucer of the *Tales*, Mandeville viewed pilgrimage not as an ideal spiritual practice become desiccated but as only one form of travel, which can and must be supplemented by a further, worldly kind of travel. I wish to show that in the *Travels* we are witnessing, as it were in a compressed form, the shifting motivations that distinguish the medieval pilgrim from the Renaissance voyager. Within this one book pilgrim piety is replaced by confessed curiosity. And that curiosity leads Mandeville to a perception of the cultural and religious diversity of the world—a world gradually seen to be larger, stranger, and more deserving of investigation, the world that in the fifteenth and sixteenth centuries thinkers and travelers (often inspired by this book) began to uncover.[9]

Mandeville's Prologue explains why Christians should go to the Holy Land and why he has chosen to describe this pilgrimage route. Christians journey to the "Lond of Promyssioun" because Christ selected it over all other lands inasmuch as it is "the herte and the myddes of all the world" (1).[10] Aristotle had said "The vertue of thinges is in the myddes," but common sense also teaches that anyone wishing to make public an announcement "wil make it to ben cryed and pronounced in the myddel place of a town," as Christ wished his Word to become known "euenly to alle the parties of the world" (2).[11] Throughout the first portion of the *Travels*, as he moves toward Jerusalem, Mandeville often reminds us that Christ's home is the focal point of every pilgrim's journey, and once in the city he will allude to the exegetical and mystical beliefs that pictured Jerusalem as the navel of the world. All good Christians also need to make the "holy viage" to "chacen out alle the mysbeleeuynge men" (2). Earlier *itineraria* to the Moslem-beseiged Holy Land normally began with this call to crusade, and Mandeville, though somewhat less vigorously, follows suit.[12] Aziz Atiya would have us understand Mandeville's *Travels* as "paramountly a work of propaganda," an exhortation to the nobility to put aside vice and unite to repel the Saracens.[13] However, unlike contemporary crusade propagandists, Mandeville is eager to describe the wonders of the East, and he displays little serious

interest in the military stance of the enemy aside from estimating
Saracen fighting strength (26). He does worry that pride, covetousness, and envy have made fourteenth-century European lords "more
besy for to disherite here neyghbores more than for to chalenge or to
conquere here right heritage" (2-3). The immorality of a lax nobility—
a perennial topic with homilists of the time—is a recurrent theme in
the *Travels*, and it may partly account for the frequent inclusion of
Mandeville's book in collections of moral treatises.[14]

But having made the standard plea for lords and "comoun peple"
to go and disperse the heathens, Mandeville turns to his real motives
for writing the book. He writes, he says, for the "many men" who
"desiren for to here speke of the Holy Lond" but have been deprived
of news because there has been for a "longe tyme . . . no generalle
passage ne vyage ouer the see" (3); he also, of course, is writing a
guidebook for pilgrims planning to visit the region. In between these
brief statements of intention, Mandeville tells us his name, says he
was born in England at St. Albans, and notes that he went to sea in
1322. His credentials as a world traveler are more imposing than
Chaucer's Knight's. He has journeyed through "Turkye, Ermonye the
Litylle and the Grete, thorgh Tartarye, Percye, Surrye, Arabye, Egypt
the High and the Lowe, thorgh Lybye, Caldee, and a gret partie of
Ethiope, thorgh Amazoyne, Inde the Lasse and the More a gret partie,
and thorghout many other iles that ben abouten Inde." Clearly he
is going to give us more than a guide to the Holy Land. His assumed
audience includes all *curiosi* waiting to be transported from the known
to the unknown world. Mandeville wants us to believe he is no vicarious encyclopedist; he everywhere makes us feel he has been there,
seen it all, and returned home to take us back with him; and he has
taken pains to convince us that what follows are his own observations,
his own experiences. Indeed, not until the last chapter is there any
explicit admission that he has also used "informacoun of men that
knewen of thinges that I had not seen myself" (228). With a further
reminder that he has traveled East "often tymes," much as Chaucer's
Knight had "riden, no man ferre,/ As wel in cristendom as in hethenesse," Mandeville calls upon other competent authorities to correct
or add to his book and begins "To teche you the weye out of Englond to Constantynoble."

Through chapters I-XIV Mandeville sketches the pilgrimage routes on a map that extends from "the west syde of the world"—specifically England, Ireland, Wales, Scotland, and Norway—to Palestine. He describes not the whole network of pilgrimage roads but only the "most princypalle stedes," because to name them all would (as he has occasion to say so often during the book) "make to long a tale" (5); and, besides, for Christians "the weye is comoun and it is knowen of many nacyouns" (39). Since the book is meant to entertain curious readers who like "to here speke of straunge thinges of dyuerse contreyes" (15) as much as to instruct potential pilgrims, these chapters offer a mixture of local history, mileage estimates (given in terms of "iourneyes"), and descriptions of cities, shrines, and relics. This initial decision to write for two audiences, the pilgrim and the expectant armchair reader, proved to be Mandeville's guarantee of popular success. As an incessant *curiosus* he was naturally equipped for the task.

His first pause along the road to Jerusalem is in Constantinople at Saint Sophia, "the most fayr chirche and the most noble of alle the world" (6). In front of the church stood a gold statue of Emperor Justinian on horseback; a round gold apple he once held in his hand, Mandeville observes, "is fallen out therof. And men seyn there that it is a tokene that the emperour hath ylost a gret partie of his londes and of his lordschipes. . . . This appulle betokeneth the lordschipe that he hadde ouer alle the world that is round." Bennett says "symbolism required that it should have fallen out," agreeing with other commentators that the apple, in Mandeville's time, was still in place, not fallen.[15] Mandeville mentions the statue, of course, because it was a pilgrims' landmark and because the moral *sentence* echoes what he says elsewhere about lords who grow too fond of the world. He understood the fallen apple as a sign of Justinian's lost empire; and the world where fallen man has lived since Adam "ete the appulle" (8) was commonly enough symbolized by that fruit in the late Middle Ages.[16] But it is clear Mandeville is also very much interested in the *roundness* of the apple; the object is not only a symbol but also the first of a series of spherical images he will discover in surveying the religious geography of the Christ-centered pilgrim world that wheels about Jerusalem. In chapter X he describes in detail the various circular structures in and around the city lying in the middle of the world. And he finds in Egypt a temple "made round after the schappe of the temple of Ierusalem" (34); the apple tree of Adam (35), whose seed produced the tree later used to make Christ's cross (8)[17]; and a fruit (in actuality the banana) the Egyptians call the apple of Paradise, which, when cut open, reveals in its core "the figure of the holy cros of oure lord Ihesu" (35).

Mandeville's eye lighted on the round object Justinian held because it suggested all this. The *mappamundi* he will tell us he saw in the Pope's chambers on his way home to England (229)(a map probably similar to the Ebsdorf and Hereford T-O maps) might have represented the earth as round and two-dimensional and depicted Jerusalem (a round or square emblem at the center), the circular maze at Crete (usually moralized as the labyrinth of this world), the garden of Eden at the top circled by a wall, and Christ's head, hands, and feet visible at the four sides of the map as though He were crucified on the globe.[18] While Mandeville generally adheres to this conception of a Jerusalem-centered world, there is a further implication in the nature of the world's roundness—but he saves that till later. The world, he will say, is round in three dimensions, not just two; a man might go all the way around it; and, strangest of all, he will probably find other men living all over it.[19] All these ideas are withheld at this early point in the book because the pilgrims are merely going to the Holy Land; it is the *curiosi* who think about circumnavigating the earth.

Only in Jerusalem could pilgrims visit the site of their Savior's crucifixion, but they might receive a foretaste of the experience in Constantinople, where the cross Saint Helen found, Christ's coat, the sponge of gall, and one of the nails were preserved. Mandeville in passing warns pilgrims against believing the monks of Cyprus, who, in order to defraud visitors, wrongfully pretend to possess half of the cross (7, 20), then describes the four kinds of precious wood used to fashion the cross. He notes, perhaps for the benefit of English readers, that Saint Helen's father and son were English kings. As for the crown of thorns, half of it is in Constantinople and the other half in Paris. Mandeville brags a bit by confiding that he has "on of tho precyouse thornes," and says, almost as if all eyes are on him and he is still examining it, that it "semeth liche a white thorn, and that was youen to me for gret specyaltee" (9). Continuing on through Greece, Mandeville informs us that men honor Aristotle at his tomb "as though he were a seynt" (12), and this reminds him that back in Saint Sophia the body of another ancient pagan, Hermogenes, was unearthed along with a tablet on which he proclaimed his belief in the Savior who would be born to Mary (12-13). He assays a short explanation of the doctrinal differences between the Greek and western churches and cheekily repeats the Greek patriarch's curt reply to Pope John XXII's demand for obedience, a reply that ended with the taunt, "*Dominus tecum quia dominus nobiscum est. . . .* Lord be with the, for oure lord is with vs" (13). Mandeville refrains from criticizing the autonomous stand of the Greeks; even when he sees that they "sellen benefices of Holy Chirche," he wryly mentions that "so don men in othere places" (14).

Sacred and worldly marvels are as numerous in the islands and seaports of the Mediterranean as on the continent. At Ephesus one can visit the grave of John the Apostle and watch it "steren and meuen as there weren quykke thinges vnder" (16). Not far off is the isle of Lango (here we are in romance territory) where a fair lady in the shape of a dragon waits for the brave knight who will kiss her and thus become lord of the region (16-18). There is Tyre, where Christ preached, and, eight miles away at Sidon, the home of Dido "that was Eneas wif" (21). After arriving at the port of Jaffa (named for Japhet, son of Noah), pilgrims can proceed directly to Jerusalem; but Mandeville interrupts to say that some pilgrims may go first to Mount Sinai through the wilderness, up to Babylon, before going to Jerusalem—and this means meeting the Saracens.

Babylon is the seat of Saracen rule, and Mandeville rehearses the history of its rulers, customs, and military conquests at some length, for the account would have interested still-hopeful crusaders as well as pilgrims wandering by the way. He gained his thorough familiarity with Islam, we are to believe, during long service at the sultan's court "as soudyour in his werres a gret while ayen the Bedoynes" (24); the sultan even offered Mandeville the chance to marry a prince's daughter, but (unlike Constance in the *Man of Law's Tale*) he refused the proprosal since it would have meant forsaking "my lawe and my beleue" (24). As an afterthought, he tells us that this city of Babylon (present-day Cairo) is distinct from that other Babylon "where the dyuersitee of langages was first made for vengeance by the myracle of God, whan the grete tour of Babel was begonnen to ben made" (28). The "tour of Babiloyne," now surrounded by desert, dragons, and serpents, was built by Nimrod, "the firste kyng of the world," the same man responsible for inventing "the ydoles and the symulacres" (28).

Mandeville guides us back from old Babylon to the new one and
the pilgrim's road, though not before mentioning the awesome names
of the Great Chan and Prester John, whose distant realms he promises
to speak of later. In a quick survey of the sweep of the Arabian desert
from east to west, he identifies Mecca ("where Machomet lyth") and,
again mindful of English and French legendary ancestry, the city of
Carthage "that Dydo that was Eneas wif founded, the whiche Eneas
was of the cytee of Troye and after was kyng of Itaylle" (30). Egypt
would have been the major attraction for pilgrims taking the southern
route to go up through Sinai, and Mandeville devotes a long chapter
to this country, combining edifying tales about a deformed desert
beast that believed in Christ and the phoenix bird who is like the
resurrected Lord with practical advice on how not to get duped when
buying balm from Saracens and his sure opinion (one very few actual
travelers disputed) that the pyramids were once Joseph's grain garners
and not, as "sum men seyn," tombs.[20]

The nearer the *peregrini* are brought to the Holy Land, the more
their progress is slowed by the increasing number of shrines and holy
places lying in their way. Mandeville has so far described two prominent overland routes from western Europe, one leading through Egypt
and the other bypassing it, and now, in chapter VIII, he pauses to
insert an alternate itinerary for pilgrims who desire a speedier journey.
This route leads by sea from Italy and includes stopovers at Sicily
(the site of Mount Etna and volcanoes that "ben weyes of Helle"),
Crete, Rhodes, Cyprus, Constantinople, Alexandria, and finally the
new Babylon. Here pilgrims who have arrived by ship join others to
go through the Arabian wasteland where "Moyses ladde the peple of
Israel" (41) on an earlier and more memorable pilgrimage. Mandeville
misses none of the historic spots along the way, he is careful to note
the exact lengths of various legs of the journey, and he adds an occasional bit of factual information (the Red Sea, for instance, "is not
more reed than another see"). We are made to notice several monasteries in the desert, particularly one lying at the foot of Mount Sinai.
It adjoins the Church of Saint Catherine, where men may go to see
the burning bush of Moses. Indeed, says Mandeville, since all the birds
of the country come there annually "as in pilgrymage" to honor the
virgin Catherine and do so lacking "kyndely wytt ne resoun," therefore "wel more oughten men than to seche hire and to worschipen
hire" (43). With the slyness Chaucer's Pardoner might have appreciated,

Mandeville the *curiosus* has here quietly rebuked the impiety of Christian pilgrims; but no reader could have done less than nod in pious agreement, since he would not learn until much later that Mandeville is ultimately concerned more with terrestrial than spiritual observations. The final stage of the trek through the desert brings the pilgrims, in succession, through Beersheba and Hebron—where Adam wept one hundred years over the death of Abel—past the dry tree that will grow green again only when "a lord, a prince of the west syde of the world" wins back the Holy Land, through Bethlehem and, then at last, only two miles farther on (about as far as Canterbury lay from Harbledown), into Jerusalem.

That city has been the reader-pilgrim's destination all along, but it would be wrong to make too abrupt an entry. Thus, Mandeville spends four chapters (X-XIII) showing pilgrims and readers the abundant sacred wonders of the Holy Land.[21] The shrines and miracles that may have edified pilgrims up to this point were merely stimuli urging them on along over the many ways that, like spokes of a wheel, "comen to on ende," Jerusalem. Nearly everything Mandeville describes in these chapters underscores that major consideration of traditional Christian geography, the actual and symbolic location of Jerusalem at the center of the world, the *orbis terrarum* comprising Europe, Africa, and Asia.[22] The lands surrounding Judea, the country about Jerusalem, exist at the four points of a compass whose center is Jerusalem: Arabia lies east, Egypt south, the Great Sea and Europe on the west, and Syria on the north (54). Within a smaller circuit lie the cities of the Holy Land, described here in terms of their distances from the city of peace.

And there are holy spots within spots in the central city of Christendom. Men's "first pilgrymage" in the city is to the Church of the Holy Sepulchre, a building "alle rownd," in the middle of which rests the tabernacle enclosing Christ's tomb. Inside the church pilgrims will also find the rock of Golgotha, on which is written in Greek and Latin, "This God oure kyng before the worldes hath wrought hele in myddes of the erthe" (Psalm 74:12). As men "gon vp to that Golgatha be degrees" they can find wonders of history miraculously condensed in a small space: the head of Adam, discovered on the rock after Noah's flood, the place of Abraham's sacrifice, and the tombs of crusaders Godefroy de Bouillon and Baldwin and other Christian kings of

Jerusalem (56). By this point in the description, none of Mandeville's readers would be amazed to learn that "in myddes of that chirche" a "compas" or circle in which Joseph of Arimathea laid Christ's body was also "the myddes of the world" (58).

It is a short walk from the Holy Sepulchre to the Temple of Jerusalem, which is similarly "alle round." Mandeville takes a moment to boast that while the Saracens usually forbade Christians to enter the temple, the sultan gave him a special pass and instructed subjects that he be allowed to "seen alle the places" throughout the country and be shown "alle the mysteries of euery place" (60). As one might expect, there are some places the pilgrim cannot go that the curious man with the right connections can. We are given the history and dimensions of the temple and the names of its builders and protectors. The remains of Biblical history to be seen around it on every side overwhelm the pilgrim: the ark containing the Ten Commandments; Aaron's rod and Moses' staff; the rock of Jacob's ladder (in Christian mystical thought, a means of ascent to heaven usually located at the navel of the earth, along with Mount Tabor, the rod of Jesse, and the cross[23]); the headquarters of the Knights Templar; Herod's house; Mount Sion; the innumerable scenes from Christ's life and passion (67-72). Mandeville concludes his tour of the Holy Land in the next two chapters (XII-XIII), offering the long-suffering pilgrim-reader a visit to the Dead Sea and towns along the Jordan, a summary of the arguments over the authenticity of a head of John the Baptist kept in Samaria, a prediction of what the Last Judgment will be like, and the information that Cain lived two thousand years before being slain by Noah's father.

In chapter XIV Mandeville closes the portion of his book devoted to the *itineraria hierosolymitana*. He admits that the routes he has shown us from England to Jerusalem are the "farrest and longest" ones, and in short order he lists three other faster and more direct routes. It is worthwhile knowing these ways, because

some men will not go the other; some for they have not spending enough; some for they have no good company, and some for they may not endure the long travel, some for they dread them of many perils of deserts, some for they will haste them homeward, desiring to see their wives and their children, or for some other reasonable cause that they have to turn soon home.[24]

We are not halfway through his book, yet already we sense that Mandeville would not count himself among those travelers who might choose safer and quicker routes. Here and there in the *Travels* he implies that he journeyed in a style befitting a knight, a friend of sultans, and at times a mercenary. He enjoyed traveling in the "gode companye of many lordes" (3) and had an unusual liking for "long travel," as his thirty-four years of journeying testifies. Later we will watch him risk not only the "perils of deserts" but a valley full of devils, "on of the entrees of Helle" (203). And at the end we will hear him grudgingly confess to having returned home not in haste but "mawgree myself . . . ayenst my wille, God knoweth" (229).

John Mandeville was no ordinary pilgrim, but a far-traveler whose guide to the Holy Land was only the preamble to an account of the longer excursions that dominate the *Travels*. He wrote a book of travels, not just another *itinerarium*, and pilgrimage was to him but one form of travel, undertaken, he realized, for various spiritual reasons and with particular destinations in mind. Pilgrims gloried in hearing saints' stories and in learning of the world symbolically fallen from an emperor's hand as they journeyed on toward Jerusalem, the city symbolic of the higher world. But Mandeville's book effectively subordinates pilgrimage to a form of travel motivated by love for this world. Ultimately, though Mandeville speaks of the divided earth as if it were two equal halves, his greater interest is not in the commonly known Christian world but in the vast, unknown, non-Christian sphere lying beyond; not in the familiar tales of saints but in anecdotes about Alexander and the Chan; not in moral significances but in empirical speculations about the round earth diverse races of men inhabit. At chapter XV Mandeville left the pilgrim to retrace his way home, while he pushed past Jerusalem. In his narrative he goes on to do what cartographers like Fra Mauro and Bianco a few generations later began to do: he decentralizes Jerusalem (and the objectives of pilgrimly travel) because his mental map of the world is much larger and his reasons for travel are other than spiritual.[25] He is eager to tell "of the marches and iles and dyuerse bestes and of dyuerse folk" in the East—"yif it lyke you," he adds, playing with our curiosity as Chaucer, turning from the solemn *Knight's Tale*, playfully apologized for the *Miller's Tale* to "whoso list it nat yheere."

Since Mandeville's exact itinerary in the rest of the book would have been of little practical use to readers, we do best to discontinue following his progress from one place to another. Besides, his *curiositas* —as I have already suggested—is really discernible from the very start of the *Travels*, not just in the second part of the book. To expose this *curiosus* disguised in pilgrim's clothing we must look all over his book at once.

At the beginning and end of the *Travels* Mandeville quite openly admits that he has written the book for people like himself who enjoy seeing and hearing about strange new things; but it is not until midway through the work that he takes the occasion to explain why he and kindred *curiosi* are the way they are. His reaction to the enormous population of Ind prompts him to remark that the people there

> han this condicoun of kynde, that thei neuere gon out of here owne contree, and therfore is ther gret multitude of peple. But thei ben not sterynge ne mevable because that thei ben in the firste clymat, that is of Saturne; and Saturne is slough and litille mevynge, for he taryeth to make his turn be the xii. signes xxx. yeer, and the mone passeth thorgh the xii. signes in o moneth. And for because that Saturne is of so late sterynge, therfore the folk of that contree that ben vnder his clymat han of kynde no wille for to meve ne stere to seche strange places.

But sloth and inertia have no such hold on Mandeville's countrymen:

> [for] in oure contrey is alle the contrarie, for wee ben in the seuenthe clymat that is of the mone, and the mone is of lyghtly mevynge and the mone is *planete of weye.* And for that skylle it yeueth vs wille of kynde for to meve lyghtly and for to go dyuerse weyes and to sechen strange thinges and other dyuersitees of the world, for the mone envyrouneth the erthe more hastyly than ony other planete. (119-120)

Mandeville's explicit coupling of curiosity with travel and of both preoccupations with Englishmen seems to have hardened into a conviction among English writers by the fourteenth century.[26] Ranulph Higden, the historian, observed that the English are

> curious, and kunneth wel i-now telle dedes and wondres that thei heueth i-seie. Also they gooth in dyuers londes, vnnethe beeth eny men richere in her owne londe othere more gracious in fer and in straunge londe. They konneth betre wynne and gete newe than kepe her own heritage; therfore it is that they beeth i-spred so wyde and weneth that euerich other londe is his owne heritage.[27]

The ever-restless palmers, said Chaucer, "longen . . . for to seken straunge strondes,/To ferne halwes, kowthe in sondry londes." In *Confessio Amantis* Gower accounted for the Englishman's wanderlust with the same astrological evidence Mandeville used:

> . . . he schal his places change
> And seche manye londes strange:
> And as of this condicion
> The Mones disposicion
> Upon the lond of Alemaigne
> Is set, and ek upon Bretaigne,
> Which nou is cleped Engelond;
> For thei travaile in every lond.[28]

This influence of the moon, which, as C. S. Lewis said, was thought to produce wandering of two kinds, traveling and lunacy,[29] also occurred to Caxton as an explanation for the wide variance of English dialects. "For we englysshe men/ben borne vnder the domynacyon of the mone which is neuer stedfaste but euer wauerynge/wexynge one season/and waneth & dyscreaseth another season/And that comyn englysshe that is spoken in one shyre varyeth from a nother."[30] Ruled by the moon and "this condicioun of mynde"—curiosity, manifested by ceaseless travel—Mandeville went forth to search the world. He could have wished it said of him as it was said of Marco Polo, that he "observed more of the peculiarities of this part of the world than any other man, because he travelled more widely in these outlandish regions than any man who was ever born, and also because he gave his mind more intently to observing them."[31]

Mandeville is the main character of the *Travels* as well as its author; he is present at the center of every experience. Sometime after 1400, in fact, the book was recast into an English metrical romance, centering on the adventures of "Sir Iohn Mavndevile."[32] Indeed, "I, John Mandeville"[33] resembles that other popular medieval hero, Alexander the Great, whose reputation in the romances as a curious wanderer may explain in part his conspicuous presence in the *Travels*. In one well-known episode from Alexandrian romance, the young king voyaged as far as the garden of Eden but was prevented from entering by gatekeepers who gave him an eye as a sign "that thine eye is not satisfied with riches, nor will thy desire be satisfied by thy roaming over the earth."[34] In one of Mandeville's own tales, Alexander's

combination of curiosity and pride earns him a rebuke from the is-
landers of Gynosophe who cannot understand why he is "so besy for
to putten alle the world vnder his subieccoun" (213). To be "busy"
is one delight of the *curiosus*, and Mandeville himself is always "busy";
for example, he stresses that he "did gret besyness" at the Chan's
court to learn the trick of making metal birds dance and sing (157).
The magicians there refused to teach him, claiming that Chinese could
"seen with ii. eyen, and the Cristene men see but with on, because
that thei ben more sotylle than thei" (157). Most Christians, knowing
what thinkers like Augustine and Bernard had said about lust of the
eyes, might meekly accept that remark as a compliment. But to Mandeville it must have been as painful a rebuff as any teacher could give an
aspiring student.

However, Chinese opinion to the contrary, Mandeville in various
ways everywhere exhibits a curious eye. In the *Travels* we have "one
of the few descriptions of Islam in the literature of medieval Europe"[35]
only because Mandeville obtained permission from the sultan to see
and learn "alle the mysteries of euery place." He prided himself on
witnessing things at first hand. He assures us he saw the spear that
killed Christ (10), that he had "often tyme seen and radd" the Koran
(96) (an unusual and questionable activity for any European of his
day), and that he personally observed the efficacy of pagan auguries
and prognostications (though, naturally, a Christian should not "putten
his beleeve in suche thinges") (123). He vouches for the existence of
Asian reeds thirty fathoms long (perhaps bamboo shoots or else the
redwood-sized reed trees mentioned in earlier Alexander sagas) and
fish that cast themselves out of the sea in homage to a king (140-42)
by stressing that he saw them "with myn owne eyyen" (140). He
takes a special detour to visit the castle of the sparrow-hawk in Arme-
nia, explaining that "This is not the right weye for to go to the parties
that I haue nempned before, but for to see the merueyle that I haue
spoken of" (108). As we are wondering whether Mandeville actually
saw all these marvels, he abruptly disarms us with candid admissions
that there are some other places he has not been to. As for the dragon-
lady of Lango, "I haue not seen hire" (16); he heard of, but never
saw, the trees of the sun and moon that conversed with Alexander
(36, 215). Yet Mandeville often credited reports of things he had
never set eyes on. As he tells us, he was just as skeptical of the Chan's

power and riches as we might be, "til I saugh it" (159); and once he had actually experienced fear in the valley of the devils "I was more deuout thanne than euere I was before or after" (205). For the curious, most of the time anyway, seeing is believing.

In other ways, Mandeville keeps reminding us that he conscientiously sought out and investigated all phenomena, both the marvelous and the more strictly miraculous (Mandeville equates these two things, in fact, throughout the book, just as de Bury treated holy and secular books as companionable storehouses of learning). He examines the crown of thorns at Constantinople to check its authenticity and verifies the Jewish plot to poison all Christianity by listening in on Jews' confessions (139). He learns that Saracens counterfeit balm and Indians falsify diamonds, figures out how to tell the genuine article in both cases, and passes along the information for other travelers (36-37, 117-18). Though at times he accepts a rumor or story because it is supported by authority, at other times he makes a point of testing opinions by his own experience. The land Christ chose to dwell in naturally sits in the middle of the world because, as Aristotle said, virtue lies in the middle way, and because a message is best spread equally to all men from the center of population. But, as Mandeville confidently adds, the centrality of Jerusalem can also be "preuen" by placing a spear into the ground there at noon and observing that it casts no shadow (134). As a *curiosus*, Mandeville always keeps an eye out for matters of scientific interest. Egypt, he says, is an ideal place for astronomers to work, since "the eyr is alwey pure and cleer" (32). He twice mentions the ingenuity of the Chinese magicians and astrologers, whose ruling authority is second only to the Chan's (157, 169-70). With apparent seriousness (we can never be sure) he claims to have taken the "smale children" engendered by "male and femele" diamonds and watered them with May dew until they grew (116). In a more practical vein, he argues after long thought, experimentation with the astrolabe, and "sotyle compassement of wytt," that "yif a man fond passages be schippes that wolde go to serchen the world, men myghte go be schippe alle aboute the world and abouen and benethen" (132).

The curious man betrays an unflagging desire to examine all that he sees; he also reveals himself by telling tales that are strange, or unbelievable, or both. Putting aside for the moment the possibility that

Mandeville's *Travels* is one gigantic tale—in the sense of a fiction, or even in the sense Mandeville's modern critics mean when they call it plagiarism—it is feasible to read the book as if it were a miscellany of tales. Pilgrims were expected to be tale-tellers (Chaucer and his Canterbury folk knew that), and the individual stories John Mandeville offers us are often as unusual as this curious book as a whole. To define what he meant by "tales," or to classify them as legends, fables, saints' lives, and romances, is unnecessary. As a *curiosus* and a believer in the heterogeneity of earthly inhabitants, Mandeville found all varieties of stories useful, and for two purposes: to amaze, but finally to enlarge his readers' outlook on the familiar and the unfamiliar worlds.

There are all sorts of tales about his new-found wondrous world that need to be recorded. He writes about an abbot's lamp that lights and quenches itself (and expresses annoyance at the monks' refusal to tell him how it happens); he describes the sea off Java that seems higher than the land and the perpetual zone of darkness in Persia that once protected Christians from heathens; but in each instance he eventually accounts for the wonder by quoting relevant passages from the Psalms about God's *mirabilia* (44, 145, 188). For a far-traveler who sees exploration as an inevitable extension of pilgrimage, God's miracles and the inexplicable marvels of God's creation are one. Mandeville satisfies the pilgrim audience's liking for anecdotes about the saints, then enthralls them with a story of the woman in the shape of a dragon who has killed two knights that feared to kiss her and, like Joyce's Earwicker, still sleeps, waiting to be restored to human form (16-18). In between a capsule life of Saint Athansius (106-7) and a skeptical report about a monk who said he climbed Mount Ararat (109) Mandeville's readers could find a tale—so far traceable to no known literary source—about "a faire lady of fayrye" who would grant men "wyssche of erthely thinges." To a rich lord who asked for her body she gave instead poverty and strife, to a Knight Templar she gave riches that eventually destroyed his Order, but to a poor boy she gave fame and wealth (107-8). The *Travels* also offered readers a selection of extracts from the romances about Alexander,[36] a tale of trees that grow and disappear in a day—truly "a thing of fayrye" (198) —and a story of the insidious Gatholonabes, the original Assassin, who lured "lusty bacheleres" into an enclosed garden that he called Paradise (200-202). Mandeville could usually match these wonders with an invention or two of his own, most notably the intriguing story "I haue herd cownted whan I was yong" about a precocious medieval Magellan who traveled all around the world till he reached home again (135). The fact that manuscripts of the *Travels* were often bound together with romances suggests one effect all these disparate tales had on readers' understanding of the book.[37] Mandeville realized perfectly well that "men han gret likyng to here speke of straunge thinges" and that "newe thinges and newe tydynges ben plesant to here" (228). Chaucer, like his curious pilgrims, knew it too. And one must wonder where on his eclectic shelves de Bury would have placed this incredible book, had he lived long enough to purchase it.

The audience's curiosity, as much as the author's, fed on novelty and strangeness. This appetite extended beyond the assorted tales of unusual human behavior and supernatural happenings to the beasts that, having escaped from maps and other manuscripts' margins, romp across the pages of the *Travels* and to Mandeville's stories about that fantastic Christian ruler in Asia, Prester John. Bestiaries must have provided Mandeville with models for many of the strange animals that dot his African and Asian landscapes, but except for the phoenix, which was undeniably "lykne . . . vnto God" (34), most of his creatures amble by without symbolic trappings. Like the pictorial zoos that crowded the medieval world maps, and like the vulgar oddities Bernard objected to, Mandeville's beasts no doubt had the straightforward appeal "of the strange and the wonderful, the appeal to the imagination of men who . . . had not ceased to dream of marvels at the far corners of the earth."[38] The legendary Prester John, whose mighty armies European Christians once expected to crush the Saracens boldly from the rear, had the same imaginative appeal. Karl Helleiner has suggested, in fact, that stories about this figure affected medieval readers much as science fiction affects modern readers; both audiences "derived vicarious pleasure from visualizing fantastic accomplishments and experiences of a race of superior beings."[39] If so, then Mandeville's further speculations about the inhabitable lands lying eastward beyond Prester John's domain (chapters XXXIII, XXXIV) would have been all the more appealing to the imagination.

Mandeville's tale-telling, added to his interest in exotic animal life and in the lore surrounding Prester John, reflects the same "awakening desire to know more of the great world and its secrets beyond the

limits of the local *patria"* that G. R. Owst has documented in English
sermon materials of the fourteenth and fifteenth centuries.[40] (Mandeville would have well understood the plan of a later Jerusalem-bound
English pilgrim, the humanist John Tiptoft, to take an artist along on
board to make accurate drawings of any strange birds, animals, and
scenes he might encounter in the East[41]—the kind of project natural-
ists of later centuries routinely carried out on voyages.) A passion for
the strange or new identical to Mandeville's pervaded the writings of
the important group of fourteenth-century English friars whom Beryl
Smalley considers incipient humanists. *Curiositas* "was devouring the
minds of educated clergy and laity alike"; it led scholars like Thomas
Waleys and Robert Holcot to indulge their taste for tales from history
and mythology with such enthusiasm that the sacred matters under
consideration became obscured by all the profane embroidery. To
these men of Mandeville's generation, almost anything "nova et
inusitata" was worth repeating.[42]

Storytellers like Mandeville thrive on novelty, and as the range of
their experience widens, their repertoire becomes richer. But at the
same time their sense of the differences among the accumulated items
of that experience forces them to examine the meaning of human
diversity. "Undoubtedly Philosophers are in the Right," Gulliver
comes to realize (for a time, anyway), "when they tell us, that nothing
is great or little otherwise than by Comparison."[43] From the very
beginning of his book Mandeville is aware that the world is composed
of "dyuerse folk and of dyuerse maneres and lawes and of dyuerse
schappes of men" (3). This fascination with diversity is present all
through the *Travels*; the curious man who makes his home in the
climate of the moon feels compelled to immerse himself in the "dyuerse weyes and to sechen strange thinges and other dyuersitees of the
world" (120). Toward the end of the *Travels* Mandeville will speak of
the fundamental unity of all men; but, being curiously disposed, he is
at first more concerned to make discriminations between cultures and
religions. He appreciates the diversity of languages (as did Chaucer),
and he senses the need (as did Bacon and de Bury) for all westerners,
not just pilgrims, to become more aware of them. Patiently, although
not too accurately, Mandeville describes the alphabets of the Greeks
(14), Egyptians (38), Hebrews (79), and Arabs (104), treating us in
the last instance with a short lecture on linguistics:

And iiii. lettres thei haue more than othere for dyuersitee of hire langage and speche, for als moche as thei speken in here throtes. And wee in Englond haue in oure langage and speche ii. lettres mo than thei haue in hire abc, and that is þ and ʒ, the whiche ben clept *thorn* and *yogh*.

An English traveler of the fifteenth century, William Wey, compiled handy (and more reliable) English-Greek, Greek-Latin, and Greek-English glossaries for pilgrims going to the Levant, but Mandeville's alphabets would have been of less real value to pilgrims.[44] They were, in both the medieval and modern senses, curiosities, and Mandeville put them in for anyone who wished merely to "knowe the difference of hem and of othere" (38).

Morton Bloomfield has pointed out that Mandeville's sense of cultural diversity—shared by Chaucer and by very few other English contemporaries—owed something to the thirteenth-century schoolmen's attempt to prove that a belief in the existence of God was implanted in all men by the light of natural reason. "The far-reaching implications of this attempt led to the belief that all men could arrive at some concept of the truth. This in turn involves the belief that to some extent other cultures are worth some consideration."[45] In a passage Bloomfield singles out, Mandeville writes:

> And yee schulle vndirstonde that of alle theise contrees and of alle theise yles and of alle the dyuerse folk that I haue spoken of before and of dyuerse lawes and of dyuerse beleeves that thei han, yit is there non of hem alle but that thei han sum resoun within hem and vnderstondynge—but yif it be the fewere—and that han certeyn articles of oure feith and summe gode poyntes of oure beleeve; and that thei beleeven in God that formede alle thing and made the world and clepen Him God of Nature . . . (227)

In a slightly earlier passage Mandeville makes the same point but with even more feeling.

> And therfore alle be it that there ben many dyuerse lawes in the world, yit I trowe that God loueth alweys hem that louen Him and seruen Him mekely in trouthe, and namely hem that dispysen the veyn glorie of this world, as this folk don and as Iob did also. . . . no man scholde haue in despite non erthely man for here dyuerse lawes, for wee knowe not whom God loueth ne whom God hateth" (214).

It is wrong, I think, to argue from these sentiments, as some have, that Mandeville doubted Christianity's superiority over other religions.[46] Rather, it seems that in these moments of reflection and summary his aim is to remind other Christians that they should love their neighbors—and also tolerate and try to understand them, Moslems and Mongols as well as Greek Orthodox. As Chaucer put it in the *Troilus*, "ecch contree hath his lawes" (II, 42). At any rate, Mandeville's interest in the strangeness of other religions follows as a corollary from his perception of cultural diversity.

This broad moral viewpoint rests heavily on Mandeville's firm belief that the earth is not only round but inhabitable "vnder as above," and is inhabited everywhere. His lengthy proofs for this idea, which are set forth in chapter XX, spring, he says, from observation, scientific calculation, and intuition. First, he asserts what most knowledgeable men had believed since classical times, that "the lond and the see ben of rownde schapp and forme" (132).[47] For Mandeville it follows that if men found the right passages they could "serchen the world . . . be schippe alle aboute the world."[48] So positive an assertion was astounding for a mid-fourteenth-century man. Nicole Oresme in the 1370s went only as far as to say that a man *might* be able to circumnavigate the earth (though he was quite sure of the time it would take: four years, sixteen weeks, and two days).[49] Mandeville says he would have been curious to undertake such a voyage himself "yif I hadde had companye and schippynge for to go more beyonde" (133). He may also have felt that inquisitive men could go around the world as easily as their governing planet the moon "envyrouneth the erth."

But having said the round earth is circumnavigable, a statement that had a profound impact on Renaissance voyagers[50] and on Renaissance geographers like Toscanelli,[51] Mandeville cannot escape the theologically unsettling conclusion: sailing around the earth one "alleweys . . . scholde fynde men, londes, and yles als wel as in this contree [Lamary]" (134).[52] Few men before or during his time would have suggested that the earth was inhabited all over or expressed the opinion so forthrightly. In 1410 Pierre d'Ailly was still reluctant to deny the authority of the Bible and Augustine and admit the antipodes were populated; and that curious pilgrim, Felix Fabri, expressed the same reservations in the 1480s.[53] Such hesitation was understandable, for all humankind, it must be remembered, was thought to reside only ㅜ ㅓ¹ e three joined continents, which were surrounded by the wide Ocean Sea and cut off from any other hypothetical land masses. Mandeville's notion thus undercut the traditional belief that all

peoples were descended from Adam and Eve and, furthermore, that
the Gospel of Jesus had been able to reach all men (Romans 10:18).[54]
Mandeville does not grapple with the theological implications of what
he has just said; instead, he proceeds to support his theory with an
anecdote about a man who *did* circumnavigate the globe—twice.[55] The
inference he draws is really an observation on human nature that will
become the foundation for his ideas about diversity and tolerance.
"For fro what partie of the erthe that man duelle, outher abouen or
benethen, it semeth alweys to hem that duellen that thei gon more
right than any other folk" (135). Good Christians, especially pilgrims,
rightly focus their eyes on Jerusalem, the sacred midpoint of the
world; but explorers who look with care and curiosity to the world
beyond Christendom come to adopt a perspective on the ways men
live and worship that the true Christian pilgrim would be uninterested
in sharing.

Mandeville's recognition that there is great diversity and contrariety
between "this half and beyond half" is important because it underlies
the total principle of organization in the *Travels*. M. C. Seymour has
allowed that the work "has an obvious autobiographical beginning and
end, and there is a sufficient number of cross-references and statements about the need for conciseness to show that the author was
working to a general design," but his opinion is that "overall there is
no intense preoccupation with the form of the book."[56] Intense it
may not have been, but Mandeville did have a definite sense of the
form of the book, a conception of its organization that depended
chiefly on his dual role as pilgrim and explorer. Structurally, he separates the goal of pilgrimage from the other distant goals of exploration.

So the book divides easily into two sections: the first comprises
the principal and secondary pilgrimage routes from England to the
Holy Land, and the second is a longer account of travels through other
parts of the world. En route and at its destination, the pilgrimage of
chapters I–XIV pauses at points of Christian worship, while the wanderings of the rest of the book take Mandeville and the reader through
regions made marvelous by secular and non-Christian news. Pilgrims
find their goal at Jerusalem where they adore the land their Savior
favored as the center of the world; their pilgrimage done, these men

are free to "turn soon home." After a chapter (XV) full of information about the crusaders' enemy, Mandeville invites us to follow him on a journey to other destinations. In the words of a thirteenth-century traveler to Asia, it is like "stepping into another world."[57] By chapter XXII we are among one-eyed, headless, and flat-faced peoples; in this looking-glass land, as Gulliver later found, there is a race of pygmies who employ normal-sized humans to labor for them. "And of tho men of oure stature han thei als grete skorn and wonder as we wolde haue among vs of geauntes yif thei weren amonges vs" (152). Farther on in this topsy-turvy region we meet the most powerful king on earth, the Chan, whose round and walled palace-city contains inside it other palaces and a hill on which sits still another palace (154-55). Going still farther, we encounter the gloriously Christian Prester John. And, at last, somewhere near the extreme eastern edge of the Asian continent, we approach the Terrestrial Paradise.

If Prester John's existence was thought miraculous and the Chan's domain unbelievably marvelous (159), then Eden is both at once. It is protected by fire "so that no man that is mortalle ne dar not entren" (220); surrounded by a wall (depicted as a golden O in the duc de Berry's *Tres riches heures*[58]); it rests on the highest point of the earth —"like a woman's breast," thought Columbus, who believed he had found it in South America and tried to enter.[59] For Mandeville the moon-driven traveler, the earthly paradise—which "toucheth nygh to the cercle of the mone, there as the mone maketh hire torn" (220)— has turned out to be his true destination. With other Christian pilgrims he went to Jerusalem, and of course he hoped some day to reach the heavenly paradise. But being an earth-bound *curiosus* he also sought, like Alexander before him, to find the terrestrial one: a place located (medieval tradition had it) at the pole exactly opposite Jerusalem.[60] Mandeville never gets inside the garden, but even in defeat his curiosity prevails:

> Of Paradys ne can I not speken propurly, for I was not there. It is fer beyonde, and that forthinketh me, and also I was not worthi. But as I haue herd seye of wyse men beyonde, I schalle telle you with gode wille. (220)

Mandeville's inquisitiveness produced not the promised guidebook "specyally" for pilgrims but a small compendium concerned mainly with earthly regions most pilgrims would never enter. The Prologue advertises a pilgrimage and something more, but by the final chapter it is the curious journey and Mandeville's curious speculations that have dominated the book. One last time he affirms that all he has written is true and that he has told it all because men enjoy hearing strange new things. Indeed, his desire to obtain a papal imprimatur and have his confession heard by the pope (228-29) may reflect some momentary worry about much of what he put in this unusual book.[61]

Mandeville's curiosity asserted itself most noticeably once he advanced beyond the Holy Land. All the concomitants of the explorer's curiosity—his pilgrim fondness for tales, his appreciation of human diversity, and his acceptance of cultural relativity—became increasingly evident with each stride into the unknown. Along the pilgrimage roads he only occasionally doubted the veracity of miracles; for the most part he held his tongue and took on faith what a Christian had no business questioning. Beyond the Christian pale, however, he allowed his speculative urges fuller rein, continually testing with his senses the workings of magic, the inferences to be drawn from the sphericity of the globe, all the phenomena of nature. His accounts of saints, relics, and events of Christian history mostly echoed received opinion, but his narration of Asian experiences depended on the claim of having seen and heard everything at first hand. There was no end of the tales to be collected and passed on about the lands of the East, and indeed the climate there brought out the best in Mandeville. Informed by the natives of Caldilhe that a particular fruit contained edible animals, he matched them with "als gret a merueyle," a description of the fruit in "oure contree" that becomes flying birds that men catch and eat. He seems to have won that exchange, for the natives thought his story so amazing "that summe of hem trowed it were an inpossible thing to be" (191). Medieval and Renaissance travelers consistently worried that readers would not believe some of their stories or discoveries, and in the process of denying that they were lying they often only confirmed the wary audience's opinion. In responding to the Caldilheans with his own barnacle geese tale, Mandeville offers us a little parable about this whole problem of credulity toward the unfamiliar. The reader may believe or disbelieve the natives' story, or Mandeville's, or both; the final effect is to broaden the mind, to encourage westerners to become as open as curious Mandeville is to the possibility of the improbable—in short, to share Mandeville's sense of the cultural diversity of man. The *curiosus* thrives on the implications of multiple points of view. Two hundred years later, Walter Ralegh reported that he had located a tribe of people in Guiana with eyes in their shoulders and mouths in their chests: just such a people as Mandeville imagined in the *Travels.* Ralegh was forced to admit that "Such a nation was written of by *Mandeville*, whose reports were holden for fables many years; and yet since the *East Indies* were discovered, we find his relations true of such things as heretofore were held incredible."[62] Ralegh tried; Mandeville—by trading the flying birds for the animal fruits and making us decide—succeeded.

Mandeville's strange, improbable world, the unknown half of the globe, however, has meaning only when gauged against the known. The pilgrimage in the first fourteen chapters of the book must of necessity come first because it provides, as it were dramatically, the background and norms against which any intelligible judgments about the non-Christian world can be made. To make a convincing case for the plenitude of the world and for his forward-looking belief that the world is more mysterious and exciting than most of his contemporaries thought, Mandeville chose to prepare them to accept the improbable by reminding and summarizing for them the understood Christian world. Thus, for example, unfamiliar eastern religious practices can be explained in terms familiar to the western Christian audience: the pagans chant prayers like ours (143, 225), they have orders of holy men and leaders corresponding to our monks (148), friars (150), bishops (103), and pope (224). Saracens kneel before the sultan's signet-ring as Christians genuflect before the *"corpus domini"* (60-61), and the people of Milke—one of the several cannibalistic nations Mandeville visits—gladly drink human blood "whiche thei clepen *dieu*" (143). Sometimes Mandeville compares non-Christians with Christians to criticize failings of the latter. The natives of Calamye in India revere the arm and hand of Saint Thomas the Apostle and let it adjudicate all "doubtable causes"; they also make pilgrimages to a gilded idol "with als gret deuocoun as Cristene men gon to Seynt Iames or other holy pilgrimages" and endure so much self-inflicted punishment "for loue of hire god. . . . that a Cristene man, I trowe, durst not taken vpon him the tenthe part the peyne for loue of oure lord Ihesu Crist" (128-29). The familiar world of Christian pilgrimage must precede the new, unpredictable, curiously seen world which follows.

Medieval readers and librarians variously responded to Mandeville by shelving his book with other works on eastern travel, or with romances, or with moral treatises and social criticism. It was bound once with Chaucer's *A Treatise on the Astrolabe* (which opens with remarks on the diversity of speech and learning in the world before describing the workings of Mandeville's favorite instrument); once it was put with the book of another *curiosus*, Richard de Bury's *Philobiblon*.[63] The *Travels* had a many-sided appeal. Moreover, it gave evidence of having been shaped out of older materials for a particular reason. Mandeville's readers could have learned much of what he told them by turning to Vincent of Beauvais or any number of Holy Land itineraries or eyewitness reports of travelers like Polo, Odoric, Carpini, and Rubroek—as in fact we know Mandeville had turned to them. But Mandeville's ingenious yoking of the two kinds of journeys offered his countrymen a different perspective on the "newe thinges and newe tydynges" they enjoyed hearing. As far as I know, it is the first "travel book" of its kind to combine a pilgrimage itinerary with an account of worldly exploration. The two worlds, two sorts of journeys, and two kinds of travelers embraced by the *Travels* and its author finally complement rather than oppose each other. Pilgrims, inevitably and historically, develop into curious wanderers: pilgrimage converts to exploration.

Christopher Columbus, the last medieval traveler, consulted his copy of Mandeville before sailing out to find China; Ralegh had it in mind while writing about Guiana; and Frobisher took along a copy of the book on his search for the northwest passage in 1578.[64] Throughout the centuries the *Travels* continued to be read, though less as an authority on Asia and more as a source of entertainment—for what Thomas Browne called its "commendable mythologie"[65] or for what one dull contemporary of Browne's called an idle man's waste of time.[66] Thomas More and Jonathan Swift were influenced by the book; Renaissance travelers quoted from it, authors of Renaissance romances and plays drew on it.[67] Samuel Johnson, facetiously or not, recommended Mandeville as a valuable guide for a friend going to China in 1784.[68] It is likely that medieval audiences read it for both amusement and instruction. As the curious John Leland said, John Mandeville was England's greatest traveler: Britain's "Ulysses," he called him.[69] Scholars of this century and the last, suspicious that "I, John Mandeville" may not have been the actual historical person he claimed to be and irritated by his unmodern habit of "plagiarizing" from earlier writers, have generally judged the book and its author to be frauds.[70] If the mysteries of "John Mandeville's" identity are ever cleared up, the facts may turn out to be of some interest. Such investigations could substantiate the theory that the *Travels* was written by someone with a different name or prove that a real John Mandeville was a great traveler. But would it not be as easy to argue that the "I" of the narrative had simply an intended fictional existence: that he was a character, a persona, like Chaucer the pilgrim, or the "I" of *Troilus and Criseyde*, or the "I" of another book of travels, Lemuel Gulliver?[71] It does not matter what the author's name was, for, finally, it is our awareness of this narrator's presence that holds us to the book, and what we sense is his inquisitive fascination with a world he wants to make us imagine. Mandeville was a reader (and perhaps, to an extent, a traveler) who wrote for other readers, not really a returned world traveler, immobilized by "gowtes artetykes," writing for other travelers. Even the tactic of worrying about whether his audience will believe his accounts (159, 191, 229 *et alia*)—whether the worry was serious or playful—works to keep us alert, to keep the readers (like Ralegh) as curious as the writer about what is possible and imaginable. Should a historical "John Mandeville" be turned up one day, it might happen that in discovering him we will lose another, equally valuable Mandeville.

The modern resolve to discount the factuality of the *Travels* is, moreover, a condescension to the medieval reader as much as a rebuke to the author. To say Mandeville was a deceiver is to imply that his readers were gullible and that he somehow possessed an intellect superior to theirs. In truth, Mandeville's book is no more susceptible to the charge of untruthfulness than Isidore's etymologies, or the bestiary's zoology, or the oddly outlined medieval maps of the world, or the selective techniques of medieval chroniclers. His and their conception of history and truth was different from ours, and not as rigorous. Etymologies, Mandeville knew, were intended to convey more than linguistic origins (and therefore "Ham" gives us "Chan"), animals had symbolic meanings that were sometimes more important than the factual ones, *mappaemundi* were artistic enjoyments for the eye and not charts meant for navigators,[72] and interest more than relevance was the criterion historians normally abided by in arranging their materials.[73] So for the same reasons that Mandeville made no solid distinctions between what we would think of as fact and fiction, his readers would have been unperturbed by the thought that the author might not really have been everywhere he claimed and might have written it all out of other men's books. He was, as John Updike somewhere says of Marco Polo, a "mental traveller," and he dreamed a world more and more medievals were ready to realize. As one medievalist has remarked in explaining the attitude toward fact and fiction shared by a contemporary of Mandeville's,

> If Holcot could attach *exempla* to real authors with no justification, may he not have invented authors as well as *exempla*? He used a medley of classical and medieval sources, medieval commentaries on classical texts in particular. The borderline between what he read and what he invented must have been thin. . . . Holcot not only pillaged antiquity and improved on it, but invented ancient tales and ancient authors when it suited him. He had the qualities of a historical romancer.[74]

Whether Mandeville copied his book from other men's books or whether he traveled as he said (and, of course, he could have done both) remains a partial mystery, but it does not pose an obstacle to our understanding of the *Travels*. The narrator and character John Mandeville had been to all those places, as much as Gulliver had been to Lilliput, risked devils in the Valeye Perilous, measured the earth, and come home to tell about it; his story would be read alongside other romances, for his exploits were as entertaining as any romance hero's. And then, as for the unknown author who must lie behind this adventurer, we still know very well what kind of man he was. Like de Bury inside his study and Chaucer inside his book of fictive pilgrimage, Mandeville was the armchair *curiosus*, whose satisfaction was gotten vicariously. Like Petrarch, who rejected an offer to accompany a friend on a Palestine pilgrimage but agreed to write a guidebook for the man (a nobleman with the curious name of Giovanni di Mandello), Mandeville chose "not to visit those countries a single time by ship, on horseback, or on foot—interminable journeys!—but to make many brief visitations with maps, and books, and imagination."[75]

It is odd that scholars have labored so long to prove that Mandeville's *Travels* was not a tale of an actual journey, that its author was a fake; and that at times other scholars, hoping to discover Chaucer's

interest in pilgrimage, have stressed that Chaucer lived in Kent, must
have been to Canterbury, knew the route well, and so forth. One almost wishes the facts of Chaucer's life were unknown and that a full
biography of a Sir John Mandeville of St. Albans existed. What is important is that both men knew what pilgrimage had meant traditionally; and although they seem to have had different opinions on the
matter, both knew that pilgrimages in their day had become vehicles
for curiosity—an urge that could be socially and institutionally detrimental *or* valuably enlightening. And what is important in reading the
Travels is to be able to see the world, a new world, through the eyes
of a blissfully curious pilgrim-explorer. Mandeville's broad humanist
perspective on this world is finally that of the following generations
of thinkers and voyaging discoverers; as Elisabeth Feist Hirsch has said
of them, "The humanists, it becomes clear, thought of Christian unity
in different terms than did the men of the Middle Ages. For them the
idea of one Christendom exploded; they put in its place a Christian
world composed of varied elements."[76]

The fellowship de Bury shared with his beloved books and colleagues
is not unlike the larger fellowship Mandeville encourages his audiences
to see among the "varied elements" of east and west, a fellowship of
understanding and tolerance based on the love God holds for all
creatures on the water-linked land mass. Chaucer's pilgrims lack fellowship, partly because of their individual curious urges; but perhaps each
one of them, given the chance to travel alone and as far as Mandeville,
would reach the goals de Bury, Mandeville, and Chaucer himself sought
in their separate intellectual endeavors, in their readings and writing,
in their travels and intersecting associations with Italy, St. Albans, and
Avignon. Possibly one more Chaucerian invention—say, an unthink-
able hybrid of learning and wayfaring called "The Clerk of Bathe"—
would best typify the feeling for nature, interest in new scientific discoveries, sense of the past, and curiosity about new lands and peoples
that characterize the kind of fourteenth-century English world the
humanist bishop, the poet, and the explorer reveal to us. With them
we are in the great age of poetry, learning, and discovery that has
already dawned.

ABBREVIATIONS

AN&Q	*American Notes and Queries*
BJRL	*Bulletin of the John Rylands Library*
ChauR	*The Chaucer Review*
EETS	Early English Text Society
ELH	*Journal of English Literary History*
ES	*English Studies*
JEGP	*Journal of English and Germanic Philology*
JHI	*Journal of the History of Ideas*
MAE	*Medium Aevum*
MGH	*Monumenta Germaniae Historica*
MLN	*Modern Language Notes*
MLQ	*Modern Language Quarterly*
MLR	*Modern Language Review*
MP	*Modern Philology*
MS	*Mediaeval Studies*
N&Q	*Notes and Queries*
NM	*Neuphilologische Mitteilungen*
PL	Migne, *Patrologia latina*
PLL	*Papers on Language and Literature*
PMLA	*Publications of the Modern Language Association of America*
PQ	*Philological Quarterly*
SP	*Studies in Philology*
TSLL	*Texas Studies in Literature and Language*
UTQ	*University of Toronto Quarterly*
YES	*Yearbook of English Studies*

NOTES

CHAPTER I

1. See William Matthews, "Inherited Impediments in Medieval Literary History," in *Medieval Secular Literature: Four Essays*, ed. William Matthews (Berkeley and Los Angeles: Univ. of California Press, 1965), p. 19; and D. W. Robertson, Jr., ed., *The Literature of Medieval England* (New York: McGraw-Hill Book Company, 1970), pp. ix-x.

2. Donald R. Howard, "*The Canterbury Tales*: Memory and Form," *ELH*, 38 (1971), 319-28.

3. "Chaucer's Reading," in *Chaucer's Mind and Art*, ed. A. C. Cawley (Edinburgh and London: Oliver & Boyd, 1969), p. 64.

4. David Knowles, *The Evolution of Medieval Thought* (New York: Vintage Books, 1964), esp. parts four and five; Gordon Leff, "The Changing Pattern of Thought in the Earlier Fourteenth Century," *BJRL*, 43 (1961), 354-72; idem, *Paris and Oxford Universities in the Thirteenth and Fourteenth Centuries: An Institutional and Intellectual History* (New York: John Wiley & Sons, Inc., 1968); two of R. W. Southern's books are especially pertinent: *Western Views of Islam in the Middle Ages* (Cambridge, Mass.: Harvard Univ. Press, 1962) and *Medieval Humanism* (New York and Evanston: Harper & Row, 1970); Heiko A. Oberman, "The Shape of Late Medieval Thought: The Birthpangs of the Modern Era," in *The Pursuit of Holiness in Late Medieval and Renaissance Religion*, ed. Charles Trinkaus and Heiko A. Oberman (Leiden: E. J. Brill, 1974), pp. 3-25.

5. Leff, "The Changing Pattern of Thought," p. 370.

6. Knowles, p. 335.

7. *Paris and Oxford Universities*, p. 295.

8. Ibid., p. 302.

9. "The Shape of Late Medieval Thought," pp. 6, 24.

10. Robert E. Lerner, *The Age of Adversity: The Fourteenth Century* (Ithaca: Cornell Univ. Press, 1968), p. 83.

11. Erwin Panofsky, *Early Netherlandish Painting: Its Origins and Character* (Cambridge, Mass.: Harvard Univ. Press, 1958), I, 170.

12. Some of the most provocative discussions are those contained in *The Pursuit of Holiness*, ed. Trinkaus and Oberman. See, besides Oberman's essay, William J. Courtenay, "Nominalism and Late Medieval Religion," pp. 26-59; but also note Paul Oskar Kristeller's rejoinder, "The Validity of the Term 'Nominalism'," pp. 65-66. Also see Oberman's earlier study, *The Harvest of Medieval Theology: Gabriel Biel and Late Medieval Nominalism* (Cambridge, Mass.: Harvard Univ. Press, 1963); and Roy Julius Van Neste, "The Epistemology of John of Mirecourt in Relation to Fourteenth Century Thought," Diss. Wisconsin 1972. I am indebted to Prof. Russell Peck for pointing me to some of these recent studies.

13. *Nicole Oresme and the Medieval Geometry of Qualities and Motions,* ed. and trans. Marshall Clagett (Madison: Univ. of Wisconsin Press, 1968), p. 12.

14. Joseph R. Strayer, "The Promise of the Fourteenth Century," *Proceedings of the American Philosophical Society*, 106 (1961), rpt. in *Medieval Statecraft and the Perspectives of History: Essays by Joseph R. Strayer* (Princeton: Princeton Univ. Press, 1971), p. 318.

15. Roberto Weiss, *Humanism in England during the Fifteenth Century*, 2nd ed. (Oxford: Basil Blackwell, 1957), p. 1.

16. Ibid., p. 9.

17. Roberto Weiss, *The Renaissance Discovery of Classical Antiquity* (Oxford: Basil Blackwell, 1969), p. 2.

18. *Medieval Humanism*, p. 60.

19. *Paris and Oxford Universities*, p. 302.

20. Beryl Smalley, *English Friars and Antiquity in the Early Fourteenth Century* (Oxford: Basil Blackwell, 1960).

21. Paul Oskar Kristeller, "The Medieval Antecedents of Renaissance Humanism," in *Eight Philosophers of the Italian Renaissance* (Stanford: Stanford Univ. Press, 1964), pp. 147-65.

22. *The Renaissance Discovery of Classical Antiquity*, p. 51.

23. *Itinerarium Syriacum*, ed. Giacomo Lumbroso in *Atti della Reale Accademia dei Lincei*, Serie Quarta, Vol. 4 (Rome, 1888), 390-403. I am now completing an English translation of this travel account.

CHAPTER II

1. J. R. L. Anderson, *The Ulysses Factor: The Exploring Instinct in Man* (New York: Harcourt Brace Jovanovich, 1970), pp. 35, 42.

2. Don Cameron Allen, *The Legend of Noah: Renaissance Rationalism in Art, Science, and Letters* (Urbana: Univ. of Illinois Press, 1963), ch. 1; George Boas, *Essays on Primitivism and Related Ideas in the Middle Ages* (Baltimore: Johns Hopkins Press, 1948), particularly the chapters on "The Original Condition of Man" and "Christianity and Cynicism"; G. K. Hunter, "Elizabethans and Foreigners," *Shakespeare Survey*, 17 (1964), 37-52, especially 44-45; Eugene F. Rice, Jr., *The Renaissance Idea of Wisdom* (Cambridge, Mass.: Harvard Univ. Press, 1958); and Howard Schultz, *Milton and Forbidden Knowledge* (New York: MLA, 1955), ch. 1.

3. Biblical references on this topic are legion. Along with the Genesis passages on original sin, various psalms, 1 John 2:16, and Paul's epistles were the parts of the Bible most often cited in expositions on curiosity. Paul's most important utterances are: Romans 1:20-23, 12:3, 12:16; 1 Thessalonians 4:9-12; 1 Timothy 6:3-10, 20. Of equal influence were his remarks on how knowledge "puffs up": 1 Corinthians 8:1, 13:4, and 2 Timothy 3:4. On "scientia inflat" also see the *Glossa ordinaria, PL* 114: 532.

4. On Christian interpretations of Prometheus and Pandora, see Schultz, p. 4, and Frederick J. Teggart, "The Argument of Hesiod's *Works and Days*," *JHI*, 8 (1947), 45-77; see Boas, pp. 186 ff. on Prometheus, and also Dora Panofsky and Erwin Panofsky, *Pandora's Box: The Changing Aspects of a Mythical Symbol* (New York: Pantheon Books, 1956), pp. 3-13. Mainly because of the influential works of Ovid and moralizations of them, medieval readers often saw the stories of the flight of Dedalus and the fall of Icarus as moral lessons about the sinfulness of learning and curious endeavors. More will be said later in this chapter on medieval treatments of Ulysses.

5. Plutarch's essay "On Curiosity" is translated by W. C. Helmbold in *Plutarch's Moralia* (London: William Heinemann Ltd., 1939), VI, 473-517.

6. *The Renaissance Idea of Wisdom*, esp. pp. 2-19.

7. Church fathers and later writers hint at the connections between *curiositas* (as an element in original sin) and man's wandering state. Ambrose thought of Adam as a man of perfect wisdom who would have been at home anywhere in the world had he not eaten of

the tree of knowledge and become an uneasy wanderer in the world (Boas, p. 43). Augustine described man's state as a restlessness that only the peaceful return to God could quiet (*Confessions*, I, 1). Hugh of St. Victor considered man's unstable, wandering life to be a punishment for Adam and Eve's wrongful desire to seek more than the perfect wisdom they were given (*De arca Noe morali, PL* 176: 619-20). In *Piers Plowman*, Langland, citing Bernard as authority, has Anima identify original sin as Adam and Eve's craving for knowledge (B-Text, Passus XV). See Morton W. Bloomfield, *Piers Plowman as a Fourteenth-Century Apocalypse* (New Brunswick, N.J.: Rutgers Univ. Press, 1961), pp. 121-22; and D. W. Robertson, Jr., and Bernard F. Huppé, *Piers Plowman and Scriptural Tradition* (Princeton: Princeton Univ. Press, 1951), p. 178.

8. *PL* 192: 827.

9. *The Legend of Noah*, p. 14.

10. Foster Watson, *Vives: On Education: A Translation of the* De Tradendis Disciplinis *of Juan Luis Vives* (Cambridge: Cambridge Univ. Press, 1913), esp. pp. 16 and 20. On Milton's view see Patrick Brantlinger, "To See New Worlds: Curiosity in *Paradise Lost*," *MLQ*, 33 (1972), 355-69.

11. Charles Page Eden, ed., *The Whole Works of the Right Rev. Jeremy Taylor, . . .* (London: Longman, Brown, Green, and Longmans, 1850), III, 79-81.

12. Vernon J. Bourke, trans. (New York: Fathers of the Church, Inc., 1953), p. 311. Quotations from the *Confessions* are taken from this translation and, except for passages from Book X, ch. 35, will be cited in the text according to Augustine's book and chapter divisions. Augustine treats *curiositas* briefly in a number of his writings, but his most thorough analysis of it occurs here. Other references to his various discussions of the temptation may be found in *PL* 46 (in the topical index to Augustine's works) and in the valuable two-volume compendium by F. David Lenfant, *Concordantiae Augustinianae sive Collectio Omnium Sententiarum* (1656 and 1665; rpt. Brussels: Culture et Civilisation, 1963).

13. In *De Genesi ad litteram*, Augustine also explains how *visio corporalis* refers to all of the senses, not only sight (*PL* 34: 459 ff.). On the connections between curiosity and lust of the eyes, see Donald R. Howard, *The Three Temptations: Medieval Man in Search of the World* (Princeton: Princeton Univ. Press, 1966), pp. 48 ff.

14. Alain de Lille later condemned this same perverse interest in the grotesque and obscene as *curiositas*; see his *Dicta Alia, PL* 210: 254-55.

15. Bede links *curiositas*, the concupiscence "corporalium rerum," with *vana gloria* (*In Lucae Evangelium Expositio, PL* 92: 370). Insofar as *curiositas* was seen as a desire for the knowledge of good and evil, it was sometimes confused with pride in the sin of Eve. See Howard, pp. 48-54. Peter Damian (*Opuscula* 58, *PL* 145: 834) seems to mix pride and *curiositas* in this way, too.

16. Augustine, *De doctrina christiana, PL* 34: 52 ff.

17. *De Praescriptionibus, PL* 2: 21; see also cols. 26-27.

18. *XL Homiliarum in Evangelia, PL* 76: 1268. According to Ivo of Chartres (*Epistulae, PL* 162: 201), *curiositas* results from restlessness and inquietude in the soul (and neither hiding in the forest nor scaling mountains can cure it).

19. On this idea, see George H. Williams, *Wilderness and Paradise in Christian Thought: The Biblical Experience of the Desert in the History of Christianity and the Paradise Theme in the Theological Idea of University* (New York: Harper, 1962), pp. 159 ff.; Jean Leclercq, *The Love of Learning and the Desire for God: A Study of Monastic Culture*, trans. Catharine Misrahi (New York: New American Library, 1962), pp. 136, 158-61; and Gerhart B. Ladner, *The Idea of Reform: Its Impact on Christian Thought and Action in the Age of the Fathers* (1959; rpt. New York: Harper, 1967), p. 143. A thirteenth-century fantasy, "The Land of Cokaygne," parodies this monastic conception of paradise, as does Rabelais's vision of the Abbey of Thélème.

20. Gerhart B. Ladner, "*Homo Viator*: Mediaeval Ideas on Alienation and Order," *Speculum*, 42 (1967), 233-59. On the importance of monastic *stabilitas* in the general

development of the medieval West, see David Knowles, *Saints and Scholars: Twenty-five Medieval Portraits* (Cambridge: Cambridge Univ. Press, 1962), ch. 1, "The Rule of St. Benedict"; and Friedrich Heer, *The Intellectual History of Europe*, trans. Jonathan Steinberg (Garden City, N.Y.: Doubleday, 1968), I, 37 ff.

21. *The Rule of Saint Benedict*, trans. Abbot Gasquet (London: Chatto & Windus, 1909), pp. 7-9. Augustine (*De Opere Monachorum*, *PL* 40: 575) had condemned "monachos vagos," as had Basil. See Paul Delatte, *The Rule of Saint Benedict: A Commentary*, trans. Justin McCann (1921; rpt. Latrobe, Pa.: Arch Abbey Press, 1950), pp. 33-35. For Bernard's commentary on the Rule and on the *gyrovagi* who "begin everything and finish nothing," see Leclercq, pp. 171-72.

22. Morton W. Bloomfield, *The Seven Deadly Sins: An Introduction to the History of a Religious Concept, with Special Reference to Medieval English Literature* (East Lansing: Michigan State College Press, 1952), pp. 69 ff.; and Siegfried Wenzel, *The Sin of Sloth*: *Acedia in Medieval Thought and Literature* (Chapel Hill: Univ. of North Carolina Press, 1967), pp. 21-24. See also Herbert B. Workman, *The Evolution of the Monastic Ideal from the Earliest Times down to the Coming of the Friars* (1913; rpt. Boston: Beacon, 1962), pp. 326-31.

23. Leaders of the mendicant orders worried about the effects of *curiositas* among their ranks too; see John Moorman, *A History of the Franciscan Order from its Origins to the Year 1517* (Oxford: Clarendon Press, 1968), esp. pp. 149, 185.

24. I use the text of *De gradibus humilitatis et superbiae* printed in *PL* 182: 941-72. There is also the valuable edition and translation by George Bosworth Burch of *The Steps of Humility* (Notre Dame: Univ. of Notre Dame Press, 1963).

25. Etienne Gilson, *The Mystical Theology of Saint Bernard*, trans. A. H. C. Downes (London: Sheed and Ward, 1955), p. 155.

26. *The Rule of Saint Benedict*, p. 34.

27. *PL* 182: 958.

28. Ibid. On the popularity of Dinah and Eve with medieval preachers, see G. R. Owst, *Literature and Pulpit in Medieval England*, 2nd ed. (Oxford: Basil Blackwell, 1961), p. 119.

29. *Elucidarium*, *PL* 172: 1119.

30. *PL* 182: 959.

31. Sermon 36, part 3 of *Sermones in Cantica Canticorum*, *PL* 183: 968.

32. *Apologia ad Guillelmum Sancti-Theodorici Abbatem*, *PL* 182: 895-918.

33. I use the translation provided by Elizabeth Gilmore Holt, ed., *A Documentary History of Art*, Vol. I, *The Middle Ages and the Renaissance* (Garden City, N.Y.: Doubleday, 1957), p. 21.

34. *PL* 182: 915.

35. *Verbum Abbreviatum*, *PL* 205: 251.

36. *De diligendo Deo*, *PL* 182: 985.

37. For representative medieval denunciations of *curiositas* in art and architecture, see Edgar de Bruyne, *Études d'Esthétique Médiévale* (Brugge: De Tempel, 1946), II, 133-45.

38. See Giles Constable, "The Popularity of Twelfth-Century Spiritual Writers in the Late Middle Ages," in *Renaissance Studies in Honor of Hans Baron*, ed. Anthony Molho and John A. Tedeschi (Firenze: G. C. Sansoni, 1971), pp. 3-28, esp. 13 ff.

39. *Summa Theologica*, I. ii, q. 77, art. 5. I use the translation by the Fathers of the English Dominican Province (New York: Benziger Brothers, Inc., 1947-48), 3 vols.

40. II. ii, q. 162, art. 4.

41. II. ii, q. 35, art. 4.

42. The extended discussion of *curiositas* which follows is from II. ii, qq. 166 (on *studiositas*) and 167 (on *curiositas*).

43. II. ii, q. 160, art. 2.

44. *De arca Noe morali*, *PL* 176: 656.

45. Josef Peiper, *The Four Cardinal Virtues: Prudence, Justice, Fortitude, Temperance*, trans.

Richard Winston and Clara Winston et al. (New York: Harcourt, Brace, & World, 1965), p. 201.

46. For instance, Bede, *In Primam Epistolam S. Joannis, PL* 93: 92; and *The Sermons of Thomas Brinton, Bishop of Rochester (1373-1389)*, ed. Sister Mary Aquinas Devlin, O.P., Camden Third Series, 85 and 86 (London: Offices of the Royal Historical Society, 1954), p. 300.

47. Boas, pp. 121-22.

48. *Middle English Sermons*, Woodburn O. Ross, ed., EETS, O.S. 209 (1940; rpt. London: Oxford Univ. Press, 1960), p. 289. W. A. Pantin, *The English Church in the Fourteenth Century* (Cambridge: Cambridge Univ. Press, 1955) has documented the important fourteenth-century reactions "against the excessive intellectualism and excessive subtlety of scholasticism" coming from not only Lollards and mystics but a broad range of clerics and laymen; see esp. pp. 132-35 and 251-52.

49. Tertullian, *Ad nationes, PL* 1: 660; Ambrose, *De officiis ministrorum, PL* 16: 64; for Aldhelm's comments in his letter to Wihtfrid see Rudolphus Ehwald, ed., *Aldhelmi Opera* in *MGH, Auct. Ant.*, XV, 229-30. More will be said later in this chapter about the mystics' viewpoint.

50. Owst, pp. 479-85.

51. "Mesure Is Tresour," in *The Minor Poems of John Lydgate*, ed. Henry N. McCracken, EETS, O.S. 192 (London: Oxford Univ. Press, 1934), p. 778.

52. See, for example, Moorman, pp. 149, 185; *The Sermons of Thomas Brinton*, pp. 221, 384; and Gustaf Holmstedt, ed., *Speculum Christiani: A Middle English Religious Treatise of the 14th Century*, EETS, O.S. 182 (London: Oxford Univ. Press, 1933), pp. 204, 232.

53. *The Seven Deadly Sins*, pp. 90-91.

54. *Summa Theologica*, II. ii, q. 167, art. 2.

55. William of Conches, *Das moralium dogma philosophorum des Guillaume de Conches*, ed. John Holmberg (Uppsala: Almqvist & Wiksells, 1929), p. 11; Richard of St. Victor, *De eruditione hominis interioris, PL* 196: 1315.

56. *Aristotle: The Metaphysics: Books I-IX*, trans. Hugh Tredennick (London: William Heinemann Ltd., 1933), p. 3.

57. Bourke, p. 352.

58. "On the Aesthetic Attitude in Romanesque Art," in *Art and Thought: Issued in Honor of Dr. Ananda K. Coomaraswamy on the Occasion of His 70th Birthday*, ed. K. Bharatha Iyer (London: Luzac, 1947), pp. 134-37. Coincidentally, Leclercq has cited as an instance of Bernard's use of *praeteritio* that very passage of the *Apologia* which I have pointed to as an example of contagious *curiositas*. Leclercq says only that Bernard "presents as an 'omission' what is, in reality, a long enumeration of things he wishes to denounce as abuses; that is what Cicero called the *praetermissio*" (p. 257).

59. *Sententiae, PL* 192: 689-90.

60. Johan Huizinga, *The Waning of the Middle Ages: A Study of the Forms of Life, Thought and Art in France and the Netherlands in the Dawn of the Renaissance* (1924; rpt. Garden City, N.Y.: Doubleday, 1954), p. 155.

61. *The Cloud of Unknowing and The Book of Privy Counselling*, ed. Phyllis Hodgson, EETS, O.S. 218 (London: Oxford Univ. Press, 1944), p. 105.

62. From Rolle's *Ego Dormio* (ll. 170-73); see Hope Emily Allen, ed., *English Writings of Richard Rolle, Hermit of Hampole* (Oxford: Clarendon Press, 1931), p. 66.

63. *The Divine Comedy*, trans. and ed. Thomas G. Bergin (New York: Appleton-Century-Crofts, 1955), p. 91. On the novelty of Dante's portrayal of Ulysses and his motives for voyaging, see Sir Ernest Barker, "Dante and the Last Voyage of Ulysses," in *Traditions of Civility: Eight Essays* (Cambridge: Cambridge Univ. Press, 1948), pp. 53-73; and W. B. Stanford, *The Ulysses Theme: A Study in the Adaptability of a Traditional Hero* (Oxford: Basil Blackwell, 1954), pp. 178-83. Benvenuto da Imola, for instance, remarked that Dante departed from the customary view of Ulysses; see William Warren Vernon, *Readings on the Inferno of*

Dante Chiefly Based on the Commentary of Benvenuto da Imola (London: Macmillan and Co., 1894), II, 385.

More typical Christian interpretations of the Greek hero may be found in *Scriptures Rerum Mythicarum Latini Tres Romae Super Reperti*, ed. G. H. Bode (Celle: E. H. C. Schulze, 1834), p. 233. Honorius of Autun saw him as a figure of the wise Christian voyager (*Speculum ecclesiae, PL* 172: 855-57), and earlier Fulgentius read the name Ulixes "quasi -olon xenos id est omnium peregrinus" (*Fabii Planciadis Fulgentii V. C. Opera*, ed. Rudolphus Helm [Leipsic: B. G. Teubneri, 1898], p. 92). The long tradition of Christian interpretations of Ulysses has been traced by Hugo Rahner, *Greek Myths and Christian Mystery*, trans. Brian Battershaw (London: Burns and Oates, 1963), pp. 341-71.

64. Ladner, *"Homo Viator,"* p. 251; John Freccero, "Dante's Prologue Scene," *Dante Studies*, 84 (1966), 1-25, esp. 16-17; Joan M. Ferrante, "The Relation of Speech to Sin in the *Inferno*," *Dante Studies*, 87 (1969), 33-46.

65. Grosseteste equates *curiositas* with "motiva," one of the seven "vis animae." See Siegfried Wenzel, "The Seven Deadly Sins: Some Problems of Research," *Speculum*, 43 (1968), 11.

66. Like Bernard's big-eyed and big-eared monk, later personifications made Curiosity a person with ears and frogs (because frogs had bulging eyes); see Samuel C. Chew, *The Pilgrimage of Life* (New Haven: Yale Univ. Press, 1962), p. 182. The ape seems to have been a common medieval representation of *curiositas*; the famous north façade sculpture of Chartres Cathedral portrays Curiosity as an ape, perhaps because the animal signified sensual pleasure and was itself an object of idle pleasure. On this sculpture, see H. W. Janson, *Apes and Ape Lore in the Middle Ages and the Renaissance*, Studies of the Warburg Institute, Vol. 20 (London: Univ. of London Press, 1952), pp. 112-13; and Adolf Katzenellenbogen, *Allegories of the Virtues and Vices in Mediaeval Art From Early Christian Times to the Thirteenth Century* (New York: W. W. Norton, 1964), p. 61. The ape, however, was symbolic of other vices besides *curiositas*; see Janson, passim; and Ernst Robert Curtius, *European Literature and the Latin Middle Ages*, trans. Willard R. Trask (New York: Harper and Row, 1963), pp. 538-40.

67. *The Opus Majus of Roger Bacon*, trans. Robert B. Burke (1928; rpt. New York: Russell and Russell, 1962), II, 728.

68. *Seneca, Epistulae Morales*, trans. Richard M. Gummere (London: William Heinemann Ltd., 1920), p. 53.

69. Ibid., p. 353.

70. *On Christian Doctrine*, ed. Marcus Dods and trans. J. F. Shaw (Edinburgh: T. & T. Clark, 1883), pp. 9-10.

71. *De diligendo Deo, PL* 182: 985.

72. *De Miseria Humane Conditionis*, ed. Michele Maccarone (Lucani: Thesauri Mundi, 1955), Bk. I, ch. xiii, pp. 18-19.

73. See Gerson's "Contra Curiositatem Studentium" in *Jean Gerson: Oeuvres Complètes*, ed. P. Glorieux (Paris: Desclée & Cie, 1960), III, 240.

74. *Letters from Petrarch*, trans. Morris Bishop (Bloomington, Ind.: Indiana Univ. Press, 1966), pp. 134-35.

75. *The Three Temptations*, p. 291.

76. M.-D. Chenu, *Nature, Man, and Society in the Twelfth Century: Essays on New Theological Perspectives in the Latin West*, ed. and trans. Jerome Taylor and Lester K. Little (Chicago: Univ. of Chicago Press, 1968), p. 11.

77. Antonia Gransden, "Realistic Observation in Twelfth-Century England," *Speculum*, 47 (1972), 42.

78. C. Raymond Beazley, *The Dawn of Modern Geography* (1897, 1901, 1906; rpt. New York: Peter Smith, 1949), I, 403.

79. John Kirtland Wright, *The Geographical Lore of the Time of the Crusades: A Study in the History of Medieval Science and Tradition in Western Europe* (New York: American Geographical Society, 1925), p. 179.

80. Ibid., p. 217.

81. Ibid.

82. W. A. B. Coolidge, *The Alps in Nature and History* (New York: E. P. Dutton, 1908), pp. 205-7.

83. See the informative note in *Mandeville's Travels: Texts and Translations*, ed. Malcolm Letts (London: The Hakluyt Society,1953), I, 106.

84. Ernest A. Moody, "John Buridan on the Habitability of the Earth," *Speculum*, 16 (1941), 415.

85. For a thorough and concise summary of previous scholarship on this matter and particularly of the views of Rossi, Billanovich, and Wilkins, see Hans Baron, *From Petrarch to Leonardo Bruni: Studies in Humanistic and Political Literature* (Chicago: Univ. of Chicago Press, 1968), pp. 17-20.

86. I have used the translation of Hans Nachod in *The Renaissance Philosophy of Man*, ed. Ernst Cassirer, Paul Oskar Kristeller, and John Herman Randall, Jr. (Chicago: Univ. of Chicago Press, 1948), pp. 43-44.

87. *The Life of Solitude by Francis Petrarch*, trans. Jacob Zeitlin (Urbana: Univ. of Illinois Press, 1924), p. 267.

88. *Boccaccio on Poetry: Being the Preface and the Fourteenth and Fifteenth Books of Boccaccio's Genealogia Deorum Gentilium*, trans. Charles G. Osgood, The Library of Liberal Arts (1930; rpt. Indianapolis: Bobbs-Merrill, 1956), p. 40.

89. Beazley, III, 420; and see Giorgio Padoan, "Petrarca, Boccaccio e la Scoperta delle Canarie," *Italia Medioevale e Umanistica*, 7 (1964), 263-77.

90. *King Alfred's Orosius*, ed. Henry Sweet, EETS, O.S. 79 (1883; rpt. London: Oxford Univ. Press, 1959), p. 17.

91. *The King's Mirror (Speculum Regale—Konungs Skuggsjá)*, trans. Laurence M. Larson (New York: American-Scandinavian Foundation, 1917), p. 142.

92. J. J. Jusserand, *English Wayfaring Life in the Middle Ages*, trans. Lucy Toulmin Smith (1889; rpt. London: Methuen, 1961); R. W. Southern, *The Making of the Middle Ages* (New Haven: Yale Univ. Press, 1961), ch. 5; Charles Muscatine, "Locus of Action in Medieval Narrative," *Romance Philology*, 17 (1963-64), 115-22.

93. See the *OED* and the *Thesaurus linguae Latinae* and the studies cited in note 2 above for discussions of the changing senses of *curiositas* in the Renaissance and after; also see Clare Howard, *English Travellers of the Renaissance* (London: John Lane, 1914), ch. 1; and Harry Levin, *The Overreacher: A Study of Christopher Marlowe* (Cambridge, Mass.: Harvard Univ. Press, 1952), pp. 176-78.

94. Quoted by T. A. Sandquist, "The Holy Oil of St. Thomas of Canterbury," in *Essays in Medieval History Presented to Bertie Wilkinson*, ed. T. A. Sandquist and M. R. Powicke (Toronto: Univ. of Toronto Press, 1969), p. 337 n 24.

95. Gomes De Azurara, *Chronicle of the Discovery and Conquest of Guinea*, trans. C. Raymond Beazley and E. Prestage (London: Hakluyt Society, 1896-99), I, 27, 29.

CHAPTER III

1. *Middle English Sermons*, ed. Woodburn O. Ross, EETS, O.S. 209 (1940; rpt. London: Oxford Univ. Press, 1960), p. 74.

2. Silvestro Fiore, "The Medieval Pilgrimage: From the Legacy of Greco-Oriental Antiquity to the Threshold of Greco-Occidental Humanism," *Revue de Littérature Comparée*, 40 (1966), 6.

3. *On Christian Doctrine*, ed. Marcus Dods and trans. J. F. Shaw (Edinburgh: T. & T. Clark, 1883), pp. 9-10. I prefer the wording in Shaw's translation of this passage to that of D. W. Robertson's translation (Indianapolis: Bobbs-Merrill, 1958).

4. Of the abundant studies on pilgrimage I have found the following to be the best: Donald J. Hall, *English Mediaeval Pilgrimage* (London: Routledge & Kegan Paul, 1966); "Pilgrimage," in *Encyclopaedia of Religion and Ethics*, ed. James Hastings (New York: Scribner's, 1951),X, 10-28; Sidney Heath, *In the Steps of the Pilgrims* (New York: Putnam's

Sons, 1951), a revision and enlargement of his *Pilgrim Life in the Middle Ages* (London: T. F. Unwin, 1911); J. J. Jusserand, *English Wayfaring Life in the Middle Ages*, trans. Lucy Toulmin Smith (1889; rpt. London: Methuen, 1961); L. Vázquez de Parga, *Las Peregrinaciones a Santiago de Compostela*, Tom. I (Madrid: Lacerra [y] Ríu, 1948); Walter Starkie, *The Road to Santiago: Pilgrims of St. James* (Berkeley: Univ. of California Press, 1965); D. T. Starnes, "Our Lady of Walsingham," *The Texas Review*, 7 (1922), 306-27; Edward L. Cutts, *Scenes & Characters of the Middle Ages*, 5th ed. (London: Simpkin, Marshall, Hamilton, Kent & Co., Ltd., 1925), esp. pp. 157-94; Francis Watt, *Canterbury Pilgrims and Their Ways* (London: Methuen & Co., Ltd., 1917). Vernon P. Helming, "Medieval Pilgrimage and English Literature to A.D. 1400," Diss. Yale 1937, is informative on pilgrimage generally, but Helming was concerned with literature only as a source of historical data. C. P. R. Tisdale, "The Medieval Pilgrimage and Its Use in the *Canterbury Tales*," Diss. Princeton 1969, offers an allegorical reading of the *Tales* (or, rather of some parts of it) but he does provide abundant bibliographical material on pilgrimage and the patristic tradition that lay behind exegetical discussions of pilgrimage.

5. See the excellent summary of pre-Christian pilgrimage practices by Sir Steven Runciman, "The Pilgrimages to Palestine before 1095," in Kenneth M. Setton, ed., *A History of the Crusades* (Madison: Univ. of Wisconsin Press, 1969), I, 68-78; and C. Raymond Beazley, *The Dawn of Modern Geography* (1897, 1901, 1906; rpt. New York: Peter Smith, 1949), I, 10-11.

6. On the idea of exodus and exile, see Jacques Guillet, *Themes of the Bible*, trans. Albert J. La Mothe, Jr. (Notre Dame: Fides Publishers Association, 1964), ch. 1; George H. Williams, *Wilderness and Paradise in Christian Thought: The Biblical Experience of the Desert in the History of Christianity and the Paradise Theme in the Theological Idea of University* (New York: Harper, 1962), chs. 1-2. Northrop Frye, *Anatomy of Criticism: Four Essays* (1957; rpt. New York: Atheneum, 1966), pp. 190-91, makes some brief but pointed remarks about these mythic themes in the Bible.

7. Also see Ephesians 2:19, Hebrews 13:2, and Acts 13:17.

8. *Commentarium in Psalmos, PL* 191: 396. Lombard's observation pertains to Psalm 38:17.

9. Williams, pp. 44-45. On a related idea in Ambrose, see Pierre Courcelle, *Recherches sur les* Confessions *de Saint Augustin* (Paris: E. de Boccard, 1950), pp. 106-17.

10. *Confessions*, IV, 16; VII, 20; IX, 13; X, 5; and XII, 16; *Enarrationes in Psalmos, PL* 36: 419, 429; also see Christine Mohrmann, *Études sur le Latin des Chrétiens, Tome II: Latin Chrétien et Médiéval* (Roma: Edizioni di Storia e Letteratura, 1961), pp. 75-76.

11. Bernard of Clairvaux, for example, succinctly expresses this feeling in his sermon, "De peregrino, mortuo et crucifixo," *PL* 183: 183.

12. The occurrence of this topos is too widespread and well-recognized to need discussion. It has been cataloged best in Bartlett Jere Whiting's *Proverbs, Sentences, and Proverbial Phrases From English Writings Mainly Before 1500* (Cambridge, Mass.: Belknap Press of Harvard Univ. Press, 1968), pp. 458-59. But see also the primary and secondary references gathered in an earlier work, Joseph Hall, ed., *King Horn: A Middle-English Romance* (Oxford: Clarendon Press, 1901), p. 154n.

13. Hall, *English Mediaeval Pilgrimage*, p. 2.

14. Donald G. Bloesch, *The Christian Life and Salvation* (Grand Rapids, Michigan: W. B. Eerdmans Publ. Co., 1967), p. 114.

15. Aquinas, *Summa Theologica*, II. ii, q. 175, art. 4; also *The Sermons of Thomas Brinton, Bishop of Rochester (1373-1389)*, ed. Sister Mary Aquinas Devlin, O. P., Camden Third Series, 85 and 86 (London: Offices of the Royal Historical Society, 1954), p. 173; and S. Gordon Wilson, *With the Pilgrims to Canterbury and the History of the Hospital of Saint Thomas* (London: Society for Promoting Christian Knowledge, 1934), p. 14.

16. According to Herbert Thurston, *The Stations of the Cross: An Account of their History and Devotional Purpose* (London: Burns & Oates, 1906), p. 3, this belief in Mary's pilgrimages became popular only after the eleventh century.

17. Gilbert Cope, *Symbolism in the Bible and the Church* (New York: Philosophical Library, 1959), pp. 52-53, and M. D. Anderson, *Drama and Imagery in English Medieval Churches* (Cambridge: Cambridge Univ. Press, 1963), pp. 150-51. For an illustration, see John Plummer, *The Hours of Catherine of Cleves* (New York: G. Braziller, 1966), plate 75. The *Glossa ordinaria, PL* 114: 352, explains the senses in which Christ was a pilgrim at Emmaus. Bonaventure reported that one Easter Saint Francis disguised himself "as a pilgrim and beggar" in imitation of "Him who on that day had appeared unto the disciples going unto Emmaus," and begged alms from the brethren of his own order. See Bonaventure's account in *The Little Flowers of St. Francis*, ed. Damian J. Blaher (New York: J. M. Dent, 1951), p. 457. See also F. C. Gardiner, *The Pilgrimage of Desire: A Study of Theme and Genre in Medieval Literature* (Leiden: E. J. Brill, 1971).

18. Helming, pp. 7-8. For a convenient bibliographical listing of the accounts of pilgrim- ages made to the Holy Land from the early centuries through the nineteenth century, see Reinhold Röhricht, *Bibliotheca Geographica Palaestinae: Chronologisches Verzeichnis der von 333 bis 1878 Verfassten Literatur über das Heilige Land mit dem Versuch einer Karto- graphie* (Berlin: H. Reuther, 1890); the revised edition by David H. K. Amiran (Jerusalem: Universitas Booksellers, 1963) is an annotated reprint.

19. *New Catholic Encyclopedia* (New York: McGraw-Hill, 1967), XII, 236-37.

20. Joseph R. Strayer, *The Albigensian Crusades* (New York: Dial Press, 1971), p. 53.

21. *New Catholic Encyclopedia*, VII, 483.

22. Cutts, p. 168; *The Pilgrimage of Arnold Van Harff Knight . . . in the years 1496 to 1499*, ed. and trans. Malcolm Letts (London: Hakluyt Society, 1946), p. xx. Dante, in *La Vita Nuova*, XL, had the experience of the Roman pilgrimage of the jubilee year 1300 in his mind when he distinguished three kinds of pilgrims: "They are called *palmers* who journey across the sea to that Holy Land, whence they often bring back palms; they are called *pilgrims* who journey to the house of Galicia, because the tomb of St. James is farther away from his own country than that of any other apostle; they are called *romers* who travel to Rome, where these whom I call *pilgrims* were going." See *La Vita Nuova of Dante Alighieri*, trans. Mark Musa (1957; rpt. Bloomington, Ind.: Indiana Univ. Press, 1962), p. 82.

23. C. Du Cange, *Glossarium Mediae et Infimae Latinitatis* (1678; rpt. Graz: Akademische Druck-U. Verlagsanstalt, 1954), VI, 270.

24. James A. Brundage, *Medieval Canon Law and the Crusader* (Madison: Univ. of Wis- consin Press, 1969), pp. 4-5.

25. *Etymologiarum libri XX, PL* 82: 390.

26. On *peregrinus*, see Du Cange; also R. E. Latham, ed., *Revised Medieval Latin Word- List from British and Irish Sources* (London: Oxford Univ. Press, 1965), p. 342.

27. Aziz S. Atiya, *Crusade, Commerce and Culture* (Bloomington, Ind.: Indiana Univ. Press, 1962), p. 17; and Paul Alphandery, *La Chrétienté et L'Idée de Croisade*, I (Paris: A. Michel, 1954), ch. 1.

28. *Gesta Francorum et aliorum Hierosolimitanorum: The Deeds of the Franks and other Pilgrims to Jerusalem*, ed. Rosalind Hill (London: T. Nelson, 1962), passim.

29. Brundage, p. 10.

30. Helming, p. 152; Brundage, ch. 1.

31. Hall, *English Mediaeval Pilgrimage*, p. 1.

32. *Die asketische Heimatlosigkeit im altkirchlichen und frühmittel alterlichen Mönchtum*, Sammlung gemeinverständlicher Vorträge und Schriften aus dem Gebiet der Theologie und Religionsgeschichte, No. 149 (Tübingen: J. C. B. Mohr, 1930); von Campenhausen's idea was earlier hinted at by Herbert B. Workman, in *The Evolution of the Monastic Ideal from*

the Earliest Times down to the Coming of the Friars (1913; rpt. Boston: Beacon, 1962), pp. 124 ff. There are some useful observations on early eremitic monasticism in Peter F. Anson, *The Call of the Desert: The Solitary Life in the Christian Church* (London: Society for Promoting Christian Knowledge, 1964), pp. 161-68, and in the introduction to Helen Waddell's *The Desert Fathers* (1936; rpt. London: Collins, 1962).

33. See above, ch. II, n. 21. In addition, see Philip S. Allen, *Medieval Latin Lyrics* (Chicago: Univ. of Chicago Press, 1931), pp. 103-5; and the observations of Jean Leclercq in "Le Poéme de Payen Bolotin Contre les Faux Ermites," *Revue Benedictine*, 68 (1958), 52-86. Workman, p. 134 n. 1, summarizes a number of medieval strictures against the *gyrovagi.*

34. On the practices of Celtic exiles, see Nora K. Chadwick, *The Age of the Saints in the Early Celtic Church* (London: Oxford Univ. Press, 1961), esp. pp. 80-83; John T. McNeill and Helena M. Gamer, *Medieval Handbooks of Penance* (New York: Octagon Books, 1965), p. 34; and H. Zimmer, *The Irish Element in Medieval Culture* (New York: G. P. Putnam's Sons, 1891), passim. Gwyn Jones, *The Norse Atlantic Saga* (London: Oxford Univ. Press, 1964), pp. 6 ff., vividly describes the habits of the Irish monastic exiles. Exile, like homelessness, denied the possibility of any return home, but it usually presumed that the monk sought a specific destination.

35. Cutts, pp. 189-90.

36. Prohibitions against clergy taking part in pilgrimages occurred repeatedly in the Middle Ages. In the eighth century, Winfrid, an English missionary to Germany, urged the archbishop of Durham to curtail pilgrimages because of the licentiousness connected with them (Heath, *Pilgrim Life in the Middle Ages*, p. 34). On ninth- and tenth-century restrictions against clergy (especially nuns) going on pilgrimage, see Louis Gougaud, *Gaelic Pioneers of Christianity: The Work and Influence of Irish Monks and Saints in Continental Europe (VIth-VIIth Cent.)*, trans. Victor Collins (Dublin: M. H. Gill & Son, 1923), pp. 32-34; on repeated warnings issued to nuns in later periods, see Eileen Power, *Medieval People*, 2nd ed. (London: Methuen, 1925), pp. 80-82. For a more general survey of the Church's disapproval of clerical pilgrimages, see Helming, pp. 150 ff.

37. Jean Leclercq, "Monachisme et Pérégrination du IXᵉ au XIIᵉ Sìecle," *Studia Monastica*, 3 (1961), 50-51.

38. Alphandery, I, 21-22; *The Sermons of Thomas Brinton*, pp. 335, 496.

39. *De Nugis Curialum (Courtiers' Trifles)*, Englished by Frederick Tupper and M. B. Ogle (London: Chatto & Windus, 1924), p. 5.

40. Evelyn Underhill, *Mysticism: A Study in the Nature and Development of Man's Spiritual Consciousness* (1911; rpt. Cleveland: World Publ. Co., 1955), p. 129.

41. *Enarrationum in Epistolas Beati Pauli, PL* 112: 331. See Dante's often cited discussion of the literal and allegorical meaning of Israel's deliverance from the Egyptians, in his letter to Con Grande, in *Dantis Alagherii Epistolae: The Letters of Dante*, ed. Paget Toynbee, 2nd ed. (Oxford: Clarendon Press, 1966), pp. 173-74. A thorough survey of the various fourfold interpretations of Jerusalem can be found in Henri de Lubac, *Exégèse médiévale: Les quatre sens de l'Écriture* (Paris: Aubier, 1959-64), I, 645-52.

42. Norman Cohn, *The Pursuit of the Millennium* (London: Secker & Warburg, 1957), p. 45.

43. *The Tale of Beryn, with the Pardoner and Tapster*, ed. F. J. Furnivall and W. G. Stone, EETS, E.S. 105 (London: Oxford Univ. Press, 1909).

44. This was the happy fate of a pilgrim in one of *The Exempla or Illustrative Stories from the Sermones Vulgares of Jacques de Vitry*, ed. Thomas Frederick Crane (London: David Nutt, 1890), pp. 59-60.

45. A complete mid-fourteenth-century version can be found in the *Manuale ad usum Percelebris Ecclesie Sarisburiensis*, ed. A. Jefferies Collins, Henry Bradshaw Society, Vol. 91 (Chichester, 1960); there is a modern English translation in Frederick E. Warren, *The Sarum Missal in English* (London: A. R. Mowbray & Co., 1913), Part II, pp. 166-73. Many modern Roman Catholic missals contain essentially the same Mass for pilgrims and travelers. Medieval

travelers, especially pilgrims, were often urged to hear Mass sometime during their journey as well as beforehand; see Edith Rickert, *Chaucer's World*, ed. C. Olson and M. Crow (1948; rpt. New York: Columbia Univ. Press, 1962), p. 268; and *The Minor Poems of the Vernon MS.*, ed. F. J. Furnivall, EETS, O.S. 118, Part II (London: Kegan Paul, Trench, Trübner, 1901), pp. 496-97. On religious services for pilgrims generally, see Heath, pp. 272 ff., and G. G. Coulton, *Chaucer and His England*, 3rd ed. (London: Methuen, 1921), p. 138.

46. There is much helpful information about the ceremony and pilgrim habits in Cutts, pp. 157-94.

47. G. R. Owst, *Literature and Pulpit in Medieval England*, 2nd ed. (Oxford: Basil Blackwell, 1961), p. 104.

48. Starkie, p. 63.

49. See, for example, R. J. Mitchell, *The Spring Voyage: The Jerusalem Pilgrimage in 1458* (London: John Murray, 1964), p. 108; and H. F. M. Prescott, *Jerusalem Journey: Pilgrimage to the Holy Land in the Fifteenth Century* (London: Eyre & Spottiswoode, 1954), pp. 110, 126.

50. On this infamous eleventh-century forerunner of the Wright brothers, see Lynn White's amusing and provocative essay, "Eilmer of Malmesbury, An Eleventh Century Aviator: A Case Study of Technological Innovation, Its Context and Tradition," *Technology and Culture*, 2 (1961), 97-111.

51. For Joinville's vow, see *Joinville & Villehardouin: Chronicles of the Crusades*, trans. M. R. B. Shaw (Baltimore: Penguin Books, 1963), p. 322; for Aeneas Sylvius's, see R. J. Mitchell, *The Laurels and the Tiara: Pope Pius II, 1458-1464* (London: Harvill Press, 1962), p. 67; for Columbus's, see Lionel C. Jane, ed. and trans., *Select Documents Illustrating the Four Voyages of Columbus* (London: Hakluyt Society, 1930), p. 166; and for Magellan's, see *Magellan's Voyage: A Narrative Account of the First Circumnavigation by Antonio Pigafetta*, ed. and trans. R. A. Skelton (New Haven: Yale Univ. Press, 1969), I, 148.

52. Hall, *English Mediaeval Pilgrimage*, p. 215.

53. *De diligendo Deo, PL* 182: 986. The entire treatise concerns the incessant erratic movement that characterizes the curious man, and Bernard does not miss the opportunity to string together puns on the words *curo, currere,* and *curiositas.*

54. See "Contra Curiositatem Studentium" in *Jean Gerson: Oeuvres Complètes*, ed. P. Glorieux (Paris: Desclée & Cie, 1960), III, 230.

55. Francis P. Magoun, Jr., "*Hymselven Lik a Pilgrym To Desgise: Troilus,* V, 1577," *MLN*, 59 (1944), 176-78; and William W. Kibler, "The Fake-Pilgrim in *Lion de Bourges*," *Romance Notes*, 11 (1969), 407-13.

56. Translated in George B. Parks, *The English Traveller in Italy* (Roma: Edizioni di Storia e Letteratura, 1954), I, 70, 75.

57. Alphandery, I, 21.

58. *Liber in Distinctionibus dictionum theologicalium, PL* 210: 850-51.

59. *Elucidarium, PL* 172: 1152.

60. *Le Roman de la Rose par Guillaume de Lorris et Jean de Meun*, ed. Ernest Langlois (Paris: Firmin-Didot, 1914-24), III, 124 ff., ll. 9493 ff.

61. Jerome, *Epistola 58, PL* 22: 580: "Non Jerosolymis fuisse, sed Jerosolymis bene vixisse, laudandum est." A ninth-century Irishman similarly upbraided Rome-seeking countrymen: "Coming to Rome, much labour and little profit! The King whom you seek here, unless you bring Him with you you will not find Him." See Kenneth H. Jackson, *A Celtic Miscellany: Translations from the Celtic Literatures* (Cambridge, Mass.: Harvard Univ. Press, 1951), p. 148.

62. Vera Hell and Helmut Hell, *The Great Pilgrimage of the Middle Ages: The Road to St. James of Compostela* (New York: C. N. Potter, 1966), p. 27.

63. Mention of these various pilgrim vices may be found in *The Book of the Knight of La Tour-Landry*, ed. Thomas Wright, EETS, O.S. 33 (London: Trübner, 1868), pp. 35-36; also in *The Tale of Beryn*, and in numerous Lollard works, most notably the recorded

examinations of William Thorpe. On pilgrims' licentiousness also see Heath, *Pilgrim Life in the Middle Ages*, p. 34; and Huizinga, *The Waning of the Middle Ages*, p. 124. The Dominican, Bromyard, in his *Summa Praedicantium* (Basle, 1484) takes up the evils of fourteenth-century pilgrim life under the topic "Ferie," vi: he denounces pilgrims' habitual tale-telling and their preoccupations with "spectaculis et pugnis," curious dress, and the temptations to lust and be lusted after.

64. *The Rule of Saint Benedict*, trans. Abbot Gasquet (London: Chatto & Windus, 1909), pp. 91 and 105; see, too, *The Rule of Saint Benedict: A Commentary*, trans. Justin McCann (1921; rpt. Latrobe, Pa.: Arch Abbey Press, 1950), pp. 418-21.

65. Starkie, p. 61.

66. Ibid., p. 69.

67. Aziz S. Atiya, *The Crusade in the Later Middle Ages* (1938; rpt. New York: Kraus Reprint Corp., 1965), p. 156 n.2. Portions of Richard II's statute of 1388 restricting the movement of pilgrims can be found in J. J. Bagley and P. B. Rowley, *A Documentary History of England* (Baltimore: Penguin Books, 1966), pp. 215-21. In *The Lanterne of Lizt*, ed. Lilian M. Swinburn, EETS, O.S. 151 (London: Oxford Univ. Press, 1917), the Wycliffite objections to the instability ensuing from pilgrimages are made clear from the list of six acceptable and "true" pilgrimages men may make: the pilgrimage of life which we all make, going to our own church, visiting the needy and giving alms, the preaching of itinerant priests, necessary travel to any place in order to be instructed in the faith, and the final pilgrimage from grave to heaven (pp. 85-87). On the adverse effects of pilgrimage on national economy and gold supply in the fifteenth century, see M. J. Barber, "The Englishman Abroad in the Fifteenth Century," *Medievalia et Humanistica*, 11 (1957), 69-75.

68. *A Pilgrimage for Religion's Sake*, in *Erasmus: Ten Colloquies*, trans. Craig R. Thompson, The Library of Liberal Arts (Indianapolis: Bobbs-Merrill, 1957), p. 57.

69. *The Wanderings of Felix Fabri* (London: Palestine Pilgrims' Text Society, 1897), I, Part 1, 49.

70. *The Praise of Folie by Sir Thomas Chaloner*, ed. Clarence H. Miller, EETS, O.S. 257 (London: Oxford Univ. Press, 1965), p. 70.

71. Herbert B. Workman, *John Wyclif: A Study of the English Medieval Church* (Oxford: Clarendon Press, 1926), II, 18; *Select English Works of John Wyclif*, ed. Thomas Arnold (Oxford: Clarendon Press, 1869-71), I, 81, 83; and III, 463.

72. *Thomae Walsingham, Quondam Monachi S. Albani, Historia Anglicana,* ed. Henry Thomas Riley, Rolls Series (London: Longman, Green, 1863-64), II, 188.

73. Probably the most detailed summary of and rebuttal to Lollard attacks on pilgrimage is that by Bishop Reginald Pecock in his *The Repressor of Over Much Blaming of the Clergy*, ed. Churchill Babington, Rolls Series (London: Longman, Green, 1860), esp. I, chs. 9 and 10. See, too, the poem "Defend Us From All Lollardry" in *Historical Poems of the XIVth and XVth Centuries*, ed. Rossell Hope Robbins (New York: Columbia Univ. Press, 1959), pp. 152-57, esp. p. 155. One hundred years later it is noticeable that the Church's defense of pilgrimage has somewhat weakened, as is apparent in *A dyaloge of Sir Thomas More knyghte: . . . wheryn be treatyd dyuers maters . . . & goynge on pylgrymage . . .* (n.p., 1530), esp. fols. xii^v-xiiii^r.

74. Gordon Leff, *Heresy in the Later Middle Ages: The Relation of Heterodoxy to Dissent c. 1250-c. 1450* (Manchester: Manchester Univ. Press, 1967), II, 584.

75. *Shakespeare's Holinshed*, ed. Richard Hosley (New York: G. P. Putnam's Sons, 1968), pp. 116-17.

76. *Mysticism*, pp. 125-36.

77. *The Vision of William Concerning Piers the Plowman . . .* , ed. Walter W. Skeat (1886; rpt. London: Oxford Univ. Press, 1968), I, 182 (B. V, 541-43), 368 (B. XII, 36 ff.), and 438 (B. XV, 44-53).

78. *Of the Imitation of Christ in Four Books by Thomas à Kempis*, trans. Justin McCann (New York: New American Library, 1957), p. 157.

79. Thurston, *The Stations of the Cross*, p. 13. It was the practice of returned crusaders to set up tableaux at home and perform what they called "the Little Jerusalem"; see the *New Catholic Encyclopedia*, XIV, 832.

80. Thurston, p. 2.

81. Sir Steven Runciman, "The Decline of the Crusading Ideal," *The Sewanee Review*, 79 (1971), 498-513.

82. On this admirer of Petrarch see Ernest Hatch Wilkins, *Life of Petrarch* (Chicago: Univ. of Chicago Press, 1961), pp. 165-66.

83. Margaret Aston, *The Fifteenth Century: The Prospect of Europe* (New York: Harcourt, Brace and World, 1968), p. 85.

CHAPTER IV

1. W. Braxton Ross, Jr., "Giovanni Colonna, Historian at Avignon," *Speculum*, 45 (1970), 533-63.

2. *Le Familiari*, ed. Vittorio Rossi (Firenze: G. C. Sansoni, 1933-42), I, 106.

3. Beryl Smalley, *English Friars and Antiquity in the Early Fourteenth Century* (Oxford: Basil Blackwell, 1960), p. 74. Much of Smalley's fourth chapter, "Patronage," concerns de Bury. There is a full account of the relationship between de Bury and Petrarch in Carlo Segre's *Studi Petrarcheschi* (Florence: Successori Le Monnier, 1903), pp. 227-56.

4. Petrarch himself commented on de Bury's unresponsiveness. See Smalley, p. 69; and N. Denholm-Young, "Richard De Bury (1287-1345)," *Transactions of the Royal Historical Society*, Fourth Series, 20 (1937), 148 (reprinted in his *Collected Papers on Mediaeval Subjects* [Oxford: Basil Blackwell, 1946], pp. 1-25).

5. The important facts of de Bury's life may be found in Denholm-Young's article; in the *DNB*; in the three-part monograph by J. De Ghellinck, "Un Évêque Bibliophile au XIVe Siècle: Richard Aungerville De Bury (1345)," *Revue d'Histoire Ecclesiastique*, 18 (1922), 271-312 and 482-508; 19 (1923), 157-200; and in A. B. Emden, *A Biographical Register of the University of Oxford to A.D. 1500* (Oxford: Clarendon Press, 1957), I, 323-26.

6. Denholm-Young, p. 150.

7. De Bury's political importance is discussed by John Lord Campbell, *The Lives of the Lord Chancellors and Keepers of the Great Seal of England* (London: J. Murray, 1846), I, 221-31; in *Richard D'Aungerville of Bury: Fragments of his Register, and Other Documents*, Publications of the Surtees Society, 119 (Durham: Andrews & Co., 1910); and by Thomas Frederick Tout, "Literature and Learning in the English Civil Service in the Fourteenth Century," *Speculum*, 4 (1929), 374-76.

8. Besides the *Philobiblon*, de Bury did leave behind a collection of various Latin letters he copied for use as models of composition; see N. Denholm-Young, ed., *The Liber Epistolaris of Richard De Bury* (Oxford: Roxburghe Club, 1950). On the medieval habit of collecting letters for use as models in letter-writing, see Charles Homer Haskins, *The Renaissance of the Twelfth Century* (1927; rpt. Cleveland and New York: Meridian Books, 1957), p. 140.

9. *The Philobiblon of Richard de Bury, Bishop of Durham, Treasurer and Chancellor of Edward III*, ed. and trans. E. C. Thomas (London: K. Paul, Trench, 1888), p. xiv.

10. Smalley, ch. 4, treats some of these figures in their relationships to de Bury, and she devotes one chapter (7) to Holcot. Denholm-Young, "Richard De Bury (1287-1345)," pp. 164-65, discusses these and lesser scholars connected with de Bury.

11. Denholm-Young, "Richard De Bury (1287-1345)," p. 158; and Emden, p. 325.

12. *Historiae Dunelmensis Scriptores Tres, Gaufridus de Coldingham, Robertus de Graystanes, et Willielmus de Chambre*, ed. James Raine (London: J. B. Nichols & Son, 1839), p. 130.

13. *Adae Murimuth Continuatio Chronicarum, Robertus de Avesbury De Gestis Mirabilibus Regis Edwardi Tertii*, ed. Edward Maunde Thompson, Rolls Series, 93 (London: Eyre & Spottiswoode, 1889), p. 171.

14. George B. Parks, *The English Traveller in Italy* (Roma: Edizioni di Storia e Lettera-tura, 1954), I, 427. Denholm-Young's introduction to the *Liber Epistolaris*, p. xxvii, shows further reason why Murimuth's opinion of de Bury should not be taken too seriously: Murimuth was habitually malicious toward contemporaries.

15. Hans Baron, *From Petrarch to Leonardo Bruni: Studies in Humanistic and Political Literature* (Chicago: Univ. of Chicago Press, 1968), p. 198.

16. *Adae Murimuth Continuatio Chronicarum*, p. 171.

17. *Historiae Dunelmensis Scriptores Tres*, p. 130.

18. Roberto Weiss, "The Private Collector and the Revival of Greek Learning," in *The English Library Before 1700: Studies in its History*, ed. Francis Wormald and C. E. Wright (London: Univ. of London, Athlone Press, 1958), pp. 114-15. De Bury's library and its possible contents are discussed by James Westfall Thompson, *The Medieval Library* (1939; rpt. New York: Hafner Publ. Co., 1967), ch. 13. Also see F. Somner Merryweather, *Biblio-mania in the Middle Ages* (London: Woodstock Press, 1933), pp. 113-31.

19. Roger Sherman Loomis, "The Library of Richard II," in *Studies in Language, Lit-erature, and Culture of the Middle Ages and Later*, ed. E. Bagby Atwood and Archibald A. Hill (Austin: Univ. of Texas Press, 1969), pp. 173-78; Millard Meiss, "The Library of Jean de Berry," in *French Painting in the Time of Jean de Berry: The Late Fourteenth Century and the Patronage of the Duke*, National Gallery of Art, Kress Foundation Studies in the History of European Art, 2 (London: Phaidon Press Ltd., 1967), I, 287-308, esp. 287.

20. See R. J. Mitchell, *John Tiptoft (1427-1470)* (London: Longmans, Green, 1938), ch. xi on Tiptoft's library; and B. L. Ullman, *Studies in the Italian Renaissance* (Roma: Edizioni di Storia e Letteratura, 1955), ch. xvii, on the manuscripts of Duke Humphrey of Gloucester.

21. George K. Anderson, *Old and Middle English Literature From the Beginnings to 1485* (New York: Collier Books, 1962), pp. 99, 100.

22. The text I use is that edited by E. C. Thomas (London: K. Paul, Trench, 1888); in the first part of his edition he prints the Latin text and in the second part his English translation. I quote generally from the translation except when it seems necessary to cite the Latin. The numbers in parentheses after citations in my chapter are those Thomas uses to designate sections in both the Latin and English versions. A more recent and superior edition of the *Philobiblon* is that of Antonio Altamura (Naples: F. Fiorentino, 1954) but because of its general inaccessibility I have chosen to use Thomas's edition instead. I have, however, checked Thomas's edition against Altamura's at all points. There is, incidentally, a factual error in Altamura's edition: in his index, on p. 157, he identifies the "glorious martyr St. Thomas" (mentioned by de Bury in ch. 19) as Thomas Aquinas, but in view of the calendar date de Bury also mentions—July 7—the "martyr" must be Thomas à Becket, an English rather than an Italian saint.

23. Denholm-Young, "Richard De Bury (1287-1345)," pp. 154-55.

24. Karl Julius Holzknecht, "Literary Patronage in the Middle Ages," Diss. Pennsylvania 1923, p. 223.

25. De Ghellinck, p. 286.

26. Moriz Sondheim, "Das Philobiblon des Richard de Bury," *Zeitschrift für Bucher-freunde*, 1 (1897-98), 325.

27. W. A. Pantin, "John of Wales and Medieval Humanism," in *Medieval Studies Pre-sented to Aubrey Gwyn, S.J.*, ed. J. A. Watt et al. (Dublin: O. Lochlainn, 1961), p. 301.

28. Jean Leclercq, *The Love of Learning and the Desire for God: A Study of Monastic Culture*, trans. Catharine Misrahi (New York: New American Library, 1962), pp. 22-23 and ch. 7.

29. *The Little Flowers of St. Francis*, ed. Damian J. Blaher (New York: J. M. Dent, 1951), p. 319. The portions of the passage I have cited in Latin are from *Le Speculum Per-fectionis ou Mémoires de Frère Léon*, ed. Paul Sabatier (Manchester: Univ. of Manchester Press, 1928, 1931), I, 200.

30. *The Ship of Fools Translated by Alexander Barclay* (1874; rpt. New York: AMS Press, 1966), I, 20, 23.

31. Other mentions of this *topos* in the *Philobiblon* occur in sections 29, 33, 34, 73, 75, 77, 129, 157, 164, and 205.

32. See Leclercq, pp. 109-13; and Ernst Robert Curtius, *European Literature and the Latin Middle Ages*, trans. Willard R. Trask (1953; rpt. New York: Harper, 1963), pp. 310-15.

33. Ernest Hatch Wilkins, *Life of Petrarch* (Chicago: Univ. of Chicago Press, 1961), p. 184.

34. *The Complaint of Nature by Alain de Lille*, trans. Douglas M. Moffat, Yale Studies in English, 36 (New York: H. Holt & Co., 1908), p. 54 (Prosa v).

35. *Historiae Dunelmensis Scriptores Tres*, p. 128.

36. Most editors and commentators now reject the idea that Holcot may have written the work, although it is possible that he had a hand in it and perhaps wrote it at de Bury's dictation. See, for instance, Smalley, p. 67 n.4; and Thompson, p. 384.

37. Smalley, pp. 102 ff., 212 ff., and 148 ff. Also see Jean Seznec, *The Survival of the Pagan Gods: The Mythological Tradition and its Place in Renaissance Humanism and Art*, trans. Barbara F. Sessions (1953; rpt. New York: Harper, 1961), pp. 11 ff. and 84 ff.

38. D. W. Robertson, Jr., *Chaucer's London* (New York: John Wiley & Sons, Inc., 1968), p. 181.

39. *The Parliament of Fowls*, ll. 24-25.

40. W. A. Pantin, *The English Church in the Fourteenth Century* (Cambridge: Cambridge Univ. Press, 1955), pp. 143, 145, 148-9.

41. R. R. Bolgar, *The Classical Heritage and Its Beneficiaries from the Carolingian Age to the End of the Renaissance* (1954; rpt. New York: Harper, 1964), pp. 240-41.

42. *The Medieval Library*, p. 386.

43. Paul Oskar Kristeller, "The Medieval Antecedents of Renaissance Humanism," in *Eight Philosophers of the Italian Renaissance* (Stanford: Stanford Univ. Press, 1964), pp. 147-65.

44. For evidence that the *ars dictandi* was being taught, written about, and used at Oxford and elsewhere early in the fourteenth century, see R. J. Schoeck, "On Rhetoric in Fourteenth-Century Oxford," *MS*, 30 (1968), 214-25. Denholm-Young, "The Cursus in England," in *Collected Papers on Mediaeval Subjects* (pp. 26-55) describes the *cursus* as it was known and used by de Bury. Briefly, it was "a system of rhythmical clausulae, according to which those who wished to indulge in fine writing would end each clause and each sentence in one of a few well-defined ways" (p. 26). It was in vogue at the papal court and chancery and became popular in civil and ecclesiastical circles in the thirteenth and fourteenth centuries. It was an artificial style—and was thought of as such in de Bury's day. For further discussion of the *cursus*, see the appendix to *Dantis Alagherii Epistolae: The Letters of Dante*, ed. Paget Toynbee, 2nd ed. (Oxford: Clarendon Press, 1966), pp. 224-27; Albert C. Clark, *Fontes Prosae Numerosae and The Cursus in Mediaeval and Vulgar Latin* (Oxford: Clarendon Press, 1910); and Henry J. Chaytor, *From Script to Print: An Introduction to Medieval Literature* (Cambridge: Cambridge Univ. Press, 1945), pp. 57 ff.

45. See, for example, Bolgar, p. 260.

46. In his chapter on "London as an Intellectual Center," in *Chaucer's London*, Robertson provides one starting point for a wider discussion of such humanism (pp. 181-83). See also my first chapter.

47. In connection with de Bury's fondness for the past and his humanist tendencies, see Gerhart B. Ladner, "Vegetation Symbolism and the Concept of Renaissance," in *De Artibus Opuscula XL: Essays in Honor of Erwin Panofsky*, ed. Millard Meiss (New York: New York Univ. Press, 1961), pp. 303-22.

48. Hans Schnyder, *Sir Gawain and the Green Knight: An Essay in Interpretation*, The Cooper Monographs, 6 (Bern: Francke Verlag, 1961), p. 27. Schnyder mentions de Bury only in passing. D. W. Robertson, Jr., *A Preface to Chaucer: Studies in Medieval Perspectives*

(Princeton: Princeton Univ. Press, 1962), pp. 307-9, touches on de Bury's book to argue that the bishop was concerned with the need for expounding the spiritual sense of Scripture.

49. See *Poetria magistri Johannis anglici de arte prosayca metrica et rithmica*, ed. G. Mari, *Romanische Forschungen*, 13 (1902), 914-15; also the remarks of Geoffrey of Vinsauf in Edmond Faral, *Les Arts Poétiques du XIIe et du XIIIe Siècle* (Paris: É. Champion, 1924), pp. 205, 211-13, and 275-76. Charles Sears Baldwin, *Medieval Rhetoric and Poetic (to 1400) Interpreted from Representative Works* (New York: Macmillan, 1928), p. 215, suggests that the use of these figures is appropriate to the elegance of the *cursus* style employed by de Bury.

50. Petrarch spoke to and listened to books in much the same way; see Wilkins, *Life of Petrarch*, pp. 20-21 and 57-58.

51. *Canterbury Tales*, I, 299-302. A. Wigfall Green, "Chaucer's Clerks and the Mediaeval Scholarly Tradition as Represented by Richard De Bury's *Philobiblon*," *ELH*, 18 (1951), 1-6, draws some parallels between de Bury himself and Chaucer's Clerk.

52. That de Bury's methods of obtaining books were not always entirely scrupulous is apparent from the *Philobiblon* itself, and an anecdote Thomas Walsingham tells about the bishop corroborates this. It seems de Bury was presented with four books (copies of Terence, Virgil, Quintilian, and *Ieronymun contra Rufinum*) by the abbot of St. Albans with the understanding that in return he would further the interests of the monastery at Edward's court. Walsingham was angered at the idea of letting books out of the cloister library, especially for such a crass reason; but he reported that de Bury returned the four volumes after he became bishop of Durham and that the monastery offered prayers for his soul when he died. Cf. *Thomae Walsingham, Gesta Abbatum Monasterii Sancti Albani*, Rolls Series (London: Longman, Green, 1867), II, 200. For some insightful remarks on de Bury's book-borrowing, see Christopher R. Cheney, "Richard de Bury, Borrower of Books," *Speculum*, 48 (1973), 325-28.

53. *European Literature and the Latin Middle Ages*, p. 328.

54. Denholm-Young, "Richard De Bury (1287-1345)," p. 137; and Emden, p. 323.

55. See Smalley, p. 69; George Saintsbury, *A History of Criticism and Literary Taste* . . . , 2nd ed. (Edinburgh: Blackwood, 1949), I, 456; and J. W. H. Atkins, *English Literary Criticism: The Medieval Phase* (1943; rpt. Gloucester, Mass.: Peter Smith, 1961), p. 141.

56. *European Literature and the Latin Middle Ages*, pp. 317, 322.

57. As far as the laity is concerned, de Bury abhors the prospect of their ever being allowed to handle books; throughout his book he derides them (48, 51, 56, 72, 224). However, Smalley (p. 29) suggests the laity of the time were more educated and *au courant* with matters de Bury was interested in than he admits. Thompson, p. 375, gives instances of laymen borrowing books; de Bury's intolerance on this point, while it may have been justified in his experience, seems a little high-minded.

58. *Historiae Dunelmensis Scriptores Tres*, p. 128.

59. *The Didascalicon of Hugh of St. Victor: A Medieval Guide to the Arts*, trans. Jerome Taylor (New York: Columbia Univ. Press, 1961), p. 130.

60. *The Opus Majus of Roger Bacon*, trans. Robert B. Burke (1928; rpt. New York: Russell & Russell, 1962), II, 776-77.

61. Quoted in Henry Osborn Taylor, *The Mediaeval Mind: A History of the Development of Thought and Emotion in the Middle Ages*, 4th ed. (London: Macmillan, 1927), II, 346.

62. Smalley, p. 152n.

63. *The Philobiblon*, ed. E. C. Thomas, introduction, pp. lxvii-lxviii. One interesting word de Bury coins is *geologiam* (174), by which he means not geology but "the earthly pursuits of law"; on de Bury's use of *geologia* as the first recorded occurrence of the word, see R. E. Latham, ed., *Revised Medieval Latin Word-List from British and Irish Sources* (London: Oxford Univ. Press, 1965). Altamura in his edition (pp. 151-55) provides a useful glossary of strange words, only a few of which are to be found in Du Cange.

64. *Canterbury Tales*, X, 418, 430ff., and 829.

65. *The Mirrour of the Blessed Lyf of Jesu Christ / A Translation of the Latin Work Entitled Meditationes Vitae Christi . . .* , ed. Lawrence F. Powell (Oxford: Clarendon Press, 1908), pp. 68-70. See also Sister Mary Immaculate Bodenstedt, *The Vita Christi of Ludolphus the Carthusian* (Washington, D.C.: Catholic Univ. of America Press, 1944), p. 111 n.99 for a discussion of Ludolphus's similar treatment of curiosity, based on the *Meditationes*, which Nicholas Love translated.

66. The sermon is printed in *Reliquiae Antiquae*, ed. Thomas Wright and James Orchard Halliwell (1843; rpt. New York: AMS Press, 1966), II, 50.

67. *A Treatise on the Astrolabe*, ll. 41-46.

68. *English Friars and Antiquity*, p. 43.

69. *Mirrour of the Chyrche* (W. de Worde, 1521), p. xviii. Edmund's opinion is repeated in *The Lay Folks' Catechism*, ed. Thomas F. Simmons and Henry E. Nolloth, EETS, O.S. 118 (London: K. Paul, Trench, Trübner, 1901), pp. 8 ff. and 103.

70. See my discussion of the *cursus* above, note 44.

71. See the *Opus Majus of Roger Bacon*, I, 279, on these influences of Mercury. Ridevall and Holcot mention Mercury as the god of merchants and thieves and eloquent men (Smalley, pp. 121, 173 n.1). Bersuire agreed and saw a meaningful pun in Mercury's name: "mercurius quasi mercatorum curius"; see Hans Liebeschutz, *Fulgentius Metaforalis* (Leipzig: Teubner, 1926), p. 61.

72. *The English Works of John Gower*, ed. G. C. Macaulay, EETS, E.S. 81-82 (London: K. Paul, Trench, Trübner, 1900-01), II, 253.

73. Curtius, p. 322.

74. For patristic and medieval background to the idea of "the mind thinking intensely of distant things" see Peter Clemoes, "*Mens absentia cogitans* in *The Seafarer* and *The Wanderer*" in *Medieval Literature and Civilization: Studies in Memory of G.N. Garmonsway*, ed. D. A. Pearsall and R. A. Waldron (London: Univ. of London, Athlone Press, 1969), pp. 62-77. I thank my colleague Prof. Alan Brown for bringing this essay to my attention.

75. *The Life of Solitude by Francis Petrarch*, trans. Jacob Zeitlin (Urbana: Univ. of Illinois Press, 1924), p. 150.

CHAPTER V

1. This and all subsequent quotations are taken from *The Works of Geoffrey Chaucer*, ed. F. N. Robinson, 2nd ed. (Boston: Houghton Mifflin Co., 1957).

2. Archbishop Arundel's interview with the Lollard, William Thorpe, is reported in *The Acts and Monuments of John Foxe*, ed. Josiah Pratt (London: Religious Tract Society, 1887), III, 268.

3. John V. Fleming, *The Roman de la Rose: A Study in Allegory and Iconography* (Princeton: Princeton Univ. Press, 1969), p. 31.

4. Ralph Baldwin, *The Unity of the Canterbury Tales, Anglistica*, V (Copenhagen: Rosenkilde and Bagger, 1955); D. W. Robertson, Jr., *A Preface to Chaucer: Studies in Medieval Perspectives* (Princeton: Princeton Univ. Press, 1962). And see, for instance, Chauncey Wood, "The April Date as a Structural Device in *The Canterbury Tales*," *MLQ*, 25 (1964), 259-71, on the *Miller's Tale*; Edmund Reiss, "The Symbolic Surface of the *Canterbury Tales*: The Monk's Portrait," Part I, *ChauR*, 2 (1968), 254-72, and "The Pilgrimage Narrative and the *Canterbury Tales*," *SP*, 67 (1970), 295-305; and C. P. R. Tisdale, "The Medieval Pilgrimage and Its Use in the *Canterbury Tales*," Diss. Princeton 1969.

5. Some valuable comments on the problems one faces in reading the *Tales* allegorically will be found in Morton W. Bloomfield, "Authenticating Realism and the Realism of Chaucer," *Thought*, 39 (1964), 335-58; and Norman Hinton, "Anagogue and Archetype: The Phenomenology of Medieval Literature," *Annuale Mediaevale*, 7 (1966), 57-73.

6. Judson B. Allen, *The Friar as Critic: Literary Attitudes in the Later Middle Ages* (Nashville: Vanderbilt Univ. Press, 1971), p. 132.

7. Paul G. Ruggiers, *The Art of the Canterbury Tales* (Madison: Univ. of Wisconsin Press,

1967), esp. p. 50n and 247 ff.; and Robert M. Jordan, *Chaucer and the Shape of Creation: The Aesthetic Possibilities of Inorganic Structure* (Cambridge, Mass.: Harvard Univ. Press, 1967), esp. pp. 11-12 and the criticism of Baldwin's thesis on pp. 112-15.

8. "Pilgrim Text Models for Dante's *Purgatorio*," *SP*, 66 (1969), 1-24, esp. 2-3. See Demaray's fuller study, *The Invention of Dante's* Commedia (New Haven: Yale Univ. Press, 1974), in which he demonstrates that "Dante's long pilgrimage throughout the *Commedia* is an imitation of an earthly pilgrimage made by countless medieval Christians to holy stations located in the Near East and Italy" (p. 4).

9. Robert O. Payne, *The Key of Remembrance: A Study of Chaucer's Poetics* (New Haven: Yale Univ. Press, 1963), ch. 5.

10. Theodore Silverstein, "Allegory and Literary Form," *PMLA*, 82 (1967), 31.

11. These matters have been discussed in a variety of places; but see the convenient summary and analysis of the problems in D. W. Robertson, Jr., *Chaucer's London* (New York: John Wiley & Sons, Inc., 1968); and R. B. Dobson, *The Peasants' Revolt of 1381* (London: Macmillan, 1970).

12. Charles Muscatine, *Poetry and Crisis in the Age of Chaucer* (Notre Dame: Univ. of Notre Dame Press, 1972), esp. pp. 14-25; and *Froissart Chronicles*, ed. and trans. Geoffrey Brereton (Baltimore: Penguin Books, 1968), p. 211.

13. More than one critic has drawn attention to this intrusive couplet about the palmers; see, for example, E. Talbot Donaldson, ed., *Chaucer's Poetry: An Anthology for the Modern Reader* (New York: Ronald Press, 1958), p. 876; Bloomfield, "Authenticating Realism," 348.

14. Thomas Merton, "From Pilgrimage to Crusade," *Cithara*, 4 (1964), 4.

15. Thomas J. Hatton, "Chaucer's Crusading Knight, A Slanted Ideal," *ChauR*, 3 (1969), 77-87, argues that the Knight fought only infidels, not other Christians; see William Spencer, "Are Chaucer's Pilgrims Keyed to the Zodiac?" *ChauR*, 4 (1970), 149-50 on the Knight as traveler.

16. See the important essay by David E. Berndt, "Monastic *Acedia* and Chaucer's Characterization of Daun Piers," *SP*, 68 (1971), 435-50. Also Robert B. White, Jr., "Chaucer's Daun Piers and the Rule of Saint Benedict: The Failure of an Ideal," *JEGP*, 70 (1971), 13-30.

17. On these and other contrasts between the two figures, see R. E. Kaske, "The Knight's Interruption of the *Monk's Tale*," *ELH*, 24 (1957), 249-68.

18. George B. Parks, *The English Traveller in Italy* (Roma: Edizioni di Storia e Letteratura, 1954), I, 352, suggests that the Wife's three trips must be an exaggeration because of the time and effort required to make even one Jerusalem journey.

19. See Robinson's notes on the *General Prologue* portraits; also H. S. Bennett, "Medieval Literature and the Modern Reader," *Essays and Studies*, 31 (1945), 11.

20. On this contrast between the Clerk and the Monk, see Joseph E. Grennen, "Chaucer's Monk: Baldness, Venery, and Embonpoint," *AN&Q*, 6 (1968), 83-85.

21. Arthur Hoffman, "Chaucer's Prologue to Pilgrimage: The Two Voices," *ELH*, 21 (1954), 1-16.

22. Ruth Nevo, "Chaucer: Motive and Mask in the 'General Prologue'," *MLR*, 58 (1963), 1-9. A similar point is made in R. T. Lenaghan's "Chaucer's *General Prologue* as History and Literature," *Comparative Studies in Society and History*, 12 (1970), 73-82.

23. *Select English Works of John Wyclif*, ed. Thomas Arnold (Oxford: Clarendon Press, 1871), II, 364.

24. *Dan Michel's Ayenbite of Inwyt, or, Remorse of Conscience*, ed. R. Morris, EETS, O.S. 23 (1866; rpt. London: Trübner, 1895), p. 187; Herbert B. Workman, *John Wyclif: A Study of the English Medieval Church* (Oxford: Clarendon Press, 1926), II, Appendix L. The mercantile aspect of pilgrimages to the Holy Land is apparent in the equal attention given by writers of travel books to both rates of currency exchange and the kinds and sizes of various indulgences; see H. F. M. Prescott, *Jerusalem Journey* (London: Eyre & Spottiswoode, 1954), p. 28.

25. On restrictions against nuns going on pilgrimage, see Eileen Power, *Medieval People*, 2nd ed. (London: Methuen, 1925), pp. 80-82. E. P. Kuhl, "Notes on Chaucer's Prioress," *PQ*, 2 (1923), 305, cites contemporary injunctions against nuns wearing rings and brooches.

26. John M. Steadman, "The Prioress' Dogs and Benedictine Discipline," *MP*, 54 (1956), 1-6.

27. Francis Manley, "Chaucer's Rosary and Donne's Bracelet: Ambiguous Coral," *MLN*, 74 (1959), 385-88.

28. For more discussion of the pattern and organization of the portraits in the *General Prologue*, see the insightful analysis by Harold F. Brooks, *Chaucer's Pilgrims: The Artistic Order of the Portraits in the Prologue* (London: Methuen, 1962).

29. The story is recounted in *An Alphabet of Tales*, ed. M. L. Banks, EETS, O.S. 126 and 127 (London: Kegan Paul, Trench, Trübner, 1904-5), p. 256; and in *Mirk's Festial: A Collection of Homilies*, ed. Theodor Erbe, EETS, E.S. 96 (London: Kegan Paul, Trench, Trübner, 1905), pp. 208 ff.

30. "De peregrino, mortuo et crucifixo," Sermo vii, *PL* 183: 183.

31. *Dan Michel's Ayenbite of Inwyt*, pp. 253-54.

32. On the various appropriate Psalms sung, see the Service for Pilgrims. (G. G. Coulton, *Chaucer and His England*, 3rd ed. [London: Methuen, 1921], p. 138, remarks in passing that pilgrims in Chaucer's day may not have bothered to attend such pilgrim services. But some authorities would be more cautious in denying that.) See Psalm 31, which was repeated twice in the Service, and also the Lesson, Secret, and Postcommunion prayers from that Mass.

33. Matthew 10:8.

34. Matthew 10:11 ff.

35. *The Acts and Monuments of John Foxe*, p. 268.

36. *The Scale of Perfection by Walter Hilton Canon of Thurgarton*, ed. Evelyn Underhill (London: J. M. Watkins, 1923), pp. 304-5.

37. Scholars have written much lately about the role of the Host in the *Tales* and especially about his capacity and standards for critical judgment of tales; see, for instance, Cynthia C. Richardson, "The Function of the Host in the *Canterbury Tales*," *TSLL*, 12 (1970), 325-44 (she argues that the Host is many things, but not a literary critic); for a bizarre approach to the issue, one that pits the Host against the Parson and sees the Host as an accomplice in Chaucer's hidden parody of the Last Judgment, see Rodney Delasanta, "The Theme of Judgment in *The Canterbury Tales*," *MLQ*, 31 (1970), 298-307. Walter Scheps's "'Up roos oure Hoost, and was oure aller cok': Harry Bailly's Tale-Telling Competition," forthcoming in *ChauR* (1975) very clearly defines the Host's critical standards.

38. On Becket's reputation as a mediator, see Paul Alonzo Brown, "The Development of the Legend of Thomas Becket," Diss. Pennsylvania 1930, esp. p. 19. Donald J. Hall, *English Mediaeval Pilgrimage* (London: Routledge & Kegan Paul, 1966), pp. 213-15, emphasizes the sense in which every pilgrimage is a journey made to obtain the intercession of a mediator.

39. It is unclear exactly when this bell was installed or when it came to be known as Bell Harry; it seems to have been named for one Prior Henry who donated it in the 1330s. See the modern pilgrims' guidebook to the shrine, *The Cathedral and Metropolitan Church of Christ Canterbury*, published by the Dean and Chapter (n.d.), p. 12; also see John Shirley, *Canterbury Cathedral* (London: Pitkin Pictorials, Ltd., n.d.), p. 24.

40. Britton J. Harwood, "Language and the Real: Chaucer's Manciple," *ChauR*, 6 (1972), talks of the Host's liquored performances as "Misrule" (p. 279); and David S. Reid, "Crocodilian Humor: A Discussion of Chaucer's Wife of Bath," *ChauR*, 4 (1970), calls the Host a "prudent lord of misrule" (p. 76). It is probably the dramatic quality of the *Tales* that consciously or unconsciously prompts us to think of Falstaffian Harry as the Vice figure of medieval drama.

41. Albert C. Baugh, ed., *Chaucer's Major Poetry* (New York: Appleton-Century-Crofts, 1963), p. 254, note to line 752, reminds us of the duties of a "marchal."

42. For the importance of the concept of contract in the Middle Ages, see J. W. Gough, *The Social Contract: A Critical Study of its Development*, 2nd ed. (Oxford: Clarendon Press, 1957), chs. 3-4; and on the use of the terms *pactum* and *foedus*, pp. 24, 34, and 37. See also M. H. Keen, "The Political Thought of the Fourteenth-Century Civilians," in *Trends in Medieval Political Thought*, ed. Beryl Smalley (Oxford: Basil Blackwell, 1965), p. 114.

43. R. W. and A. J. Carlyle, *A History of Mediaeval Political Theory in the West* (Edinburgh: W. Blackwood & Sons, 1903-36); Vol. 5; *The Political Theory of the Thirteenth Century*, pp. 471-74; and Vol. 6: *Political Theory from 1300 to 1600*, pp. 154 ff. and 519-23.

44. Gough, p. 46. On the emphasis late-medieval thinkers gave the principle of mutual consent and contract in political relations, see Walter Ullmann, *A History of Political Thought: The Middle Ages* (Baltimore: Penguin Books, 1965), pp. 147, 162, and 203 ff.

45. Sidney Heath, *Pilgrim Life in the Middle Ages* (London: T. F. Unwin, 1911), p. 18. Keeping pacts is of crucial importance in, for instance, *Sir Gawain and the Green Knight*, as John A. Burrow has demonstrated in *A Reading of Sir Gawain and the Green Knight* (London: Routledge & Kegan Paul, 1965). Burrow compares the poet's treatment of contract-keeping with Chaucer's in the *Franklin's Tale* (p. 25).

46. See the fine essay by Alan T. Gaylord, "Friendship in Chaucer's *Troilus*," *ChauR*, 3 (1969), 239-64; also see Robert S. Haller, "The *Knight's Tale* and the Epic Tradition," *ChauR*, 1 (1966), 67-84.

47. "The *Knight's Tale* as an Impetus for Pilgrimage," *PQ*, 43 (1964), 526-37.

48. Jordan, *Chaucer and the Shape of Creation*, ch. 7; Richard Neuse, "The Knight: The First Mover in Chaucer's Human Comedy," *UTQ*, 31 (1962), 299-315; and Paul T. Thurston, *Artistic Ambivalence in Chaucer's Knight's Tale* (Gainesville: Univ. of Florida Press, 1968), esp. ch. 2.

49. Charles Muscatine, *Chaucer and the French Tradition: A Study in Style and Meaning* (1957; rpt. Berkeley: Univ. of California Press, 1964), pp. 175-90; John Halverson, "Aspects of Order in the *Knight's Tale*," *SP*, 57 (1960), 606-21; Jeffrey Helterman, "The Dehumanizing Metamorphoses of the *Knight's Tale*," *ELH*, 38 (1971), 493-511; and Kathleen A. Blake, "Order and the Noble Life in Chaucer's *Knight's Tale?*" *MLQ*, 34 (1973), 3-19.

50. So argues Maurice Keen, "Brotherhood in Arms," *History*, 47 (1962), 1-17.

51. For the traditions Chaucer drew on in using clerks for "quiting," see Sheila Delany, "Clerks and Quiting in the *Reeve's Tale*," *MS*, 29 (1967), 351-56.

52. Charles Owen, "Chaucer's *Canterbury Tales*: Aesthetic Design in Stories of the First Day," *ES*, 35 (1954), 49-56. For some further analyses of the relationships between the first two tales and between the tales of the Reeve and Miller, see William C. Stokoe, Jr., "Structure and Intention in the First Fragment of *The Canterbury Tales*," *UTQ*, 21 (1952), 120-27; Bernard F. Huppé, *A Reading of the Canterbury Tales* (Albany: SUNY Press, 1964), pp. 85-88; and Ruggiers, pp. 55 ff.

53. J. V. Cunningham, "Conventions and Structure: The Prologue to the *Canterbury Tales*," in *Tradition and Poetic Structure* (Denver: Alan Swallow, 1960), p. 71; see also Frederick Tupper, "The Quarrels of the Canterbury Pilgrims," *JEGP*, 14 (1915), 256-70, on feuding between several pilgrims.

54. Gerhard Joseph, "Chaucerian 'Game'-'Earnest' and the 'Argument of Herbergage' in *The Canterbury Tales*," *ChauR*, 5 (1971), also discusses the contraction (and expansion) of time and space, although his essay is concerned with only the Knight's and Miller's tales.

55. Joseph L. Baird, "Law and the *Reeve's Tale*," *NM*, 70 (1969), 679-83; Paul A. Olson, "The *Reeve's Tale*: Chaucer's *Measure for Measure*," *SP*, 59 (1962), 1-17.

56. I follow the Ellesmere MS ordering of the *Tales*. For a convincing recent argument in favor of the Ellesmere arrangement (opposing Pratt's earlier thesis), see Lee S. Cox, "A Question of Order in the *Canterbury Tales*," *ChauR*, 1 (1967), 228-52. E. Talbot Donaldson, who followed the Ellesmere ordering in his anthology (*Chaucer's Poetry*), has since explained

in detail his reasons for doing so; see "The Ordering of the *Canterbury Tales*," in *Medieval Literature and Folklore Studies: Essays in Honor of Francis Lee Utley*, ed. Jerome Mandel and Bruce A. Rosenberg (New Brunswick, N.J.: Rutgers Univ. Press, 1970), pp. 193-204.

57. W. W. Lawrence, *Chaucer and the Canterbury Tales* (New York: Columbia Univ. Press, 1950), p. 22, represents the usual opinion; he sees the quarreling of these two pilgrims as an important part of the work but does not believe their dispute has anything to do with the discussion of marriage. John H. Fisher, "Chaucer's Last Revision of the 'Canterbury Tales'," *MLR*, 67 (1972), 249, offers the most recent restatement of the traditional view that the two tales "break the continuity of the Marriage Group." Francis Lee Utley, "Five Genres in the *Clerk's Tale*," *ChauR*, 6 (1972), 200, suggests that critics embarrassed by the presence of these two tales here "might consider linking themes beyond sovereignty: order, rhetoric, and gentilesse" as ways of integrating the tales into the group.

58. Thomas Jay Garbáty, "The Monk and the *Merchant's Tale*: An Aspect of Chaucer's Building Process in the *Canterbury Tales*," *MP*, 67 (1969), 20.

59. On the significance of rash promises and the breaking of vows in this tale, see Alan T. Gaylord, "The Promises in *The Franklin's Tale*," *ELH*, 31 (1964), 331-65.

60. *A Preface to Chaucer*, pp. 376-77.

61. On marriage as a symbol of order, see Michael Wilks, "Chaucer and the Mystical Marriage in Medieval Political Thought," *BJRL*, 44 (1961), 489-530.

62. *Select English Works of John Wyclif*, I, 83.

63. *The Book of the Knight of La Tour-Landry*, ed. Thomas Wright, EETS, O.S. 33 (London: Trübner, 1868), pp. 35-36.

64. *The Book of Margery Kempe*, ed. Sanford B. Meech and Hope Emily Allen, EETS, O.S. 212 (1940; rpt. London: Oxford Univ. Press, 1961), p. 180.

65. This is suggested in the *Roman de la Rose*, ll. 8833-38; see also *The House of Fame*, I, l. 116 and Robinson's note.

66. *The Minor Poems of John Lydgate*, ed. Henry N. McCracken, EETS, O.S. 192 (London: Oxford Univ. Press, 1934), pp. 459-60.

67. *The Fifteen Joys of Marriage*, trans. Elisabeth Abbott (London: Orion Press, 1959), pp. 128, 134, and passim.

68. *A Preface to Chaucer*, p. 128.

69. B. D. H. Miller, "Chaucer's General Prologue, A 673: Further Evidence," *N&Q*, N.S. 7 (1960), 404-6. See also D. Biggins, "Chaucer's General Prologue, A 673," *N&Q*, N.S. 6 (1959), 435-36, who anticipates Miller in arguing that *burdoun* is a sexual pun. Biggins cites earlier and later literary punning on this and similar words.

70. Ann S. Haskell, "The St. Joce Oath in the Wife of Bath's Prologue," *ChauR*, 1 (1966), 85-87.

71. This is J. V. Cunningham's thesis in "The Literary Form of the Prologue to the *Canterbury Tales*," *MP*, 49 (1952), 172-81. The article was reprinted in Cunningham's *Tradition and Poetic Structure*.

72. For an ingenious analysis of the possible joke involved in the interchange between the Host and Pardoner and the significance of that joke in relation to Becket's breeches, which hung as a relic at Canterbury, see Daniel Knapp, "The Relyk of a Seint: A Gloss on Chaucer's Pilgrimage," *ELH*, 39 (1972), 1-26.

73. *The Romance of the Rose*, trans. Harry W. Robbins, ed. Charles W. Dunn (New York: Dutton, 1962), pp. 452, 453. Gerhart B. Ladner, "*Homo Viator*: Mediaeval Ideas on Alienation and Order," *Speculum*, 42 (1967), 248-49, treats other medieval poetic uses of the "pilgrimage to love" motif.

74. See Beverly Boyd, "The Wife of Bath's Gay *Lente*," *AN&Q*, 1 (1963), 85-86; for two responses to her view that Lent simply means spring, see J. F. Cotter, "The Wife of Bath's Lenten Observance," *PLL*, 7 (1971), 293-97; and D. L. Higdon, "The Wife of Bath and Refreshment Sunday," *PLL*, 8 (1972), 199-201.

75. Edward L. Cutts, *Scenes & Characters of the Middle Ages*, 5th ed. (London:

Simpkin, Marshall, Hamilton, Kent & Co., Ltd., 1925), p. 162.

76. For comments on the summoner's curiosity, see Richard Hamilton Green, "Classical Fable and English Poetry in the Fourteenth Century," in *Critical Approaches to Medieval Literature*, ed. Dorothy Bethurum (New York: Columbia Univ. Press, 1960), pp. 125-28.

77. Utley, "Five Genres in the *Clerk's Tale*," 214.

78. S. K. Heninger, Jr., "The Concept of Order in Chaucer's *Clerk's Tale*," *JEGP*, 56 (1957), 393; Muscatine, *Chaucer and the French Tradition*, esp. p. 195.

79. On January's abuse of the sacrament of marriage and his false pilgrimage to the garden of desire, see Stanley Stewart, *The Enclosed Garden: The Tradition and the Image in Seventeenth-Century Poetry* (Madison: Univ. of Wisconsin Press, 1966), pp. 173-74. On curiosity in the *Franklin's Tale*, see Harry Berger, "The F-Fragment of the *Canterbury Tales*: Part II," *ChauR*, 1 (1967), 139, 146-47.

80. On the positioning in the *Tales* of Fragment VI, see Robinson's notes to them; Fragment VII, as Cox and Donaldson have shown, would almost certainly seem to follow rather than precede the Marriage Group; and Fragment IX-X, the tales of the Manciple and Parson, was meant to end the work as it exists. In addition to my reasons for suggesting that these last two tales are linked thematically there is the argument of Wayne Shumaker, "Chaucer's *Manciple's Tale* as Part of a Canterbury Group," *UTQ*, 22 (1953), 147-56.

81. See the essays by Cox and Donaldson.

82. Paull F. Baum, *Chaucer: A Critical Appreciation* (Durham, N.C.: Duke Univ. Press, 1958), pp. 74 ff. thinks the tales of Fragment VII comprise a "surprise group"; Alan T. Gaylord, "*Sentence* and *Solaas* in Fragment VII of the *Canterbury Tales*: Harry Bailly as Horseback Editor," *PMLA*, 82 (1967), 226-35, argues that the art of story-telling is a theme which holds the group together.

83. On *chilyndre* and *porthors* see the *OED*; on the latter word also see (under *portiforium*) R. E. Latham, ed., *Revised Medieval Latin Word-List from British and Irish Sources* (London: Oxford Univ. Press, 1965), p. 360.

84. For other treatments of the issue of sex and money in the *Shipman's Tale*, see Albert H. Silverman, "Sex and Money in Chaucer's *Shipman's Tale*," *PQ*, 32 (1953), 329-36; and Janette Richardson, "The Facade of Bawdry: Image Patterns in Chaucer's *Shipman's Tale*," *ELH*, 32 (1965), 303-13.

85. "The Design of the *Canterbury Tales*," in *Companion to Chaucer Studies*, ed. Beryl Rowland (Toronto: Oxford Univ. Press, 1968), p. 196.

86. *An Apology for Lollard Doctrines Attributed to Wicliffe*, ed. James H. Todd (London: Camden Society Publications, 1842), pp. 106-7.

87. *A Preface to Chaucer*, p. 369.

88. *Chaucer and the Canterbury Tales*, pp. 132-33.

89. Donald R. Howard, "Chaucer's Address to the Court: The *Knight's Tale* and *Melibee*," paper read at the 1965 MLA Convention; incorporated in his forthcoming book, *The Idea of the Canterbury Tales*.

90. Gardiner Stillwell, "The Political Meaning of Chaucer's *Tale of Melibee*," *Speculum*, 19 (1944), 433-44.

91. Paul Strohm, "The Allegory of the *Tale of Melibee*," *ChauR*, 2 (1967), 32-42.

92. Two instructive essays on the meaning of a tale or fable as implicitly suggested in the *Nun's Priest's Tale* are Stephen Manning, "The Nun's Priest's Morality and the Medieval Attitude Toward Fables," *JEGP*, 59 (1960), 403-16; and Walter Scheps, "Chaucer's Anti-Fable: *Reductio ad Absurdum* in the *Nun's Priest's Tale*," *Leeds Studies in English*, 4 (1970), 1-10.

93. See, for instance, R. G. Baldwin, "The Yeoman's Canons: A Conjecture," *JEGP*, 61 (1962), 232-43; and K. Michael Olmert, "*The Canon's Yeoman's Tale*: An Interpretation," *Annuale Mediaevale*, 8 (1967), 70-94.

94. On "talking too much" as the central concern in the *Manciple's Tale*, see Wayne Shumaker, "Chaucer's *Manciple's Tale* as Part of a Canterbury Group"; Donaldson, *Chaucer's*

Poetry, p. 947; and Richard L. Hoffman, *Ovid and the Canterbury Tales* (Philadelphia: Univ. of Pennsylvania Press, 1966), pp. 195-96.

95. Chaucer makes a similar point about tales, news, and rumor in *The House of Fame*, III.

96. E. Talbot Donaldson, "Medieval Poetry and Medieval Sin," in *Speaking of Chaucer* (London: Univ. of London, Athlone Press, 1970), p. 173.

97. Paul Strohm, "Some Generic Distinctions in the *Canterbury Tales*," *MP*, 68 (1971), 325.

98. To have a member of the clergy deliver a sermon at the end of a pilgrimage seems to have been a common practice among pilgrims going to the Holy Land, at least in the late Middle Ages; see, for example, R. J. Mitchell, *The Spring Voyage: The Jerusalem Pilgrimage in 1458* (London: John Murray, 1964), who notes that upon arrival in Palestine the English priest William Wey addressed the shipload of pilgrims on the theme "Peregrinus es" (p. 106).

99. On the significance of this for the *Tales*, see John M. Steadman, "Chaucer's Thirty Pilgrims and the Activa Vita," *Neophilologus*, 45 (1961), 224-30. Also see Ray C. Petry, "Social Responsibility and the Late Medieval Mystics," *Church History*, 21 (1952), 3-19.

100. *Enarrationes in Psalmos*, *PL* 36: 419; *Liber in Distinctionibus dictionum theologicalium*, *PL* 210: 850-51.

101. *The Acts and Monuments of John Foxe*, p. 267.

102. For the common definition of Jerusalem as *visio pacis*, see Henri De Lubac, *Exégèse médiévale: Les Quatre sens de l'Écriture* (Paris: Aubier, 1959-64), I, 646-47 and references in the notes there; see II, 313, for interpretations of Babel and Babylon based on Biblical comments. On the supposed etymological determinations that link Babel-Babylon, see C. Spicq, *Esquisse d'une histoire de l'exégèse latine au moyen âge*, Bibliothèque Thomiste, XXVI (Paris: J. Vrin, 1944), p. 240; and George Boas, *Essays on Primitivism and Related Ideas in the Middle Ages* (Baltimore: Johns Hopkins Press, 1948), pp. 190-91.

103. *Dante Alighieri: Monarchia*, ed. Gustavo Vinay (Firenze: Sansoni, 1950), pp. 32, 94-96, 30.

104. *Of the Imitation of Christ in Four Books by Thomas à Kempis*, trans. Justin McCann (New York: New American Library, 1957), p. 125.

105. Olive Sayce, "Chaucer's 'Retractions': The Conclusion of the *Canterbury Tales* and Its Place in Literary Tradition," *MÆ*, 40 (1971), also notes the appropriateness of the Parson's whole treatise about sin, penance, and confession to the idea of pilgrimage (236).

106. There are some useful comments on Aquinas's discussion of marriage and *amicitia* in T. P. Dunning's essay on the *Parson's Tale*, "Chaucer's Icarus Complex: Some Notes on His Adventures in Theology," in *English Studies Today*, Third Series, ed. G. I. Duthie (Edinburgh: Univ. of Edinburgh Press, 1964), pp. 89-106.

107. *Erasmus: Ten Colloquies*, trans. Craig R. Thompson, The Library of Liberal Arts (Indianapolis: Bobbs-Merrill, 1957), p. 91.

108. The rare portrayal of *Curiositas* opposed to Justice has been briefly discussed by H. W. Janson, *Apes and Ape Lore in the Middle Ages and Renaissance*, Studies of the Warburg Institute, Vol. 20 (London: Univ. of London Press, 1952), pp. 112-13. Janson suggests that curiosity's conquest of justice makes sense if justice is understood to mean righteousness; thus, the sculpture might be a depiction of Adam and Eve's loss of original righteousness. See my second chapter, note 66.

109. See Paul Alonzo Brown, "The Development of the Legend of Thomas Becket," Diss. Pennsylvania 1930, passim.

110. *The Sermons of Thomas Brinton*, p. 414.

CHAPTER VI

1. Hugo Lange, "Chaucer und Mandeville's Travels," *Archiv für das Studium der neueren Sprachen*, 173 (1938), 79-81; Josephine Waters Bennett, "Chaucer and *Mandeville's Travels*," *MLN*, 68 (1953), 531-34. These articles were superseded by the discussion of Chaucer's and

the *Gawain*-poet's debt to Mandeville in Josephine Waters Bennett's *The Rediscovery of Sir John Mandeville* (New York: MLA, 1954), pp. 221-27. Bennett's book, for a time out of print, has been reissued (New York: Kraus Reprint Co., 1971).

2. Marianne Mahn-Lot, *Columbus*, trans. Helen R. Lane (New York: Grove Press, 1961), p. 54.

3. The Cotton version of the *Travels* is found in British Museum MS Cotton Titus C. xvi. It was first printed in 1725 and has been edited in modern times by A. W. Pollard (1900; rpt. New York: Dover, 1964; modernized spelling); by P. Hamelius, EETS, O.S. 153 and 154 (London: Oxford Univ. Press, 1919 and 1923); and by M. C. Seymour (Oxford: Clarendon Press, 1967). Seymour, who has become the current authority on the textual problems associated with the *Travels*, is presently preparing an edition of the so-called Defective Version, which was made in England before the Cotton version. The fullest treatment of manuscripts and editions is to be found in Bennett, *Rediscovery*, pp. 265-385; Seymour, pp. 272-78, condenses Bennett's enormous amount of information into a convenient list. See also Seymour's "The English Manuscripts of *Mandeville's Travels*," *Edinburgh Bibliographical Society Transactions*, 4 (1966), 169-210.

4. In his edition (p. xiii) Seymour says that the *Travels* was written originally in French on the Continent and "probably" not by an Englishman; in his introduction and notes and in articles on various manuscript versions of the *Travels* he has discussed his reasons for believing "Mandeville" was a name made up by the author, who (for some reason Seymour has not yet divulged) wanted to convince people he was English. Bennett, who believes that Mandeville was probably English, discusses earlier theories of the author's identity and nationality, pp. 89 ff. J. D. Thomas, "The Date of *Mandeville's Travels*," *MLN*, 72 (1957), 165-69, concludes that the work was composed between 1356 and 1366. Arpad Steiner, "The Date of Composition of *Mandeville's Travels*," *Speculum*, 9 (1934), 144-47, had put it slightly later, between 1365 and 1371. Seymour, in his new edition of *The Metrical Version of Mandeville's Travels*, EETS, 269 (London: Oxford Univ. Press, 1973), p. xvi, repeats his belief that the book was first composed on the Continent, c. 1357, and that the first copy of the work probably appeared in England about 1375. On the sources of the *Travels*, see Bennett's plentiful treatments, Seymour's commentaries in his 1967 edition, and Malcolm Letts, *Sir John Mandeville: The Man and His Book* (London: Batchworth Press, 1949), esp. pp. 29-33.

5. In addition to Bennett's and Letts's books, see Donald R. Howard, "The World of Mandeville's *Travels*," *YES*, 1 (1971), 1-17; and C. W. R. D. Moseley, "The Metamorphoses of Sir John Mandeville," *YES*, 4 (1974), 5-25.

6. *Rediscovery*, p. 53.

7. Hamelius's notes to his edition are replete with suggestions that Mandeville merely copied from other travel writers. The remark by C. Raymond Beazley, *The Dawn of Modern Geography* (1897, 1901, 1906; rpt. New York: Peter Smith, 1949), III, 320, is rather typical of the way geographers and historians of travel have viewed the *Travels*: "... except for the student of geographical mythology and superstition, it has no importance in the history of Earth-Knowledge." Zoltan Haraszti, "The Travels of Sir John Mandeville," *The Boston Public Library Quarterly*, 2 (1950), 306-16, speaks of "the deceitfulness of the author." J. H. Parry, *The Age of Reconnaissance* (New York: Mentor Books, 1964) admits that the book "did more to arouse interest in travel and discovery, and to popularize the idea of a possible circumnavigation of the globe" than any other medieval travel book, but it was still a collection of "lying wonders" which had little value for serious explorers (p. 24).

8. Various scholars have commented on the two-part structure of the book, usually to stress that the pilgrimage portion is worthwhile and credible while the rest of the book is fanciful nonsense; see, for example, Kenneth Sisam, ed., *Fourteenth Century Verse & Prose* (1921; rpt. Oxford: Clarendon Press, 1967), p. 94. But Howard, "The World of Mandeville's *Travels*," has detected significant, purposeful reasons for the author's decision to juxtapose the two parts.

9. Parry, p. 24. C. W. R. D. Moseley is currently preparing a lengthy study of the strong influence Mandeville had on Renaissance voyagers.

10. I use Seymour's edition (Oxford: Clarendon Press, 1967) and cite page references (in Arabic numerals) and chapter references (in Roman numerals) within parentheses in the body of my text.

11. B. G. Koonce, *Chaucer and the Tradition of Fame: Symbolism in The House of Fame* (Princeton: Princeton Univ. Press, 1966), pp. 152-53, treats some of the medieval associations between Jerusalem and the *centrum* or *medium* of the world. He cites Bersuire's gloss on Joel 3 which sounds very much like Mandeville's remark about publishing news from the middle of a town.

12. Aziz S. Atiya, *The Crusade in the Later Middle Ages* (1938; rpt. New York: Kraus Reprint Co., 1965), ch. VIII.

13. Ibid., p. 163.

14. The popularity of such criticisms is demonstrated by G. R. Owst, *Literature and Pulpit in Medieval England*, 2nd ed. (Oxford: Basil Blackwell, 1961), pp. 287-331. Mandeville berates the nobility for their sinful lives often in the book, but the sermon he says he heard from the sultan (100-102) is probably the strongest statement of this sort in the work. And when the sultan has finished, Mandeville adds some more complaints of his own. For evidence that the *Travels* was looked upon as a moral treatise and was often bound with such works, see Bennett's appendix on MSS and editions, pp. 265 ff.; and Seymour, "The English Manuscripts," 172-75.

15. *Rediscovery*, pp. 51-52. In their critical notes, Hamelius and Seymour cite reports of eye-witnesses who saw the apple in the statue's hand; also see the long note on the matter in *The Buke of John Maundevill*, ed. George F. Warner, Roxburghe Club (Westminster: Nichols and Sons, 1889), p. 158. The notes in Warner's edition of the Egerton MS are invaluable.

16. It is difficult to say when the Latin words *malum* and *pomum* began to mean apples specifically and not just fruit in general; at least by the twelfth century the forbidden fruit had been translated as meaning apple (as in the sculpture of Eve in St. Lazarus Cathedral at Autun). The metaphor of the fallen world as an apple could only occur once the fruit Eve and Adam ate had been understood to be an apple. Richard of St. Victor relates lust of the eyes to the apple (*Sermo 43, PL* 177: 1015). Nicholas Bozon (c. 1300) says the world is like a cedar-apple—sweet on the outside but bitter within; see *Les Contes Moralisés de Nicole Bozon Frère Mineur*, ed. L. T. Smith and P. Meyer (Paris: Firmin-Didot, 1889), p. 109. *The Book of Vices and Virtues*, ed. W. Nelson Francis, EETS, O.S. 217 (London: Oxford Univ. Press, 1942) equates the apple with the world and opposes it to heaven (p. 80). Mandeville, like Bozon, mentions the apple that is bitter within from the cinders God rained down on Sodom (74). In *Piers Plowman* we are told that "Adam and Eue eten apples vnrosted" (B, V, 612); see also *St. Erkenwald*, 1. 295; *Cleanness*, 1. 241; and *Pearl*, 1. 640.

17. There is a succinct explanation of the growth of this popular medieval legend by Hugo Rahner, "The Christian Mystery and the Pagan Mysteries," in *The Mysteries: Papers from the Eranos Yearbooks*, ed. Joseph Campbell, Bollingen Series XXX, Vol. 2 (New York: Pantheon Books, 1955), pp. 369 ff., esp. 384-85.

18. These features are found variously on the Ebsdorf and Hereford maps. Seymour (Cotton edition, p. 258) mentions some other maps that may have been available to Mandeville in Rome during his supposed visit there. There are good reproductions of the Ebsdorf and Hereford maps in Leo Bagrow, *History of Cartography*, rev. by R. A. Skelton (London: C.A. Watts, 1964), plates E and XXIV. Letts, *Sir John Mandeville*, ch. xi, has drawn a number of parallels between pictures on the Hereford map and certain descriptions found in Mandeville.

19. Mandeville's preoccupation with round objects and the roundness of the earth may have been an esoteric concern of some significance to him. There is a strange story that comes down from the sixteenth-century antiquarian, John Leland: he said that he saw an undecayed apple enclosed within a crystal orb among the relics at Becket's shrine at Canterbury and was told it had been a gift from Mandeville (*Commentarii de Scriptoribus*, ed. Antonius Hall [Oxford, 1709], I, 368).

20. In his edition (p. 236) Seymour says Mandeville was sharing a popular European "credulity" which genuine travelers (who reported the pyramids to be tombs) did not hold to. However, in my reading I find that a great number of medieval and Renaissance travelers, many of them otherwise reliable observers, called the pyramids the granaries of Joseph; among them were an anonymous 1350 traveler, Marino Sanuto, Frescobaldi, Sigoli, and Pero Tafur.

21. For a summary of the places usually visited in the Holy Land, see John G. Demaray, *The Invention of Dante's* Commedia (New Haven: Yale Univ. Press, 1974), ch. 1.

22. On the various associations of the three known continents with the Trinity, see George H. Williams, *Wilderness and Paradise in Christian Thought: The Biblical Experience of the Desert in the History of Christianity and the Paradise Theme in the Theological Idea of a University* (New York: Harper, 1962), pp. 169-71. G. R. Crone, *The World Map by Richard of Haldingham in Hereford Cathedral circa A.D. 1285* (London: Royal Geographical Society, 1954), p. 24, says the tripartite division of the earth was not a biblical concept but began with the Romans, perhaps Sallust.

23. See Eleanor Simmons Greenhill, "The Child in the Tree: A Study of the Cosmological Tree in Christian Tradition," *Traditio*, 10 (1954), 323-71, and esp. 335-37 on the idea of Jerusalem as the navel of the world; and Mircea Eliade, *Images and Symbols: Studies in Religious Symbolism,* trans. Philip Mairet (New York: Sheed and Ward, 1961), ch. 1.

24. Half of this passage is missing from the Cotton MS and what I have quoted here appears in another version of the *Travels*, the Egerton MS. I quote from Pollard's edition, which includes it (p. 83); the spelling has been modernized.

25. Fra Mauro's world map dates from the mid-fifteenth century; in placing Jerusalem off-center, he apologized for abandoning the ancient tradition; see G. R. Crone, *Maps and Their Makers: An Introduction to the History of Cartography* (1962; rpt. New York: Capricorn Books, 1966), pp. 54-55. On Bianco's map and its implications, see R. E. Skelton, Thomas E. Marston, and George D. Painter, *The Vinland Map and the Tartar Relation* (New Haven: Yale Univ. Press, 1965), pp. 124-26.

26. Bennett, *Rediscovery* (p. 9 n. 14), says "Wyclif, Gower, and Higden all comment on the Englishman's love of travel, and Chaucer gives his knight that characteristic, but all of these comments were written after the *Travels* had begun to circulate." She does not describe the love of travel as *curiositas*.

27. *Polychronicon*, ed. Churchill Babington, Rolls Series (London: Longman and Co., 1869), II, 169. I quote from Trevisa's translation of Higden.

28. *The English Works of John Gower*, ed. G. C. Macaulay, EETS, E.S. 81-82 (London: K. Paul, Trench, Trübner, 1900-1901), II, 253.

29. C. S. Lewis, *The Discarded Image: An Introduction to Medieval and Renaissance Literature* (Cambridge: Cambridge Univ. Press, 1964), p. 109.

30. *The Prologues and Epilogues of William Caxton*, ed. W. J. B. Crotch, EETS, O.S. 176 (1928; rpt. Oxford: Oxford Univ. Press, 1956), p. 108.

31. *The Travels of Marco Polo*, trans. Ronald Latham (Baltimore: Penguin Books, 1965), p. 10.

32. M. C. Seymour's edition; see note 4 above.

33. C. W. R. D. Moseley notes that the inclusion of phrases like "I John Mandeville" occurred with more frequency as the work became more popular and more copied—although he admits that the sense of an authority addressing us is present already in the earliest versions; see "Sir John Mandeville's Visit to the Pope: The Implications of an Interpolation," *Neophilologus*, 54 (1970), 79.

34. Mary Lascelles, "Alexander and the Earthly Paradise in Mediaeval English Writings," *MÆ*, 5 (1936), 39.

35. Atiya, p. 165.

36. On Mandeville's familiarity with Alexandrian romances, see the notes in Seymour's edition (1967), pp. 209, 211, and 254.

37. Bennett, *Rediscovery*, pp. 83-84. Polo's travel account was composed with the aid of a professional romance-writer, who may have added romance material to Polo's factual record.

38. Grover Cronin, Jr., "The Bestiary and the Mediaeval Mind—Some Complexities," *MLQ*, 2 (1941), 196.

39. "Prester John's Letter: A Mediaeval Utopia," *Phoenix*, 13 (1959), 56-57. The best recent study of the impact Prester John had on the medieval European consciousness is Vsevolod Slessarev, *Prester John: The Letter and the Legend* (Minneapolis: Univ. of Minnesota Press, 1959).

40. *Literature and Pulpit*, pp. 173-76.

41. R. J. Mitchell, *The Spring Voyage: The Jerusalem Pilgrimage in 1458* (London: John Murray, 1964), p. 42.

42. "Thomas Waleys O.P.," *Archivum Fratrum Praedicatorum*, 24 (1954), 74-76. The phrase "nova et inusitate" occurs in a fourteenth-century moralist's attack on *curiositas* in sermons; see Th.-M. Charland, *Artes Praedicandi: Contribution à l'Histoire de le Rhétorique au Moyen Age* (Paris: J. Vrin, 1936), p. 316.

43. *Gulliver's Travels*, in *The Prose Works of Jonathan Swift*, ed. Herbert David (Oxford: Basil Blackwell, 1941), II, 71.

44. *The Itineraries of William Wey*, ed. G. Williams, Roxburghe Club (London: J. B. Nichols and Sons, 1857), I, appendix.

45. Morton W. Bloomfield, "Chaucer's Sense of History," *JEGP*, 51 (1952), 310-11.

46. Hamelius was convinced that Mandeville's book embodied a running attack on the papacy, and he argued that Mandeville was possessed of a covert unorthodoxy; see his commentary and notes, passim. Margaret Schlauch, *English Medieval Literature and Its Social Foundations* (Warsaw: Panstwowe W. Naukowe, 1956), p. 196, finds in the *Travels* a deliberate burlesquing of the Christian religion. See Howard, "The World of Mandeville's *Travels*," for another theory of what Mandeville was trying to do in polarizing Eastern and Western religions.

47. For a short summary of classical and medieval opinion on the shape of the earth, see Charles W. Jones, "The Flat Earth," *Thought*, 9 (1934), 296-307.

48. Bennett observes: "Mandeville's assumption that the laws of nature operate on the other side of the world is a fundamental part of his belief that it is possible to sail all the way around it" (*Rediscovery*, p. 36).

49. *Nicole Oresme le livre du ciel et du monde*, ed. Albert D. Menut and Alexander J. Denomy, trans. Albert D. Menut (Madison: Univ. of Wisconsin Press, 1968), pp. 576-77.

50. See Parry, *The Age of Reconnaissance*, p. 24, Bennett, ch. 15, and Moseley's forthcoming study.

51. Toscanelli corresponded with Columbus (who read Mandeville); Columbus also was stirred by d'Ailly's remarks (c. 1414) that the ocean might be navigable, if winds were fair. On the indirect influence of Mandeville and late-medieval geographical thinkers on those of Columbus's generation, see Thomas Goldstein, "Geography in Fifteenth-Century Florence," in *Merchants and Scholars: Essays in the History of Exploration and Trade*, ed. John Parker (Minneapolis: Univ. of Minnesota Press, 1965), pp. 9-32.

52. See Arthur C. Cawley, "'Mandeville's Travels': A Possible New Source," *N&Q*, N.S. 19 (1972), 47-48; he finds in Macrobius a likely source for Mandeville's comments on the antipodeans (ch. XX).

53. *Imago Mundi by Petrus Ailliacus*, trans. Edwin F. Keaver (Wilmington, N.C., 1948), ch. 7; *The Wanderings of Felix Fabri* (London: Palestine Pilgrims' Text Society, 1897), III, 376.

54. For a full explanation of this problem, see Edmundo O'Gorman, *The Invention of America: An Inquiry into the Historical Nature of the New World and the Meaning of Its History* (Bloomington, Ind.: Indiana Univ. Press, 1961), pp. 54-55; Don Cameron Allen, *The Legend of Noah: Renaissance Rationalism in Art, Science, and Letters* (Urbana:

Univ. of Illinois Press, 1949), pp. 113 ff.; and Bennett, *Rediscovery*, pp. 233 ff.

55. Scholars have not pinned down the source of Mandeville's tale of the Norwegian who twice circumnavigated the globe, although it has been suggested that Adam of Bremen (or some other writer who mentioned accounts of early voyagers) could have reminded Mandeville of Viking sailors. Any number of sources, oral or written, might exist. I am currently preparing a study on the probable influence of Gautier de Metz's *Image du Monde* on Mandeville's notions and especially on Mandeville's anecdote. It may be that the now lost *Inventio Fortunatae*, a written account of a voyage by an Englishman (possibly Nicholas of Lynne) to the Arctic area during the mid-fourteenth century, was known to Mandeville and influenced him on this whole issue of circumnavigation.

56. Seymour, introduction, p. xvii.

57. The phrase occurs in an account contained in *The Mongol Mission: Narratives and Letters of the Franciscan Missionaries in Mongolia and China in the Thirteenth and Fourteenth Centuries*, ed. Christopher Dawson (London: Sheed and Ward, 1955), p. 93.

58. For a convenient representation, see plate 89 in D. W. Robertson, Jr., *A Preface to Chaucer: Studies in Medieval Perspectives* (Princeton: Princeton Univ. Press, 1962).

59. *Relations des Quatre Voyages Entrepris par Christophe Colomb . . .* , ed. M. F. de Navarrete (Paris: Treuttel et Wurtz, 1828), III, 32.

60. On the tradition that Eden lay opposite Jerusalem, see Charles S. Singleton, "A Lament for Eden," in *Journey to Beatrice: Dante Studies 2* (Cambridge, Mass.: Harvard Univ. Press, 1958), pp. 141-58. For a summary of traditional views about Eden as a remote or nonexistent spot, see A. Bartlett Giamatti, *The Earthly Paradise and the Renaissance Epic* (Princeton: Princeton Univ. Press, 1966), ch. 1; and on Mandeville as representative of the medieval view about terrestrial Eden, see Howard Rollins Patch, *The Other World According to Descriptions in Medieval Literature* (Cambridge, Mass.: Harvard Univ. Press, 1950), pp. 164-73.

61. See Moseley, note 33 above. Whatever the "tretys" was that Mandeville says he showed the pope on the way home—and assuming he might have stopped at Avignon, if not Rome—it obviously was not the finished version of the *Travels*. It is clear from the Prologue and the last chapter that while the work may have been sketched out by the man during his journeys (and perhaps shown to the pope in some rough draft), the complete book was, as Mandeville says at the end, "fulfilled" later. Of course, if the author never traveled or never visited the pope, all this is just more of the apparatus of the fiction.

62. *The Discovery of Guiana*, in *Voyages and Travels Ancient and Modern*, ed. Charles E. Eliot (Boston: The Harvard Classics, 1920), pp. 359-60. See Bennett, *Rediscovery*, p. 245.

63. Bennett, *Rediscovery*, pp. 82-84; Seymour, "The English Manuscripts of *Mandeville's Travels*," 200 (the *Travels* bound with Chaucer's *Astrolabe*); and Bennett, *Rediscovery*, p. 299 (the *Travels* bound with the *Philobiblon*).

64. *The Three Voyages of Martin Frobisher*, ed. Vilhjalmur Stefansson (London: The Argonaut Press, 1938), II, 77.

65. *Pseudodoxia Epidemica*, in *The Works of Sir Thomas Browne*, ed. Geoffrey Keynes (Chicago: Univ. of Chicago Press, 1964), II, 54.

66. See Louis B. Wright, *Middle-Class Culture in Elizabethan England* (1947; rpt. Ithaca: Cornell Univ. Press, 1958), p. 86.

67. See Bennett, *Rediscovery*, pp. 237-38 (on More), pp. 255-56 (on Swift); see W. T. Jewkes, "The Literature of Travel and the Mode of Romance in the Renaissance," in *Literature as a Mode of Travel* (New York: The New York Public Library, 1963), pp. 13-30; C. W. R. D. Moseley, "Richard Head's 'The English Rogue': A Modern Mandeville?" *YES*, 1 (1971), 102-7; and Moseley's "The Lost Play of Mandeville," *The Library*, Series 5, 25 (1970), 46-49.

68. *Johnsonian Miscellanies*, ed. George B. Hill (New York: Harper & Bros., 1897), II, 387.

69. *Commentarii*, pp. 366-67.

70. The name "Mandeville" and the various dates mentioned in the manuscript versions continue to be major targets for those intent on figuring out the author's identity. Beazley (III, 320-21)—apparently following a suggestion of Warner's—remarked that perhaps the name Mandeville was derived from a satirical French romance, *Mandevie*, written by one Jean du Pin about 1340. Seymour repeats this idea and also notes that the date Mandeville gives as his time of departure from England—Michaelmas Day (September 29), 1322—was probably taken from the itinerary of William of Boldensele, another fourteenth-century traveler (introduction, p. xvi).

71. Letts, *Sir John Mandeville* (p. 125), notes that in one eighteenth-century edition of the *Travels* the date 1372, which appears in some fourteenth-century versions of the work, was inadvertently altered to read 1732; and there is a remark in that edition to the effect that "Mandeville is turned into another Gulliver." *Gulliver's Travels* was published in 1726, the year after the famous first printing of the Cotton MS version of Mandeville.

72. Lewis, p. 144.

73. On this point see William J. Brandt, *The Shape of Medieval History: Studies in Modes of Perception* (New Haven: Yale Univ. Press, 1966), ch. 2.

74. Smalley, "Robert Holcot O.P.," *Archivum Fratrum Praedicatorum*, 26 (1956), 82.

75. *Letters from Petrarch*, trans. Morris Bishop (Bloomington, Ind.: Indiana Univ. Press, 1966), p. 261.

76. "The Discoveries and the Humanists," in *Merchants and Scholars*, p. 40.

INDEX

THE JOHNS HOPKINS UNIVERSITY PRESS

This book was composed in Aldine Roman type by Horne Associates, Incorporated, from a design by Susan Bishop. It was printed on 50-lb. Cream White Bookmark paper and bound in Columbia Bayside Linen cloth by Thomson-Shore, Inc.

Library of Congress Cataloging in Publication Data

Zacher, Christian.
  Curiosity and pilgrimage.

  Includes index.
  1. English literature—Middle English, 1100–1500—History and
criticism. 2. Pilgrims and pilgrimages in literature. 3. Curiosity
in literature. I. Title.
PR275.P45Z3   820'.9'001   75-36929
ISBN 0-8018-1778-1

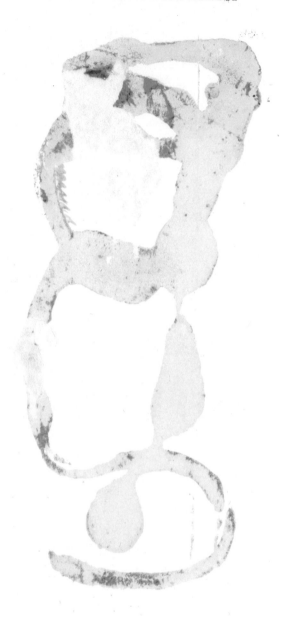